# Developmental Group Care of Children and Youth: Concepts and Practice

# THE CHILD & YOUTH SERVICES SERIES:

EDITOR-IN-CHIEF

JEROME BEKER, *Director and Professor, Center for Youth Development and Research, University of Minnesota*

# Developmental Group Care of Children and Youth: Concepts and Practice

Henry W. Maier, PhD

The Haworth Press
New York • London

*Developmental Group Care of Children and Youth: Concepts and Practice* has also been published as *Child & Youth Services*, Volume 9, Number 2 1987.

The Haworth Press, Inc. 10 Alice Street, Binghamton, NY 13904-1580
EUROSPAN/Haworth, 3 Henrietta Street, London WC2E 8LU England

**Library of Congress Cataloging in Publication Data**

Maier, Henry W. (Henry William)
   Developmental group care of children and youth.

   Bibliography: p.
   Includes index.
   1. Children — Institutional care — United States. 2. Group homes for children — United States. 3. Child development — United States. I. Title.
HV863.M35      1987      362.7'32'0973      87-7421
ISBN 0-86656-655-4
ISBN 0-86656-834-4 (pbk.)

To
Child and Youth Care Workers
Anywhere

# ABOUT THE AUTHOR

*Henry W. Maier, PhD,* has been Professor at the University of Washington, Seattle, Washington, for over 28 years as well as a visiting professor at several universities in North America and overseas. He was twice a Fulbright Scholar in Great Britain and New Zealand. Significantly, in his professional career he worked as a child care worker for many years; subsequently, he served as a child and youth care work supervisor. While at the university he continued his interest in and identification with the fields of child and youth as well as family care. These themes are evident in his teaching, consulting, and numerous workshops and training seminars. He has written articles, chapters, and books pertaining to a better life for the development of children, adolescents, and their caregivers.

# Developmental Group Care of Children and Youth: Concepts and Practice

Child & Youth Services
Volume 9, Number 2

## CONTENTS

# Foreword

Henry W. Maier has long been viewed as one of a very small group of leaders in the professional development of the child and youth care field, and as a distinguished member of an even smaller group who have successfully bridged the gap between academic knowledge and its application by practitioners. He is always in demand, therefore, at conferences in the field, and his writings are widely used by direct care workers, their supervisors, program administrators, and academic colleagues. Both in person and through his writings, he is a natural teacher, and his writings in recent years have appeared in most of the leading publications in the field. This range, however, has made it somewhat inconvenient to use his work systematically for teaching or other purposes, and some of the most significant work has not previously been published at all.

It was suggested by several interested colleagues, therefore, that a collection of Henry's recent published and unpublished articles most closely related to group care work with children and youth be provided in one volume, and we are excited to be able to do that in the *Child & Youth Services* series. Here are Henry's ideas about human development in the group care context, about the perceptions of children and youth, about the environments in which we work with them, about the role of the worker, about relationships, about the preparation of child and youth care workers, about caring for the caregiver and, most of all, about the meaning of care and the "nuts and bolts" of how to do it well. As always in his work, recent research and thinking in human development are reflected in his practical approaches.

The ideas are presented in the full depth and richness of his style, yet with all his warmth and clarity. The book may find its place primarily as a text for courses in the field but should also be useful as a handbook for child and youth care workers on the job and an orientation for anyone not familiar with the field—new workers, allied professionals, academics, informed laypersons, and others. That Henry has chosen, despite my initial reservations, to include a paper we wrote together as the final contribution to this book indeed honors me. I hope that readers will make full use of the opportunity the book provides to become immersed in the thinking of Henry Maier, one of the most vibrant, creative, and humane figures in child and youth care work today. We will all be the richer for it, particularly the young people with whom we work.

*Jerome Beker, EdD*
*Editor,* Child & Youth Services
*Professor and Director*
*Center for Youth Development and Research*
*University of Minnesota*

# Preface

At the beginning of 1985, after six years writing and teaching about practice in group child and youth care settings, I left university life to return full-time to the Walker Home and School in Needham, Massachusetts. As a new program administrator, I was immediately struck by how much more complicated the business of therapeutic group child care had become. Child care professionals at Walker School and, I believe, throughout the group care field are confronted by a confusion of equally powerful points of view as they try to do their jobs.

— First, particularly given the increasingly difficult, multihandi-capped children placed in our care, it is clear that no one theoretical system is sufficient to guide day-to-day practice. As we make key clinical decisions, we often struggle to combine concrete behavioral objectives with longer term goals generated by psychodynamic or systems considerations, just as valid as the need to teach new behaviors. The result is not always comfortable, or clear as a blue print for effective intervention.
— With reference to the families of the children and adolescents we serve, public policy and the impact of a growing number of new practice theory formulations challenge both practitioners and parents to reframe residential group care as family-centered and family supportive. This perspective is exciting in theory because it breaks down the stereotypical barriers between parents and child care workers in the name of creating a sense of permanence for every child in group care. Yet it is also disturbing as it demands program change, reallocation of resources and innovative partnerships where real power is shared with parents within the institution.
— From most public and private community funding and regula-

tory agencies, the child care professional continues to endure the pressures of increased demands for accountability and decreased willingness to provide adequate fiscal support. Often the effect of this outside pressure on child care workers is indirect, creating tension within the agency between line workers and program administrators who are so in tune with the need to reduce costs and risks of liability as to be perceived as out of touch with the real needs of the clients.

— From the perspective of non-familial child care as a social institution, child and youth care work in the United States is still a faintly suspect semi-profession, and direct care workers still lack adequate social status, adequate pay and, much too often, an adequate share of decision-making power within the group care agencies built around their work. At the very least, this sociological anomaly complicates effective direct care practice. At worst, whole agencies struggle to recruit and maintain even marginally competent direct care professionals, while significant numbers of child care workers struggle with powerlessness and cynicism in their work.

All of these points of view are relevant to practice in group child care settings. The problem for the child care worker and the program administrator alike is to achieve some sort of integrative focus — what Albert E. Trieschman called a "unifying something" — as a basis for building a coherent helping environment. The extraordinary achievement of this elegant volume of essays by Henry W. Maier is that it goes a long way toward providing just such a unifying something for professional child care work.

Professor Maier takes what he calls a developmental perspective to reframe the basic challenge of residential group care whatever the age of the clients or the specific objectives of the setting: "In what way can group care, that is, non-familial living, assure children a developmental progress similar to that of children growing up within regular family care settings?" (Chapter I, p. 9). The answers provided in this collection of separate papers written during the last ten years are based on a consistent and deceptively simple idea: *The heart of the matter is the making of human connections and the giving and receiving of basic care.* One way or another, each of the twelve essays develops the idea that the essential preoccupation of child care work is and should be "the interactive symphony of caring": how and why children at different developmental stages react differently to caregivers; how giving and receiving basic care is shaped by space, by organizational structure, and by the demands of society as a whole; and, most of all, how the mutuality of caring and the connectedness between caregiver and child or adolescent define the humanity of every child care environment.

Professor Maier is a synthesizer. He plays with seemingly disparate ideas as "thinking screens," just as he used to ask his jaded and faintly uneasy graduate students at the University of Washington to play in the classroom as a more real way of exploring the intricacies of child development. Part of the fun of reading this book is to look at child care work variously through the lens of Parsons' (1964) sociological formulations, or Barker's (1968) ecological psychology, or change theory and classical behavioral psychology. Yet the reader should make no mistake, this is not an "academic" book. Henry Maier's thinking screens are meant to be practical, and most of the time they succeed admirably. The real contribution of this book for the practitioner is that it cuts through the confusion of competing values and competing points of view to focus on the *care* at the heart of child care work. Speaking as a program administrator too often caught up in the buzz of survival issues to keep this in mind, I am very grateful.

*Richard W. Small, PhD*
*Executive Director*
*Walker Home and School*
*Needham, Massachusetts*

# Developmental Group Care
# of Children and Youth:
# Concepts and Practice

# Developmental Group Care of Children and Youth: Concepts and Practice

# Introduction:
# Group Care Utilizing
# a Developmental Perspective

## WHAT IS THIS BOOK ALL ABOUT?

This publication is meant for persons involved in the *care* of children and adolescents. It will hopefully be useful for child and youth care workers and others who are concerned with the growth and development of our younger generation. The following chapters deal with the essential developmental requirements of young persons as they mature – and more specifically with the development of those children and adolescents who must spend a major portion or all of their daily lives in group care settings. Children and adolescents in group care, just as their age-mates living in their own or foster family homes, are engaged in the life processes of development; they are striving and being challenged to achieve growing maturity. The notion of maturity is an elusive concept, but it is clear that the periods of child- and adolescenthood are the years within the human developmental life span in which the thrust to develop is viewed as the central energy investment.

This publication focuses on the *developmental* requirements of children and adolescents in relation to the care they receive while they are in non-familial, group living situations. Additionally, needed care for the caregivers in order that they can effectively provide the kind of caring involvement that children or youth require is highlighted. This requisite is too often forgotten (Chapters IV, IX, and X).

## A DEVELOPMENTAL PERSPECTIVE

The following chapters advocate that helping professionals – child and youth care workers, counselors, social workers, nurses, and others—need to relate and to work with children and adolescents as developing beings. Regardless of whether the young people are placed in the group setting due to personal complications, societal stress situations, or both, and whether they are registered in a residential program or for "ordinary" alternative care in a day care, latchkey, or other equivalent part-time setting, they remain youngsters with developmental requirements the same as those of their contemporaries who are in the care of their own families.

The author submits that it is important that we have progressed to the point where we think and speak of "children with difficulties" rather than designating these youngsters as "difficult children." The distinction is more than a semantic exercise. For example, when we encounter the old term, "learning-disabled children," we find that such categorization tends to narrow the child's dimensions, as if the child were a differently developing person to be set apart in our thinking (and perhaps in how we respond to the situation) from other children.

Yet a developmental perspective also requires the recognition and understanding of each individual's status and progression in various spheres of development. Above all, it is paramount for children striving toward mastery to experience solidly the personal involvement and continuous support of the caregivers, a point to which we shall return below. Such support includes acknowledged freedom to struggle on one's own. Developmental progress emerges from the interplay between the individual's developmental readiness and actual functioning amidst ongoing environmental challenge (Maas, 1984). It necessitates ascertaining specifically how each individual is functioning in his or her ongoing life situation—and what each one needs to experience in order to progress. Progression in competent development builds upon a sense of efficacy of that which has been learned, usually occurring by means of minute accomplishments and only occasionally on the basis of a major breakthrough. When individuals experience their own part in their mastery, they have learned (Bandura, 1977). Then, as in the old truism: what is learned is used.

It is important to remind ourselves that a developmental approach does not permit preoccupation with "deviant," "pathological," or "defective" behavior or development in the face of situationally ineffective, untimely, and other difficult responses. When an individual's affect, behavior, and cognition are evaluated as distinct processes, care workers can rely on their knowledge of predictable patterns of developmental progression instead. For example, a ten-year-old boy's tendency "to go to pieces" whenever he feels personal contacts or events are not manageable is sometimes designated as an "emotional disturbance," "regression," or behavior "stuck" at an earlier level, all of which denote "deviancy." However, the boy can more constructively be understood and observed as one who wants to master his ongoing life encounters but is at a loss when he finds himself incapable of conceiving and predicting what is going on. Consequently, he is unable to respond so as to manage his immediate life challenges effectively. He seems to need assistance in learning to predict and identify subtle opportunities or moments of change and what can be done within them. We can then turn to our developmental knowledge: How are such capabilities acquired and how can an individual's capabilities be broadened so as to incorporate the required competencies?

This developmental perspective might be more understandable if we apply it to our own lives. When we find ourselves in extremely frustrating situations, we may make such responses as stamping a foot, kicking an object in our path, exploding with severe language, or freezing up as if paralyzed. Our response may be behavioral, cognitive, or emotional, more likely, two or all three of these (Maier, 1976).

In such moments, we do not regress. We mobilize our waning energy into bodily or symbolic bodily expressions. We act in a basic, fundamental way that usually assures us a launching platform from which to try again with renewed responses. What helps us as adults in these situations? It is the reliance on a level of functioning which is fundamental to us, equivalent to employing the first gear in a car when the motor (energy) sputters. Downshifting into first gear allows the motor to revive and, ultimately, to progress to smoother speeds, rather than to stall completely. The same holds for developmental functioning. Essential in this process of helping is the certainty that one is not alone, that care will be provided by a person who is significant to the child.

The developmental approach, as elaborated in the first chapter, is introduced here not only as the author's preferred orientation and as one presently gaining prominence in the other human helping fields

and behavior studies (Maier, 1986a), but also and more importantly, for its useful application in child and youth care and treatment.

## CARE AS THE INTEGRATING
## AND SOLIDIFYING ACTIVITY

Most important, as Bronfenbrenner and Weiss (1983) remind us,
is "the enduring, irrational involvement of one or more adults in
care and joint activity with that of the child" (p. 398). Bronfenbrenner (1977) calls out even more emphatically, "Every child needs at
least one person who is really crazy about him [or her]"
(p. 5). These observations stress the vital position of the central
caregivers and the importance of their intense interaction with the
receivers of the care they give. Strong, intimate caregiver-receiver
meshing assures the development of attachment and an emergent
sense of freedom. Additionally, our growing concern for assuring a
sense of permanency for children and youth who find themselves
with multi-parents, multi-homes or multi-care situations can be
more solidly implemented by fostering attachment experiences in
short- and long-term contacts. The curious paradox that secure attachment leads to greater developmental freedom is more clearly
explicated in subsequent chapters (I, II and, especially, V).

Central in care work are the care activities, the give-and-take interactions between child and caregiver. Caregivers are those who
are predictably on hand, in particular when needed: the adults with
whom one shares ordinary daily happenings; those present for routines and the minutiae of everyday life such as getting up, turning
off to go to sleep, and sharing meals; and those who are the source
of learning about past and future events. Caregiving also involves
support, as well as control and restraint. Additionally, caregivers
provide stimulation and new challenges as well as refuge from pressures. Care workers teach through modeling or direct guidance and
serve as figures willing to be experimented with and ready to learn
from the child. All these and more of the components of care interactions — direct activities, indirect environmental care components,
and applicable interventive techniques — are explored (Chapters II,
VI, and VII).

The child or youth care worker position and role are pivotal in the lives of young people in care. How the role and functions are perceived by children and adolescents in care from their emerging cognitive perspective is the theme of Chapter III. Care workers' status, position, and roles within their work settings and in the human service field in general are discussed in detail in Chapters IX and X.

## GROUP CARE AS A SUPPLEMENT TO FAMILIAL CARE

Group care services such as residential around-the-clock or part-time care provided in day care or latchkey programs constitute an extension of the child's family life (Davis, 1981) through alternate care.

Group settings provide the context for rendering care and can offer a multiplicity of life experience, including continuous variation through intimate and casual peer contacts. through encounters with a wide spectrum of adults, and through rich program offerings. Numerous examples are set forth in the opening chapters. In groups, children and, especially, adolescents can learn from each other and risk new ways for handling old problems, or new problems can be encountered as familiar, shared challenges. In Chapters II and VII, the group setting is viewed as both the context and the means for care. Some of the contextual aspects of care, namely the powerful impact of various spatial arrangements, are emphasized in Chapter VIII, "The Space We Create Controls Us." While a developmental perspective presumes attention to each individual's ongoing functioning and projected learning progressions, the group approach is still very much in order. Young people can be fully understood and responded to only in the context of their interactions.

When we deal with children or adolescents, it is important to be aware of ethnic and cultural diversity, and to respond with understanding, respect, and appropriate differentiation to these important elements. There is, however, an underlying commonality of fundamental requirements of human beings everywhere, although technical details might vary. For example, caregivers of different ethnic subgroups may differ as to what constitutes a proper diet and acceptable eating behaviors, " . . . but nearly all believe children should be fed regularly and well" (Polansky, Ammons &

Weathersby, 1983, p. 345). In fact, commonality goes far beyond this. Proper child care anywhere recognizes the necessity that a child seeking affection should receive it. And virtually no subcultures within the American rainbow of ethnicities would condone personal or institutional abuses (Polansky, Ammons & Weathersby, 1983).

Although conflicts that arise in group care situations may be rooted at least partially in cultural or ethnic differences, and these dimensions require the caregivers' full vigilance, it is also important to be aware of the tension that can develop through conflict between the demands of personal care in groups and organizational maintenance requirements. The strain inherent in providing individualized care within an established organization is appraised and analyzed in Chapter IX.

## THE CHILD AND YOUTH CARE WORKER AS A DEVELOPING PERSON

There is no doubt that, with all the energy invested in care work with children, adults themselves gain personally and professionally from these intimate involvements. In short, the older and the younger generations experience an interweaving of rhythms in this mutual interaction of giving and taking in the shared search for a future. This sense of mutuality is ever present, although the focus of the following pages is primarily on the adults' activities as care providers.

The training of child care workers by means of supervision on the job and the widening of horizons of thought as well as the emergences of current and prospective issues are addressed in the final two chapters.

Finally, while the author hopes that readers will find stimulation and will learn from the material presented here, he also trusts that they will find original and even greater satisfaction and learning from their own work with children and youth. Care work is really rooted in the nitty gritty: in give-and-take encounters, in play with children, in the attempts to maintain control at moments of conflict, in such routines as attending to the "food traffic" at mealtime, and in just being there while quietly learning from the young people how they are doing in mastering or struggling to master a small interaction. It is in this submergence in daily life activities that we truly discover what the children or adolescents, and we ourselves, are all about. To those who are on the "front line," in the thick of child or adolescent care work, this volume is dedicated.

*Henry W. Maier, PhD*

# Chapter I

# Children and Youth Grow and Develop in Group Care

*In what way can group care, that is, non-familial living, assure children a developmental progress similar to that of children growing up within regular family care settings?* The following conversation can serve as an illustration of the kind of issues to be encountered *wherever* young people spend their daily lives.

On returning home from school, the author's nine-year-old son, Peter, was overheard questioning his mother:

> Mom, how come you don't go to work like other mothers? . . . I was just wondering. I guess it's okay that you don't work. But why did *I* have to come home to change my clothes? I like it when you make me my crackers and jelly. How do other kids get their snacks?

What Peter is really wondering is how children receive *care* in the absence of their central caregivers. This is the very issue which is fully reviewed throughout this chapter. The focus is how children and adolescents have their primary developmental care requirements fulfilled when such care has to take place temporarily or for extended periods away from familial settings.

Peter's questions allude to four important aspects of caregiving. First, that the judgment about who is a "proper" caregiver is *culturally* determined. One likes to live one's life in a way that is similar to others in one's own socio-cultural group ("Mom, why are you at home when other parents are not!"). Second, care as a *per-*

An earlier version of this article was presented at the Study Group in Residential Care, Haifa, Israel, 1982. The article appears here with permission of the Study Group sponsors.

**9**

*sonalized* experience, is a basic human desire. (Peter likes personally prepared crackers and jelly.) Third, personal care emerges from *give-and-take interaction.* (Peter responds to his mother's giving which enlivens her giving. He also assures his mother that she is "okay" even if she is not "at work" like other mothers.) And fourth, a *questioning of the care received* is part of the process of accepting that care ("Why do I still have to come home and change after school?").

Peter's first question: "Mom, how come you don't work like other mothers? . . . " articulates his concern that his life is different from those of other children. This notion is central to the chapter. A nine-year old "is able to conceptualize the quality of his or her rearing and is sensitive to the differences in the environment between self and other children" (Kagan, 1974, p. 889). Children are apt to evaluate differences as negative and may conclude that something is wrong.

> Thus, the child's conclusion that he or she is not valued by adults depends in part whether the form of rearing is different from that of the majority. If the vast majority of children in a society were raised by surrogates . . . there would be no reason to worry about the consequences of that practice, for the culture would accommodate to whatever special traits were associated with universal rearing. (Kagan, 1974, p. 889)

We shall deal with those developmental issues in order to find ways to assure keen sensitivity to differences and explore ways to assure full developmental life experience for children and youth within the context of non-familial living.

The reader is first introduced to a major developmental premise about the interdependence of human beings and their needs for basic attachments. Care workers are then defined as the most likely "attachment objects" in group care in the light of contemporary research findings on attachment formation and human development. This is followed up with examination of the developmental perspective, a singularly emerging perspective in psychology, social work, and child care (Maier, 1986a). The direct implications of such knowledge for the practice of group care is explicated in this chapter; with the latter sections of it leading the reader into "steps" of practice, based on interpretation of the developmental stance. This orientation has much direct applicability to beginnings such as placement, starting counseling or group sessions, and the fostering of attachment formations. Separate segments on "grouping residents developmentally," dealing with questions of "consistency," and appropriate program activities for children and adolescents are detailed at the end of this chapter. Throughout, current knowledge is cited as the bases for specific guidelines and interventive techniques for direct care workers in conceptualizing and implementing effective practice.

## DEVELOPMENT AND CARE

Children and youth, whether in their own homes, day care, or around-the-clock group care settings, have the same basic life requirements for personal care, social and intellectual stimulation, leeway for creativeness and, above all, a sense of rootedness. Thus, the application of knowledge about *human development* as it applies to the major caregiving activities with the child or youth is particularly pertinent. Consequently, the focus in what follows is not on existing practice in group care (e.g., Arieli, Kashti & Shlasky, 1983; Whittaker, 1979); rather it is on what could be accomplished in group care on the basis of contemporary human development knowledge.

Nurturing care experiences are essential for the healthy development of all children (Ainsworth, 1972; Bronfenbrenner, 1979), but these experiences are even more urgently needed by children and youth lacking secure and permanent roots. Being placed in day or residential care, or even going away to school or camp, may weaken a child's previous linkages and cause a search for new attachments. We are reminded of instances where, in the absence of a valid caregiver, individuals create substitutes. For example, children in concentration camps became caregivers for one another when other alternatives were absent (Freud & Dann, 1951). Rhesus monkeys attached themselves to wiremesh "mothers" in the absence of their mothers (Harlow & Menus, 1977). It is in the providing of such nurturing care that care workers, frequently perceived as generalists, are actually [or should be] specialists (Barnes & Kelman, 1974, p. 12). They are the "social engineers" for nurturing care experiences. Other services, such as education, recreation, counseling, and health care are supplements to this kind of fundamental caring.

## Interpersonal Dependence as a Major Life Spring

Interpersonal dependence is an ongoing force in human exist-ence. Throughout our lives, we tend to depend on one or several central persons — parent or an alternate caregiver, a partner, or friends — for intimate, mutual care experiences. Dependence on *per-sonal* nurturance is as essential as our dependence upon food and shelter. Thus, we do not develop from a state of dependence to one of independence; development is a continuous process and move-ment occurs from one level of dependence to another (Maier, 1986d). Certain caring persons — e.g., parent, elder, or significant friend — tend to remain an ongoing part of our lives whether or not they are in close proximity.

In non-familial living situations, child care workers provide the main source and substance of care experience and are the pivotal people in the residents' daily lives (Pecora & Gingerich, 1981). They are the people most accessible and instrumental in providing care; they are Peter's care persons with "jellied crackers." The child care worker, as the target of the residents' demands, is taken for granted, criticized, and cherished all at the same time. For the child, the care worker provides the essential *experience* of being cared for, of learning how to respond and to interact and, finally, to develop the capacity for extending caring to others.

## The Direct Care Worker as the Pivot of a Caring System

In non-familial settings, many persons tend to share in children's lives and progress. However, only the designated primary care-givers, the direct care workers, carry the full obligation for and personal involvement in providing "caring care." These institu-tionalized caregivers, like the parents or foster parents in a home setting, are the nurturers who provide life's necessities, sustained presence; and intimate care. This nurturance has considerable sig-nificance in that the caregivers are the immediate representatives of societal norms and are a child's personal backup in the residential living unit or family and in the world outside. In part, this is so central because individuals do not learn their coping behaviors or their mores, social drives, or values from the larger society. Children learn a particular culture and a particular moral system only from those people with whom they have close contact and who exhibit that culture in frequent relationship with them. (Washington, 1982, p. 105)

Thus, the core care persons constitute three basic structural components: (1) the central person for caring and attachment formation; (2) the major norm conductor for primary group life; and (3) the legitimate representative of the norms of the larger context, including the ones of the immediate setting. Consequently, the care worker is always in the business of building a relationship, setting norms, and maintaining a linkage with society.

While focusing on the role of caregivers, one must emphasize the *experience*; because care has not only to be delivered but to be experienced as caring; it is not enough simply to "deliver" the elements of caring without the "message" of having "received." Hearing such messages, or experiencing the care that is offered to them, is particularly difficult for many of the youngsters in group care. They may want and reject it at the same time, and this push/pull is what makes direct care work so complex.

In addition, care workers are constantly faced with this challenge — to provide children or youth with the *experience* of being cared for in the course of the daily activities — in the face of limited time, energy, and skills. Something as routine as requesting a child to put on fresh socks can be expressed as an act of caring; inquiring about a day in school can be experienced as genuine interest rather than as intrusion. Perseverance in the face of repeated rebuffs and tolerance of one's own less than perfect approaches expressing concern (with the hope that the message is picked up) lies at the heart of child care work, and this is one of the human service disciplines' most difficult challenges.

That the caring activities of residential workers have not received the degree of scrutiny and support they deserve is not surprising, for such fundamental personal involvement tends to impede organizational requirements (Maier, 1985a; Parsons, 1964; Resnick, 1980). For instance, allowances made for a child's tardiness in being ready for school because the child is temporarily overwhelmed raise concern about the orderliness, uniformity, and managerial efficiency of the institution. Actually, care and control are interconnected and cannot be divided into separate functions (Harris, 1980). Therefore, the child's tardiness may be viewed as an essential personal variation that will lead eventually to a greater measure of punctuality for this child, but this may also create apparent disorder in the observable scheme of group management as schedules are disrupted and other residents seek similar exceptions for themselves or attack the beneficiary of this exception. Such conflicting strains need to be understood as a natural part of residential child and youth care work (Maier, 1985a), in which constant attention is needed to ways of establishing and maintaining a balance between the requirements of nurturing care and what is needed to keep the system functioning. Experience suggests that, in the absence of such attention, system maintenance priorities tend to become dominant.

## A DEVELOPMENTAL PERSPECTIVE

Child and youth care workers will do well to anchor their work in developmental psychology (Beker & Maier, 1980; Bronfenbrenner, 1979; VanderVen, Mattingly & Morris, 1982). To emphasize a developmental approach represents a break from previous attempts by child care workers to adopt behavioral, psychodynamic, or experiential theoretical stances of other professions. It means taking the lead in an emerging trend that moves away from personality and behavioral formulations toward a developmental perspective (Maier, 1986a; Whittaker, 1979).

This body of knowledge establishes a discernable progression of development (Maier, 1978; Jones, Garrison & Morgan, 1985; Smart & Smart, 1977). The actual timing and rate of specific steps of developmental progress vary from child to child as the nature of life experiences differ from one socio-cultural context to another. Nevertheless, developmental knowledge can serve as a guiding foundation in the pursuit of effective child care work. From this perspective, a child with unusual, that is, untimely behavior is viewed in terms of how this behavior fits into his or her developmental progression rather than as "deviant" (Bronfenbrenner, 1979; Kagan, 1978; Segal & Yahraes, 1978). The emphasis on "ordinary" development is important, for it demands from us an astute appraisal of the child's behavior; how this person manages particular life situations. The worker thus gains an understanding of the individual's pattern of coping — an invaluable basis for discerning what the next developmental task should be. Caring work means helping to meet an individual's developmental requirements rather than a focus on working to undo or to correct unwanted behaviors.

For example, a big, boisterous Steven, 13, demands continuous adult approval as if he were a mere four-year old; he goes to pieces when he feels slighted. A developmental point of view looks at what Steven *is* doing rather than what he is not doing (i.e., not acting like a 13-year old or not "fitting in"). His demands for continuous adult approval and his temper tantrums when things don't go his way are not "deviant" behaviors as much as efforts to reach out to adults and to get continuous assurance that he is succeeding in his efforts. When Steven is confident of his ability to make contact with adults, when he has "practiced" doing it and succeeded over and over again, this aspect of his development will be part of him and he will be off and running with another developmental task. "Promotion of competence and normal growth and development" as a treatment objective is discussed by Denholm, Pence, and Ferguson (1983), who state that this goal "can provide a concensus necessary for a collaborative effort of staff, the child in care, and parents, which (otherwise) often creates an adversary relationship between parent and child, and brings out decisive differences in staff."

Working from a developmental perspective demands not only that a practitioner have a background knowledge of human development, but also he or she be able to observe and to verify what residents are doing and to ascertain their ongoing competencies—how each is actually managing his or her life. This attention to what a child or youth is doing might sound self-evident. Yet, in everyday accounting of children's behavior, it is a common practice to report what youngsters are *not* doing. For example: "He doesn't pay any attention to what I tell him!" The latter reveals only the caregiver's expectation, but not the child's way of handling her or his situation. In the illustration just cited, the child kept on doing what he was absorbed in and this may provide a clue to the situation. It may be necessary for the worker to gain his momentary attention before dealing with a secondary message. Moreover, in order to fully ascertain a child's progression in managing life events, the concern needs to be with the "how" rather than the "why." An explanation, whether real or assumed, may satisfy a worker's puzzlement, but it will rarely mobilize a sense of what action to take next. The "how" will open a path for the next steps of interaction; the "why" leads to an interpretation, possibly empathic understanding, and an explanation for action, but little specificity regarding what should actually be done.

### Developmental Work:
### Building on Small Increments of Change

Development occurs by small steps through the minutiae of ordinary human interactions, and within the context of events (Elkind & Weiner, 1978). An understanding of development in this way can mobilize residential care personnel to utilize activities that, however insignificant they may appear, have powerful impact for change. Such interactions as the wink of an eye, a clear and honest expression of disagreement, or a hand on the shoulder can represent most significant work with a child. It is important to keep in mind that concrete care involves flexibility, adapting personal care and management to the situation at hand. Consequently, care work interactions need to be situational rather than behaviorally specific. A momentary backrub, for example, may at one time create instantaneous closeness, but at another time result in an explosive "bug off." The reaction will depend upon the situational timing.

In many ways, the care worker is like a street-worker[1] with a roof overhead. The worker is *there*. Workers are present not only for order or personal emergencies; they are there as agents of growth and change. They enter situations directly, as requested by the youngsters or as the worker deems it advisable, just as streetworkers do. While life proceeds smoothly, resident workers may join the children's or youths' activities to share in their lives, their fun, and their joint opportunities to widen their experience. At rough spots, in anticipation of difficulties or in an actual crisis, they also become directly involved in order to assist the youngsters in "reaching the shores safely through troubled waters." Most important is the fact that residential group care workers, as do streetworkers, need to be where the youngsters are, and to do their work where the action is.

The understanding of human development and its progression by minute but discernable steps has important implications for interventive (treatment) planning. The work emphasis is translated into operational steps (process work) for fostering change rather than outcome objectives or treatment goals per se. The focus is on what to do *right now*, in the next minute or hour, rather than what is to be accomplished eventually. The latter is an important consideration for overall planning, of course, but it falls short of operationalizing the actual task. For example, the important intervention for a distressed 13-year old is what she and the worker can do immediately to ease her situation, such as discussing her worries and working together to identify and initiate a first step that will begin a change in her problematic situation. The long-range goal of assisting her to become a "more spontaneous" teenager, while not negated, is in the background at this time.

## First- and Second-Order Change

Child and youth care practitioners may find it useful to clarify for themselves whether they deal with developmental change of first- or second-order (Maier, 1984; Watzlawick, Weakland & Rich, 1974, pp. 10-11). An analogy would be water becoming warmer or colder; this is a first-order change. Water turning into ice or steam constitutes a second-order change. First-order change is incremental, a linear progression to do more or less, better, faster, or with greater accuracy. Practice, reinforcement, and time will be the most likely approaches for facilitating sound developmental change of this kind. Activities are tangible, usually verbal interactions between the caregiver and the young person involved.

Second-order change, on the other hand, involves a nonlinear progression, a transformation from one state to another. The aim would be to enable the individual to behave, think, or feel differently. Within the second-order change approach, applicable practice tools might be modeling, confrontation, conflict work, reframing and, most important, the introduction of decisively different personal experience over time. Second-order change requires greater creativity and prolonged investment of time and contact by caregiver and receiver (Maier, 1984). A crucial task of care workers is to be clear as to which order of change they are striving to create. Typically, residential care and treatment work calls for second order change, since it demands substantial intervention and leads to transformational new learning.

## Specific Enhancement of Change

Strategies for change are most effective when they are matched with the child's level of operation. The objective is to enhance the child's development along its ordinary path. For instance, fear of being overlooked or left out tells us about a child's current operating level. It needs to be understood that a child will be able to wait longer when he or she has a broader notion of time. One potentially effective change strategy in assisting a child to move developmentally forward is for the caregiver to act *as if* he or she expects a desirable event or behavior to take place (Vygotsky, 1978). That is, to respond to a child *as if* the child were moving intentionally toward a desired goal. Thus, in working with a teenager who has difficulty speaking up to authority figures, the caregiver might suggest spontaneously, "Let me know what your teacher arranges with you when you ask her to be excused from school to check out your job possibility." This is a time-honored approach that has been employed by parents and other caring adults; it can serve the same purpose in child care work.

## Nonlinear Approach to Child Care Work

In applying a developmental perspective, it is essential to think of human development as nonlinear. Practice experience has made us aware of the many ups and downs in a child's life, as growth and progress proceed over a zigzag course. Basic to residential care are the variations in the course of the day when children require greater latitude in time or space or contact. Starting the day, waiting for meals, mail time, and going to sleep, are all important moments for children that require extra staff involvement and time (Trieschman, Whittaker & Brendtro, 1969). At these moments, children may function on a more fundamental level; such fluctuations constitute a natural part of the cycle of growth. Such variations in self-management do not constitute a breakdown in self-control, and child care staff sometimes need to create interventions that are in tune with the children's earlier basic levels of functioning.

With so much emphasis in many child care settings placed on growth and improvement, it is particularly important to remember that ordinary development proceeds in nonlinear patterns. There are periods in everyone's lives when old issues re-emerge. In infancy, during pre-school development, and in early adolescence, building relationships and reaching out to a larger world remains the main focus. At each stage, the theme is similar — risking, exploring, bonding. Similarly, there is cyclical variation in children's attitudes towards details and in their sense of order, all of which have direct implication for how we relate to them, such as how we implement demands for the maintenance of their belongings. Before intervening, it is important that we assess whether we are dealing with fundamental issues or merely temporary phases.

As another example of nonlinear variation, recent research findings strongly suggest that there is a "vulnerable age phenomenon" for youngsters in geographical transition (Inbar, 1976). Children around the age periods of 5 to 7 and 13 to 15 whose primary living arrangements had been relocated and who also had to adapt to a culturally different secondary setting (e.g., a different school) were less successful in their educational and vocational pursuits than those who either relocated at a different age or did not relocate at all.[2] These tentative findings remind us to explore sensitively the children's experience of transitions when they must move into culturally different systems through being placed in residential programs at these ages of apparent high vulnerability.

Thus, the recognition of a nonlinear, cyclical pattern of human development is more than an intellectual exercise. It is a very practical stance. Each event in the constellation of behavior needs to be viewed *contextually* for what it means in terms of each individual's progression. As frustrating as it may be for the workers, a messy room is not just a messy room! In Michael Cole's words: "It all depends!" (Cole, 1979, p. x).

## *"Beginnings" in Residential Work*

Beginnings particularly reflect the cyclical nature of development. In the beginning of life, infancy, as well as in the formation of new interpersonal relationships, in the management of new situations, and in moments of crisis we find that a predictable progression is re-enacted. This understanding of beginnings can serve as a profound resource in our approach to beginnings in children's placement.

Beginnings in early life as well as later are essentially *body* experiences. Thus, it is important to provide a newcomer with a welcome that has physical as well as verbal components. This involves assisting the newcomer with the physical process of settling in by encouraging relaxation and providing opportunities for establishing private space.[3] Guarantee of and active support for private space, providing "ownership" of a bed, personal box, or corner: all these are fundamental to new beginnings (Bakker & Bakker-Rabdau, 1973; Maier, 1981, pp. 42-45).

Next, "action space" takes on importance. Newcomers want to *do* things and to show what they can do rather than to be impacted with what they cannot do. Simultaneously, they become concerned over who is going to be with them, who will be taking care of them. Once assured that there is an array of caregivers, they become concerned with what these workers do. Awareness of this progression may help care workers to increase their effectiveness. While we all have a natural eagerness to explain our roles to a newcomer, we need to save this for the time when a new person can *hear* it. Again, the worker's spontaneity and timing are crucial.

### Transitional Objects

At moments of dislocation and relocation, transitional objects serve as linkage between old and new, and tend to assist in making the unfamiliar familiar (Winnicott, 1965), as they do in early childhood. Before admission, young people should be encouarged to bring along transitional objects—a blanket, a teddy bear, an old sweater, their old hat or other cherished and seasoned object. (Linus with his blanket comes instantly to mind!) Child and youth care workers, themselves, can be "transitional objects" when they help with a child's transitions from one life situation to another, eventually from residential placement to the outside community (Maier, 1981, p. 39).

### Transformational Objects

Like transitional objects, transformational objects are reminders of a previous time but have the added significance of being reminders of earlier "monumental" achievement and growth. Such symbols or "trophies" might be a driver's license, a ticket from a dance, a team or club (or gang) jacket, a poster from a rock concert, a funky T-shirt, or other memorabilia from home. Transformational objects are entirely based upon a youngster's choice. Most likely, they are more treasured than anyone without analogous needs and experiences can possibly imagine.

## THE DEPENDENCE CYCLE

As previously discussed, all children and youth require secure dependence upon reliable adults in order to develop into dependable adults themselves. Research findings in the past decade clearly establish that a dependent and nurturing attachment leads to greater readiness to branch out and proceed on one's own (Sroufe, 1978). In fact, children whose highly responsive parents have "pampered" their dependency are the ones who are least fretful. These children ultimately achieve secure *independence* in the same behaviors where they earlier had clamored for support (Ainsworth, Bell & Stayton, 1974; Brunner, 1970). Interestingly, *dependence begets independence*. In child care work, dependence support and nurturance are fundamental ingredients of care.

To permit such knowledge to be applied, group care programs must be structured so that staff have as one of their central and ongoing tasks to provide not only immediate support but nurturance of the dependency of those in their care (Maier, 1981, pp. 30-32). We need to be mindful that, at the beginning of new experiences or at points of crisis, a child's dependence upon physical support and nurturance is primary. To be able to depend on dependence feels good and helps to promote development. Effective care work necessitates a program which provides countless opportunities and resources for rendering *concrete* caregiving.

Once a person feels assured that dependency needs will be met, self-mastery ("me-do-it") becomes alive as a developmental issue. In residential care situations, this frequently occurs after the individual has seemingly "fit-in so well." Youngsters will suddenly rebel, such as by rejecting well-meant suggestions although these were earlier accepted. They act not unlike the two-year old who insists on self feeding. As in the case of the two-year old, this rebellion is an indication of a growth spurt rather than a slight to the institution. It does provide a delicate challenge in group care settings, however: how to support self-mastery while maintaining a sense of values and order. For example, the balance may entail supporting of a child's determination to dress as he or she chooses, while making clear the expected dress code on the unit. Again, as this new phase is supported, the struggle over self-mastery becomes less of an issue (e.g., a youngster will no longer view staff involvement as a personal affront but as potential assistance).

Getting support when trying something new and reaching beyond previous mastery into new areas of experience are, for many residents, basic and ongoing developmental issues. In residential programming this means that a range of activities in play and work, variations in routines, contacts with peers and adults, and events within and outside of the institution need to be arranged and supported. Hopefully the worker can understand and evaluate the *trying* rather than expecting success with each new venture. Eventually the trying will become doing, and doing will become succeeding. It is the *process* along the way that needs support (Maier, 1982b).

## *ATTACHMENT DEVELOPMENT AND ATTACHMENT BEHAVIOR*

Attachment is as basic a life requirement as the more traditionally cited food, shelter, and clothing. Attachment involves a state of mutual dependence felt by individuals, experienced but not necessarily manifested behaviorally. Attachment provides a sense of rootedness. Genuine attachment experiences are vital for sound development; in fact, for mental health and life anywhere (Brazelton, 1981; Bronfenbrenner, 1979; Rutter, 1979).

Attachment behaviors, as contrasted to feelings of attachment, are really frantic efforts to obtain close attachment. Such behaviors are at times appropriate, and other times awkward or even unpleasant; nevertheless, they are neither "deviant" nor totally undesirable because, in essence, they reflect urgent relationship enhancement efforts. These behaviors represent an investment of energy to build or rebuild processes of attachment when a person experiences these to be absent or in a state of flux. Attachment behaviors may be seen in such proximity-seeking or attention-getting acts as clinging or running away, asking self-evident questions, or demonstratively ignoring a person. Attachment development proceeds in a cyclical (nonlinear) way. After an apparent linear progression, when attachment between individuals seems to be in a process of forming, the attachment experience is particularly vulnerable to any variation in the relationship (Maccoby & Masters, 1970).

At such points, attachment behaviors are not only more pronounced, but also strong indicators of fear that the attachment will be interrupted. For child care, this means that the relationship between worker and the child or youth becomes even more sensitive and important *after* the young person has been with the worker for some time and at a point when things seem to be "going so well between them" (Rodriguez & Hignett, 1981). It is at this point that a youngster may place "unusual" demands on the caregiver and act as if trust is absent. Relationship formation cannot be gauged on a timetable basis nor can availability be scheduled in a linear way. Much staff time and energy needs to be available for cyclic and spontaneous "renewing."

For residential programming, these observations may require revamping institutional policies and training residential workers in such a way that attachment-seeking behaviors can more easily be dealt with for what they are: a desperate striving for more human contact and closeness. Child care work could then focus upon enriching children's attachment experiences rather than merely struggling with their attachment behaviors (Maier, 1981, pp. 32-34; Rutter, 1979).

## GROUPING RESIDENTS DEVELOPMENTALLY

The stress upon developmental progression might appear to suggest that it is advisable to group children according to developmental readiness rather than by age. On the contrary, if we are thinking in a nonlinear way, then programming cannot rest upon any one fixed index of a youngster's development. We know from experience, for instance, that some children temporarily need to live as if they were much younger — in fact, they may demonstrate this need by preferring the company of much younger children. The progress of others in the unit would be hampered if the unit's programming were fully adapted to that younger level. We also need to remain mindful of the fact that some children tend to progress more readily when their learning is modeled and supported by highly respected peers who are at a slightly more advanced level of development (Elkind & Weiner, 1978).

Research findings, it is useful to point out, indicate that stronger and more capable children are apt to be able to get more attention on their own. Programming of all kinds tends to be adjusted to meet their interests and requirements, while those who are less able to influence their surroundings tend to be controlled and ignored (Rutter, 1981). We need to keep this in mind so that we continuously reappraise and restructure activities on the unit to involve all children regardless of their current development stages and tasks. When children's ongoing capabilities present a strong divergence between developmental and chronological age, then it becomes of particular importance to reconstitute programming within a *normalization* perspective (Horejsi, 1979; Maier, 1981, pp. 52-54).

## CONSISTENCY AND THE PROVISION OF CARE

Consistency in child care is advocated in all child psychologies. Choices occur in the conception of what constitutes consistency, however, and how consistency is achieved. Do we mean consistency in values, in affect, or in behaviors of the caregivers? Do such expectations apply to both caregivers and care receivers? Or does consistency apply, as advocated here, to the child's experience of predictability based on the efficacy of his or her own actions? This latter conception shifts the emphasis from behaviors and values to focus on the child's perceptions of behaviors and their meanings. In other words, consistency is most useful when viewed from the child's frame of reference. Thus, consistency means a predictable environment in terms of the child's capacity to assess it. A residential setting provides a consistent environment when residents can predict the outcome of their actions. For them, the conception of the situation as consistent depends upon a meshing, a congruence in the definition of events and in expectations between the staff members and young people involved (Division of Youth, 1978).[4]

### Consistency Applied to Child Care Practices

Children view their workers as consistent when, for example, bedtime is specified within the youngsters' own time framework. For young children, this may be "after snacks" or "when the big hand of the clock is at" . . . , etc. For developmentally older, school-age children, "consistent" bedtime may be dictated by rules that have been discussed by the workers and the youngsters. For adolescents, consistency is experienced through the workers' capacity to be flexible to meet the demands of each situation rather than through adherence to a fixed schedule. A ten o'clock bedtime might not, for example, be perceived as consistent if applied equally on a school night, on the night before vacation, and when other contextual variables make the established bedtime a difficult factor.

If we were to study current residential care practices, adaptability to the demands of the situation seems likely to be a more common practice than consistent adherence to schedules. That is, when workers are busy, when tempers are high, or when youngsters are happily engaged in activities, established bedtimes may frequently be superceded; a similar situation applies in most spheres of life in group care and in the world outside. Irregularity of the rules might be questioned by youngsters in any of these situations. However, their appreciation of their workers as predictable and dependable persons will be directly related to their workers' readiness to disregard a legalistic interpretation of consistency and follow developmental and contextual demands instead. Thus, it is suggested here that effective child and youth care work requires consistency that is in keeping with a child's developmental understanding and individual requirements rather than through steadfast, generalized rules.

## DEVELOPMENTAL PROGRAMMING

### For School-Age Children[5]

School-age children are at a developmental stage where they push forth simultaneously on three fronts: personal competence development, the development of close peer associations, and the development of encounters with the outside world, including business, transportation, entertainment, the arts, sports, youth movements, and of course, education, as well as others.

### Competence Development

For program planning on a developmental basis, it is important to create continuous opportunities for *doing*, both individually and with others. Children at this stage require support, time, space, and equipment for developing body coordination such as running, dancing, throwing, and tumbling. They are also ready to expand their knowledge in all directions. Learning through experimentation is important at this point and should take place in such developmentally appropriate spaces as workshops, laboratories, gyms or backstage. Less appropriate to their developmental requirements are study halls and formal settings.

Most important in care work, the children's concerns and energies tend to be vested in proving their competence to themselves and to others. They are bent on doing better than before. We may mistakenly interpret competitiveness of this period as the child's negation of others (White, 1972), but it actually represents a desire to improve and stretch one's self. Workers' sensitivity to this personal striving can help to create new avenues for planning and pursuing play, study, and work situations that are developmentally appropriate and that allow children to *experience* their improvement.

*Close Peer Association*

   Also of concern to children in this period in their development is the building of peer associations so as to deepen their social worlds. Peer relationships and interests fluctuate at this point, creating a curious dilemma in group care. Residential mates (as with siblings in a family) are not necessarily the ones whom a child considers to be peers or playmates. Frequently, the familiarity and self-protection inherent in intense group living make it difficult for residential peers to become personal pals. Contacts with peers beyond the residential living group become a necessity. Daily interactions between children, whether in the group living unit or outside of it — hassling, testing, building "brawn," skill and bravado, uniting, separating, clustering, or isolating may be crucial to a child's development, even though the manifestation of these activities may not always be in harmony with the orderly life of a unit.

   Children not only need love and care, but they also want and need to be responsible for others, to learn to love and to care (Kobak, 1979; Maas, 1980). Such learning appears earlier in development as well, but it is confirmed socially at this stage when the child is no longer limited to the home base. Consequently, expanding friendships away from the living group and greater generosity and helpfulness towards others outside the "family" are natural indications of growing up rather than evidence of a child's lack of appreciation or loyalty for the "home front." Residential workers, as well as parents, need to remind themselves that a "helping hand" is usually first fully exercised away from home. (Charity actually begins *away* from home.)

   Care workers with this age group are challenged to pursue a dual course: to be a child's own special worker and, simultaneously, to be the children's group leader. While this dual task may appear to be overwhelming, it can also offer a rich and potent program resource. In fact, these dual responsibilities can be well integrated within a developmental perspective, where an individual's gains and adaptations are always envisaged within a social context. In group care, a child's requirements need to be met within the context of the group; conversely, a group can progress only as the members flourish within it.

   Ordering, organizing, and establishing rules that can be generalized are of great concern to children in this developmental period (Piaget, 1951). Much of their interest in setting up collections or charts of one form or the other, their play, and their conversations with one another involve the dynamics of sorting, ordering, and organizing their collections, interactions, or ideas into hierarchical wholes. Their interest in such complicated games as: "Dungeons and Dragons" and in charting the progression of favorite athletic teams and players, or of friends within friendship cliques, are illustrative of these trends. Thus, many of the peer interactions of school-age children involve elaborations of rules and procedures. They seem to need to experiment with rules, and require many opportunities to try them out, and to work continuously on interpersonal dilemmas. Thus, much of a care worker's efforts may go into finding an elusive fit between predictable and extraordinary ways of doing things.

## Encounters With the Outside World

Children of school age are also in transition developmentally, between managing in their primary systems (home or residential unit and primary school) and being able to find their way within secondary systems (businesses, recreation, and entertainment, transportation, secondary school, and other community systems). They are absorbed in mastering new situations and environments, "entering the world." Caregivers are challenged to become involved and show interest in a child's secondary systems (Garbarino, 1982; Garbarino & Stocking, 1980).

It is also essential for school-age residents to have full individual experiences in shopping, traveling, and in experiencing other places beyond the residential confines. Encouraging children and actively participating with them in such branching out endeavors should be viewed as part of the caregivers' regular work. Research suggests that a child's comfort in the use of secondary settings is severely diminished when these settings are not shared with his or her caregiver (Inbar, 1976). We need to be mindful of the fact that the quality of care in residential work is enhanced, therefore, when a child experiences a worker's concerns and care in a variety of settings — at the residence, in the park, at school, downtown, and in other settings (Garbarino, 1982). It appears that the ultimate impact of such shared experience remains with the child after he or she leaves the group care setting.

The life of the school-age child has thus far been pictured as primarily a life of activities and events. True. However, the worker-child relationship continues to be most important. When hungry or tired, in moments of crisis or boredom, when happy or distressed, children, like Lassie on TV, will consistently return to the care of "home." Even if it appears that children have little use for their caregivers, when they hurriedly dash off after a meal or abruptly end a conversation, they *do* want and need their caregivers to be at hand. Workers must be provided with enough institutionally acknowledged time so that they can be part of children's lives in ways that extend beyond residential boundaries (Garbarino & Stocking, 1980).

### With Adolescents

*Time, Space, and Structure for Searching and Questioning*

Development can be characterized as a progression of doing more with more people — doing more with more people in more places — and doing more with more people in more places at more varied times. This *expanding progression* certainly holds true for adolescent development. Many experienced youth workers may wisely add that, for adolescents, the "doing more" often leads to a kind of bottomless pit, as if there were no end to their requests, wishes, and at times, their involvements in manifold activities. Actually, there is an end, because everyday events will never fully allow these plans and wishes.

Programming developmentally *with* youth presents a strange paradox: adolescents want a life full of happenings, yet planning and preparing "is such a drag!" The worker must constantly decide whether to program (to plan for them and to be prepared) or not to program (to let things happen and let the consequences be a learning experience). An additional struggle is who should carry out the major responsibilities for activities. Formal or informal deliberations at this stage often end up as discussion about whether or not to talk, whether or not to plan, and whether or not certain people ought to "mind their own business!" Such "discussion" is developmentally on target for this group, even if the planning leads no further than a preliminary "let's think about it." In the youngsters' preadolescent years, similar tumultuous planning sessions centered around the establishment of rules and procedures for getting things done, but for adolescents the central issue is the discovery and the exploration of alternatives. The apparent negativism, the ridiculing, and the preoccupation with what *not* to do, are also adolescents' constructive efforts at developing new boundaries and directions for themselves. Caustic inquiries and sarcasm are less an evaluation of the world around them than an indication of their uneasiness about their place in it. Because they feel some discomfort in this world, a place created and delegated as their own is a basic requirement of this age group.

We note also that adolescent residents in particular need the freedom, support, and materials to create private spaces in bedrooms (Maier, 1981, pp. 42-45; 1982a). Youth care workers can convey an active interest in adolescents by noticing their ways of decorating their private space. A sense of "rootedness" is also experienced by residents when they are involved in the management, daily procedures, outfitting, and decorating of their unit. Life beyond the residence becomes equally important in establishing a sense of "rootedness." The world of adolescents also includes school, shopping, community, and special activities such as sports or popular music. A worker will often need to help teen residents to expand their experiences in these spheres.

Youth workers need time to be involved in much discussion and attentive listening in order to understand adolescents' thoughts and questions and to engage with them in a search for solutions. "Rapping" helps the adolescents develop and provides a major avenue for them to test and build peer relations. They consequently require ample time, space, and sanction for sporadic rapping, sometimes with and sometimes without adult involvement. Rapping, we know well, proceeds more readily when the participants are comfortable, sustained with nibblies, and able to interact informally. We also need to remember that sharing a youngster's account of events in school or listening to a new record can be at least as urgent and significant as a care worker's managerial tasks or as completing reports.

The outside world can be partially brought into the unit by posters, catalogues, visitors, TV viewing, and verbal accounts. Outside experiences, moreover, require continuous rehearsals within the unit. Practicing dancing steps, discussing potential purchases, conversations about dates, appointments with a principal or prospective employer—these are all outside experiences that may require rehearsing in the safe "harbor" of the unit. Rehearsals may be verbal or through some form of role playing. Much of a caregiver's energies need to be invested in rehearsing with adolescents a variety of life experiences that are apt to be encountered away from unit supervision. Thoughts, feelings, moral values, and various behaviors all need to weighed and practiced.

Additionally, caregivers need to bring some of their personal experiences to work to share with adolescents. Such sharing is important because adolescents need to experience an adult as a whole person. Such sharing also brings added experience repertoires onto the unit and serves to provide bridges between adolescent and adult worlds and between the work outside and that of the residential unit.

## Personal Relationship Encounters

A second guiding principle in programming developmentally with adolescents is to provide an arena for helping them with primary relationship skills (Maier, 1965). Group life serves as a rich laboratory for helping adolescents establish effective relationships, deal with conflict, and survive disagreeable interpersonal situations. A conflict over who sits where, or the realization that several group members "cannot stand each other," may cause institutional tension, but such situations can serve as opportunities for learning how to deal with such problems in the future. Good programming means spontaneously exploiting the developmental features of ongoing group life situations. Spontaneity in care is "one of the most 'therapeutic' characteristics of residential 'care'" (Carlebach, 1983, p. 8).

An important life experience for adolescents is to be able to accomplish tasks through their own labor and to be able to see visibly their contributions to others. Tasks within the residential unit can provide such opportunities, as long as they are special tasks, tailored to the youth's own level of readiness, rather than routine daily chores. Attending to a long awaited repair or improvement in the unit, raising vegetables, or taking care of a pet or special unit machinery are examples of challenging work opportunities. Moreover, effective programming also requires attention to the inclusion of work opportunities outside of the residence. Gardening jobs, shopping, newspaper delivery, babysitting, dog-walking, or other odd jobs in the neighborhood are a few possibilities. Volunteer work in form of giving a hand to the physically disabled at a senior citizen center or in work and play with younger children also reflect the important ingredient of "giving to others." Work or volunteer service tasks are to be envisaged as developmental opportunities when young people are ready to progress in that direction, rather than purely as rewards for developmental achievements.

Adolescents' interactions with their direct care workers, as do those of younger children, involve struggles about dependency/independency and authority issues. The challenge for the care worker is to present himself or herself in different roles and to provide youths with a variety of interpersonal encounters so that worker and youth relate differentially: sometimes as a pal, sometimes as a partner in mutual undertakings, most of the time, however, as the guiding committed elder.

Growing into new relationship systems and augmenting old ones take place not only on the unit, but in the adolescents' relationships with their families as well. These changes require more than periodic contacts by mail, phone, or occasional get-togethers.[6] Regular contacts and involvements with youths' families and other important adults and peers from home as needed so as to draw them into residents' daily lives. Residential care should be conceived as an extension rather than a replacement of the family.[7]

Family members or friends from "back home" may be asked to join in for meals, work parties, recreational activities, and serious deliberations. These involvements not only help families stay in touch, but provide opportunities for relationship patterns to change over time. Most relevant is the fact that adolescents tend to evaluate events and people through the eyes of peers. The discovery of parents as ordinary, struggling human beings (and for a parent to see one's child as not too different from others) can occur more easily through observation. A joint outing, a residential "all-fun evening," a picnic, a painting, or fix-up work party can provide growth ("therapeutic") experience.

In summary, adolescent development occurs through a variety of intimate and communal experiences, through regular life encounters, and through continuous exposure to new life situations. Adolescents learn a particular culture and the awareness of other cultures and basic values only from those people with whom they have vital interactions and meaningful relationships (Washington, 1982, p. 105).

## CLOSING COMMENTS

This chapter poses a challenge for child and youth care workers, in many ways the same challenge faced by every parent, grandparent, foster parent, and babysitter. Children's issues are the same regardless of where the child resides. For children and youth in socially engineered, non-familial settings, child and youth care workers provide life's essentials and more. They are the ones who are always available until children don't need them any more. Workers are keenly aware, as well as uncertain, of how important they are in the children's growing-up struggles and always must work toward the bittersweet eventuality of letting them move on, while starting anew with "fresh" arrivals (adapted from Furman, 1982, p. 16).

Child care workers are pivotal in non-familial care. Yet, their roles as societal caregivers remain essentially unrecognized. Ultimately, it will be necessary to provide for them the same societal recognition that has been granted to other complex professionals involved with human health and safety, such as air traffic controllers and surgeons. Child and youth care workers require full societal and organizational support through well circumscribed on-duty hours and an income which can assure them a reasonable personal life. Moreover, experience suggests that child and youth care workers themselves must actively pursue these essentials, thus modeling the kind of personal and group development and interpersonal competence required to enhance the lives of the young people in their care. Only then can they fully invest their energies in serving the developmental demands of those children and youth for whom society has given them such major responsibilities.

## NOTES

1. Street gang work by social group workers and other services workers has been effectively utilized in helping adolescents and youths in finding more purposeful adventures (Spergel, 1971). The perspective suggested here was once defined as "marginal or life space interviews" (Long, Stoeffler et al., 1972; Wineman, 1959).

2. Success or lack of success was evaluated longitudinally compared with that of siblings who faced the same transitions at a different point of their development (Inbar & Adler, 1977).

3. The same factors apply in assisting individuals at moments of crises. The requirements for bodily comfort vary considerably for children, adolescents, and for adults, but regardless of age, beginnings are fundamentally body experiences.

The opposite is also true. The message that persons are *not* welcome is quickly conveyed by denying comfort to persons' bodies through denial of seating opportunities, crowding, and obliteration of private space. Police stations, prisons, and some of the welfare service waiting rooms in the U.S. are cases in point.

4. It is noteworthy to add here the findings of a recent Oregon study where residents in a Secure Treatment Center found to be most receptive and compliant to a consistently *managed* program tended to end up more frequently in the "failure" group, while the ones with more

demanding behavior, if they found staff members who were responsive to their provocations, ended up more frequently in the "success" group (Benning, 1981).

5. A section on programming for pre-school age or developmentally akin children is purposely omitted as the subject is well covered in the literature of day care, nursery school work, literature on kibbutzim, and on residential treatment of severely disturbed as well as autistic children.

6. We use purposely the term *get-together* in place of "visits" at home or parental visits at the residence (or school) as it is misleading to speak of a child's "visit" home or to a parent, or family "visiting" his or her child.

7. A similar approach and activities are also applicable in work with younger children.

Chapter II

# Essential Components
# in Care and Treatment
# Environments for Children

## I. A QUICK GLIMPSE AT LIFE IN A RESIDENTIAL
## CARE AND TREATMENT SETTING

"John and I are going out to kick the ball."

"Good idea! In a while I'll try to come out too and get in a few kicks. I need a whiff of fresh air too. Have fun," responded their care worker, Sheila Thomas. She was pleased over her brief conversation with Chris and John. She thought to herself: "I did it! I was able to allow them to leave with a feeling of my interest in their doings and I managed to omit my usual admonishments about staying out of trouble and wandering away. Still, John and Chris will know that I will be nearby."

Sheila Thomas, the 35-year-old child care worker of this unit, was jarred out of her reflective mood when she noticed that Matt, in explosive anger, was moving his possessions out of his room. She quickly learned that Matt was at odds with his rommmate, Al, whose possessions were mixed up with Matt's. "If only each child could have his own personal closet space," thought Sheila. She returned with Matt to their room. She wanted to be certain that she dealt with both of them as she struggled over their differences. The worker felt sure that Matt's outburst was a mere spark of a more persevering rage festering in him and possibly in Al as well. She

This article originally appeared in Ainsworth, F. and Fulcher, L. C. (Eds.). (1981). *Group Care for Children: Concepts and Issues*. London: Tavistock. Reprinted by permission of Tavistock Publications.

thought: "If I could deal solely with Matt, he could be quickly appeased. And it would be so much easier. But neither one of us would then confront his continuous tensions. I also know that I can't fully resolve their difficulties in sharing, but for children at this age I can work on it."

Sheila Thomas called to the boys outside that she saw they had quite a ball game going; she still hoped to go out later. She also commented on the good play space they had chosen. Sheila congratulated herself for the fact that she managed to point out to Chris and John what they can do rather than a negative message such as "Keep away from the rose bushes!"

Sheila took a deep breath and moved on into the troubled den, fully aware than an on-the-spot counseling session would unearth more trouble than Matt's immediate complaint suggested.[1] It was also her chance to be an effective care worker rather than a busy guardian. The session was a hot one. It took all her energy to avoid quick solutions. Sheila's counseling session was unlike the ones by social workers or other counseling professionals, where all other activities are assumed to be suspended while client and counselor closet themselves away as if their worlds were confined solely to the interviewing room. On the contrary, life for all three—Matt, Al, and Sheila—goes on. They could hear the television blasting away from the living/dining room. "Is the television really too loud? Or is the issue instead that there's actually no suitable space for television viewing as long as it has to compete with the continuous clatter of table tennis on the adjacent sun porch? Maybe I should have the courage to fold up the table tennis. Its racket adds more din and confusion than it contributes to the boys' relaxation. We should be able to find a better source for group play and recreation."

It was hard for Sheila to concentrate on Al's and Matt's dilemma with life vibrating beyond the interview situation throughout the living unit. Yet, she also knew that to deal with problems as they occurred amidst the flow of life was more realistic and opened up avenues to the counseling process as well as enriching their lives immediately. She sat down with the boys and openly empathized with Al and Matt for their uneasiness over living away from home and for having to mingle with so many new faces. Nevertheless, that was the way it was; they had to be at the residential center. She explored with them how together they could make an undesirable situation more bearable. All three would struggle over the boys' desire to be home and the subsequent anguish of recognizing that their return would not materialize for some time.

Their deliberation was interrupted by severe shouts from the direction of the unit's kitchen.

"Your mother!"

"Your mother, yourself!"

"Your mother loves the bottle more than you!"

A vehement but tearful retort: "My mother'll take me home as soon as she finds a job. You'll see!"

Sheila knew that she could only deal with one situation at a time. Most important in her work was the challenge to handle a single situation fully rather than try to respond superficially to all eruptions. Her thoughts momentarily wandered away: "Lucky therapists who can deal with one problem at a time in their insulated interview rooms."

Sheila beamed as if a lightbulb had gone on. "I am better off here. I can make strides to lessen the boys' unhappiness. There seems to be something in common in the struggles of the kids in this unit and that in itself helps me understand what needs to be done as life goes on." Turning to Matt and Al she helped these two to explore the confusions and quandaries about their respective home situations. They did seem to be facing many uncertainties and much ambiguous information. Sheila began to respond with greater certainty herself. She could assure them that she or their social worker would try to obtain clear answers as to whether they could count on a visit home soon. She also inquired as to what were the most important questions for them. While she promised action, she also empathized with their sense of hurt and unhappiness for having to live in an institution. She then explored with them what they could do right then in order to ease their immediate life situation. Sheila expected them to continue to be roommates. She voiced her concern over Al's difficulties in getting along with others and Matt's short "fuse."

Matt and Al were helped by Sheila with immediate behavioral tasks which each one could manage. Sheila likewise learned what she could do to make unit life more bearable for them. Her focus was upon becoming more adequate rather than avoiding or mitigating more difficulties. Sheila decided to remember: "Progress also means new troubles. When they'll be ready to play with the others, then their limited social skills and awkward body coordination will

require renewed help in getting themselves included in group play."
She smiled to herself: "I can just imagine that some day I will wish
we were back to the days when I had only to deal with individual
temper tantrums."

By this time all unit residents had returned from school. There
was neither time for the worker to reflect on her session with these
two lonesome roommates nor to have a respite for a cup of tea. She
was well aware that each child required her special care. Even if a
child in her unit actually presented no difficulties, it still would be a
time for child care intervention. Sheila had learned that such a resident may either have adapted too conveniently to institutional life
and require urgent assistance with his or her developmental progress
or the child might need an advocate on approaching his or her return
to regular family life.

At this point the worker was certain that each of the unit's ten
preadolescent boys were all troubled children; they required residential care. Sheila made sure that she had individual contacts and
brief chats with each about their particular concerns or interests. It
was not easy for her to focus upon their concerns. Her head was
buzzing with messages, reminders, and tasks she must relay to
them. It was very tempting to tell each what he had to do, just to get
these concerns off her chest. She was proud that she managed to
hold back new demands plus her disappointments over the boys'
unfinished jobs. She wanted to be sure to welcome each boy as an
individual person of the group rather than as a resident of a joint
household. The reminders must wait until a time when re-entry into
an unwanted place had been achieved and some of the strain of a
day in school had worn off. (Snacks and a period of loafing with
few behavioral demands are instrumental for a successful re-entry
phase—Maier, 1979, pp. 162-64.)

The child care worker's concerns for the children in her unit were
interlaced with communication among fellow staff members. Sheila
had to be sure to brief Tom Smith, the other worker for the afternoon and evening shift. She felt that in the past two hours she had
put in a full day's work; yet more than half of her eight-hour working time was still ahead. One of the hardest tasks had to be tackled.
She had to list to Tom all the unfinished tasks without becoming
defensive, appearing inadequate, or blaming the kids. At the same
time it was good to know that there was another adult to share the
load. But as she knew too well, another adult also meant more de-

mands by the children and a heightening of rivalry for each worker's time and good will.

As the phone rang again (easily the seventh call since lunch), Sheila's secret response was: "Let Tom answer it." She then noticed Tom fully engaged in fixing a boy's flashlight. Simultaneously, other youngsters shared with him their latest jokes. She was pleased to witness the happy bantering; she was also annoyed that she had to jump in again as the unit's phone-answering service. "Tom should do some of the work here!"

A call from the main office; the dentist in town has an unexpected open hour. He could see Clyde for his emergency appointment.

> Clyde can go on his own. He knows the way to the dentist's office. Shall I give him the bus fare or shall I go with him? It would give us some private time together. He'll have some painful work done. I know he is scared. To call on one of the volunteers wouldn't quite be the same. If I were to go with him I would be with him at a time he needs somebody nearby. It would be quite different from the times I tend to "stand over" him so that he gets on with the tasks at hand. We could also work in some shopping errands; an experience he needs and tasks I have to do anyhow.

An essential decision has to be made by Sheila. Even if Clyde is capable of going on his own, the worker knows that Clyde will develop more adequately if he has additional caring experiences built into his immediate self-management. Clyde can handle many tasks within the confines of institutional management. At the same time he is trying too hard to manage on his own. He lacks the common experience of turning for support when support is needed. He also has not had opportunities for casual shopping ventures. Sheila's decision to have Clyde go or not on his own is no longer a managerial choice; it has turned into a clinical decision.

In the foregoing pages we have witnessed life on the forefront. We gained a glimpse of a typical afternoon hour at a residential care unit where the child care worker had not a second to spare nor an inch to waste.

Child care, coupled with spatial arrangements, crises handling amidst regular program activities, life events within the center, and life beyond its walls, all these factors make up the residential service provided to children and youth in care. The nature of the care offered to these children shapes their lives, and the children in turn shape the actual mode of care provided. Moreover, this mutually intertwined caring experience is not merely determined by the interactions between care givers and care receivers. Of equal impact is their physical setting, the material goods at their disposal, and above all, the external forces and institutions which support and negate their efforts. These outside systems, whether they are the child welfare agencies and communal institutions, the neighborhood and wider community, or the laws and society's conceptions of children's developmental requirements, all serve as salient partners in child care work. These systems define the grand design, the contemporary world scene in which we grow and live.

The subsequent pages of this chapter will cover in detail the very intricate interplay of care giving and care receiving within the context of group settings. The issues before the reader will be covered under the following four major subheadings: (1) the personal ingredients of care giving and care receiving, (2) care giving and care receiving functioning in the physical environment, (3) group living as an everyday life experience, (4) residential life as a prelude to and extension of a child's home and community life.

## II.  CARE GIVING AND CARE RECEIVING AS A SYMPHONY OF HUMAN INTERACTIONS

### What Constitutes Caring?

*Care* is a very personal experience for both the care giver and the cared-for person. Each needs the other. Each, within the process of caring, becomes more firmly attached and paradoxically takes on a greater range of freedom from the other (Maier, 1982b). For instance, a child care worker's efforts in helping Ray, a 9-year old, to ward off the experience of being teased by the other children in group care, brings this child and his worker closer together. In this example the worker does not express pity to Ray for feeling severely hurt over his peers' teasing. Instead, the worker introduces a new game to Ray and two other boys standing nearby. She invites them to play a game of "So What?" with her. This worker had just invented the game on the spur of the moment. In this spontaneous game, each one, including the worker, takes alternately the role of teaser and teased. The worker tries to set up a number of playful situations in which she lures each one into participating. While being teased in varying degrees, the teased-one must maintain his "cool" and remain able to respond matter-of-factly with "So what?" As Ray experiences the fun of becoming engaged with the peers of his unit, he practices a more effective behavioral response and discovers in his child care worker a person who is interested in him. (Behavior rehearsals as an interventive method will be more fully taken up in Section IV of this chapter.) Ray experiences closeness to this caring adult and a new closeness to his peers. We note that while this worker consciously refused to curtail the teasing, the mutual playful activity supported Ray.

Curiously, the very feeling of the worker's concern enables Ray to risk more and subsequently to leave the worker and the unit to join the outdoor activities. The worker, in turn, needs special opportunities for becoming close and enmeshed in a child's ongoing life situation in order to be able to enact her genuine care.[2] This particular child care worker is able to validate her role and feel in the groove of *doing* child care work. With her closeness to Ray achieved, the worker also has found an added sense of freedom. She and Ray are perhaps ready to relate to each other on a more meaningful level and to delve into additional difficulties. They might now deal with the immediate object of the boys' teasing: Ray's personal problem of being called "diaper boy" and "night floater," reflecting that he wets his bed at the age of 9. Perhaps the worker can now retain Ray's cooperation in conquering his enuresis.

The foregoing incident, an ordinary daily occurrence in residential group life, is not meant to imply that a child care worker's single interventive step can bring about a scenario of successful treatment events. Rather, the example is cited here as an illustration that the minutiae of everyday child care work provide the backbone for change. In the critical incident just cited, the worker might have been very tempted to remind Ray that if he were to stop wetting his bed the teasing would subside—a very logical position, but unsound for Ray's emotional needs.[3] Psychologically, Ray would have temporarily felt even more deserted by the very resource he sought for help. He would have experienced an act of detachment at a moment when he reached out and needed anchorage. We note that the worker skillfully assisted Ray in overcoming some of his personal hurt and isolation while she helped him enhance his personal skills. Little time and energy was allocated to Ray for telling his woes to a

sympathetic listener. Instead the worker entered the scene respon-
sively, assuming responsibility in assisting Ray to move beyond the
present dilemma. He gained ground in handling conflict without
falling prey to others' taunting (a sport typical of this age). As a
group care worker the challenge remains to help the children with
their effectiveness in meeting daily interpersonal crises rather than
to try to avoid or to abolish conflicts. In fact, asking Ray's peers to
halt their teasing would mean to ask them to disengage from Ray.
The worker's role is to increase the mutual interaction of the group
members as well as to include an effective caring concern and a
possible program for Ray's efforts to manage a dry bed.

In the preceding case illustration the child and worker became a
bit clearer about respective tasks at hand. Simultaneously, they became more attached to each other. Each one needs the other for his
or her own competency development and verification: Ray, in the
process of relating to peers in conflict situations, and the worker in
the process of effective group care. Caring involves a process of
being responsive *to* and responsible *for* someone (Wrenn, 1972). It
is the activity of being *responsible for* others which differentiates
the caring activities of group workers from other caring persons
(neighbors, friends, teachers, etc.). It is the worker's role to be a
change agent and to impact the children's personal development.
The quality of care is not so much a singular question of how the
workers feel about the children as it is how they translate their care
into actions. What they actually *do* signifies the care they manifest
as this is enacted in their role as care specialists.

### Gauging Temperament

Differences in temperament have become more clearly understood through recent studies in early infant care. Time spent in caring for young infants is viewed as a constant give-and-take between
the infant and her or his care giver. In infant tending we witness a
blending of the baby's temperament and the care giver's particular
disposition at the moment. Infant and care giver jointly find their
mutual fit (Lewis & Rosenblum, 1974; Schaffer, 1977). The same
holds true for older children and their care givers. In fact, this give-
and-take process for tuning in and locating a joint rhythm occurs in
the attachment formation in all ages of life (Maier, 1982b). This
process of tuning in and finding common strands of attachments is
one of the essential features of child care work with all age groups.

Let us start out with an illustrative example. The child care worker Harriet Costigan was having dinner with her table of eight pre-adolescent girls. Early in the course of the meal she nodded to a child across from her to convey concern. Almost simultaneously Harriet moved out of reach all items but fork and plate for Meg, the child on her immediate left. She quickly put the fork in the hand of Meg who had reverted to finger feeding. A girl at the other end of the table had also begun eating with her hands. Harriet noticed it but let it go. She knew that this particular girl was temperamentally a slow-paced but bright youngster who essentially related visually to others. The child's continuous surveillance kept her well appraised of what was going on; however, only strong stimulation would prompt her to act. In contrast, Meg was prone to react to the slightest stimulation with heightened activity. Harriet was wise to remove extraneous items at the moment, lest Meg be sidetracked from eating. Her worker also knew that for this child the fingering of food was not only poor manners, it would also spontaneously escalate to squashing food and eventually to throwing it.

We can better understand the differential handling described above, if we examine recent findings suggesting that persons are born with and are apt to maintain a particular temperament. Different temperaments require different handling. In early infancy, variations in babies' temperaments cause care givers to respond discriminately toward them (Thomas, Chess & Birch, 1968; Escalona, 1968). Follow-up longitudinal research further brings out that specific temperaments persist at least through the childhood years and may even continue throughout a person's life (Thomas & Chess, 1977).

Our personal experiences as well as observations of friends may help us verify that differences in temperament are clearly evident in the way adults participate at social gatherings. Some adults quickly find themselves in the midst of the group, aggressively meeting others. Some conceive of themselves as full participants in the gathering while remaining at a distance, physically removed but visually keenly engaged in the ongoing events. To expand further, in the past ten years we have learned from research on young children's modes of interaction that although there are no classifications of temperament, there is a vast spectrum of temperamental expressiveness. On the one end are children (and possibly adults) who tend to soak up with their senses what is going on around them as if they were *"living radars."* At first impression they appear to be very placid and inactive individuals. However, on further examination they reveal themselves to be active stimulus-scanners. Their eyes are continuously on the go. Their style of relating to the world around them is predominantly visual; they prefer to be a little apart from the events in which they are engaged.

In contrast, individuals on the other end of this temperament spectrum initiate and seem to thrive on continuous physical contact and bodily experience. These bodily active children (or adults) tend to find continuous stimulation in happenings and encounters within their immediate life space. One environmental interaction leads to another. The smallest variation or new stimuli is noted and responded to. These stimulus-impacted youngsters seem to be in perpetual motion and can well be described as the *"go-go children."*

Findings from the research of both Thomas, Chess and Birch as well as Escalona can be readily applied to the group care scene (Thomas, Chess & Birch, 1964 and 1968; Thomas & Chess, 1977; Escalona, 1968. Also see Segal & Yahraes, 1978, p. 41-51; Cameron, 1978; Schaffer & Emerson, 1964 and Schaffer, 1977).

We learn from these studies that more bodily active infants, the "go-go children," immediately engage themselves with whatever is within reach. For them each stimulus becomes a call for action. It is not surprising that their care givers, primarily their parents, spontaneously tended in these studies to channel and limit stimuli input. For example, while feeding a baby, the parent was apt to protectively cover the child's hands. In the crib it was common to present them with only one or two toys to avoid overstimulation. While bathing the baby the parent avoided splashing lest the infant start a tidal wave!

By contrast, the infants we have described as "living radars" adopt a markedly different approach to life events. They take hold of their environment visually. They tend to scan thoroughly their surroundings while also relying upon other sensory (tactile and taste) input. Their actions are typified by focusing, getting hold by sight rather than grasp, using their finger tips rather than gross muscular movements to sense their environment. In turn, their care givers were decisively more apt to increase their stimulation within the field of action. The infants were splashed while bathing. They were cooed to and bodily bounced about. They were deluged with toys and other gadgets in their cribs to enhance the range of life experiences. Parents intensified stimuli input while also granting them a wider buffer zone.[4] In short, these parents had intuitively responded to their infants' major communication style.

What was the eventual outcome of these two groups of children? Differential handling for different kids but satisfactory outcomes for both! Almost all of these children, the "go-go" and "living radars" alike, developed into well balanced adults. This satisfactory development was probably enhanced by the care givers' intuitive handling, of accommodating to their infants' temperaments.

The descriptive accounts of these parents' interactions with their young children has relevance for work with older children living in group care settings. Imagine school age children in a group home setting coming into the dining area for their main meal. Some tend to come to the table as if playing a game of rugby. They reach for food while inquiring: "What's there to eat?" The natural adult response then might be to focus on one thing at a time: "Sit down!" "SIT!" "SIT DOWN!", accompanied by the worker's restraining movements. Simultaneously other children approach the table just as eagerly, perhaps slower in their movements while thoroughly surveying the table. They immediately spot things to their dislike and over distance voice their objections. The worker's reaction would be to ask them to sit down first, simultaneously calling attention to alternate attractions with pleasurable possibilities in order to widen these children's experiential scope (stimuli input).

For child care work the knowledge that children possess different temperaments and that these variations herald specific caring interactions can help us recognize the necessity for care givers and care receivers to mutually find their fit. Care workers have to allow themselves time for discerning a child's temperament. They have to observe and to experience both those children for whom personal involvement requires body contacts and reduction of stimulative input, and those children for whom personal closeness is expressed over distance and requires visual and other stimuli. In short, different strokes for different blokes. Most important, the institutional work settings have to assure the group care staff sufficient time so that managerial tasks do not compete with this kind of selective caring activity.

These recent findings make questionable some of our established emphasis upon standardizing expectations of behavior and consistent handling of the group of children in care. We have noted that similar treatment of children has a different relevance for each child. If children do vary in temperament, then they logically secure for themselves different life experiences from their care givers (Brazelton, 1977; Lewis & Rosenblum, 1974). Child care workers can tune in quite readily to their children's particular care requirements.

For child care workers to expect of themselves or be required by the program design "to be laterally consistent" is neither a natural nor a desirable objective. Contemporary child development.knowledge suggests that the focus in care has to be upon finding a proper enmeshment with the unique child and to proceed accordingly, seeking a mutual fit of that child and his or her care giver rather than trying to adhere to identical behavioral responses for all the children within one group.

## Rhythms of Care

At moments in which individuals find themselves fully in rhythm with one another — dancing, singing, hand clapping, in sexual activity, in a game of table tennis, in the rapid interplay of ideas in a rap session — these moments of rhythmic exchange provide an experience of close togetherness for the persons involved. Rhythmic activities seem to confirm the experience of repetition and continuity of repetition — and with it a sense of permanency and a promise of predictability (Maier, 1978b: pp. 36-43). The individual participating in rhythmic activity experiences a quality of mutual unity and interdependence (Brazelton, Koslowski, & Main, 1974; Lewis & Rosenblum, 1974; Maier, 1978b, 1979; Schaffer, 1977).

In early childhood much of the care givers' and infants' energy goes into a kind of "dance" where each one tries to fall in step with the other in a cyclical pattern (Hersh and Levin, 1978, p. 3). In this process of mutual inclusion, both search for a way to establish and to maintain a joint rhythm. Rhythmicity is moreover the hallmark of infant toys and activities. Rhythmic experiences, such as rattling a rattle, playing patty-cake, listening to lullabyes, or rocking jointly, bring infant and caring adult into a single frame of joint action. These experiences seem not to be limited to early child developmental periods but tend to be essential for effective interpersonal relationships throughout life. In a number of studies of this phenomenon, rhythmic interactions have been noted as the "molecules of human behavior" and basic to all human communications (Byers, 1972; Condon, 1975; Maier, 1979).

In group care individuals are brought together for varying time spans, where each seems to have his or her own rhythm without having been previously "tuned" to the others' style of life. Opportunities have to be created for these participants to discover common rhythms.

Frequently the children themselves create such moments – and occasionally to their caring adults' consternation. Sing-song slogans, for instance, are most contagious for their rhythmic patterns; they tend to be chanted far beyond the outsider's endurance, while the chanters themselves experience a deep sense of unity. It is not surprising in periods of tension that the single rhythmic banging of a spoon at mealtime, perhaps an accidental occurrence, is apt to be picked up in a flash by a whole group. It is the very search for belongingness which makes rhythmic unity such a desirable factor at moments of severe uneasiness in a residential unit. The same contagious ingredients may be observed in the rhythmic chanting or clapping at rallies – and even more so, in demonstrations.

Group care workers can make valid use of this knowledge of the power of rhythmicity. A worker may want to utilize rhythmic interactions as a means for becoming a more vital part of the unit by initiating such exchanges as tossing a ball, singing, dancing, or jam sessions, engaging in a modern "shake" (the exchange of several rhythmic alternate handclaps in place of the traditional handshake) or finding a common rhythm in speech, body movements or head nodding. At moments of tension, a familiar record with an inviting rhythm, the tossing around of a quickly exchanged beanbag or a slowly floating balloon can more readily lead to rhythmic togetherness and relaxation than a worker's well meant words of admonishment. In these moments of joint rhythmicity, participants have opportunity to experience a sense of unity and anchorage.

*Rituals* in many ways constitute an institutionalized form of psychological rhythmicity. Rituals represent a cultural confirmation of a repeated practice, while the participants experience a deep sense of togetherness. In group care, and for children and youth in general, rituals have particular significance as long as they are the children's rituals rather than adult ordained routines. Rituals, more likely than not, arise out of some spontaneously repeated practice. In one group care program, each child gave an old statue in the corner a pat or slap before getting ready for bed. This ritual represented an essential event for the children, eventually becoming just as important as the worker's nightly goodnight bidding or personal pat.[5]

Each institutional unit can probably list its own significant rituals. Examples cannot be cited here. Rituals have to emerge on their own and require the workers' full support as important events in their children's lives, even if they may appear rather ridiculous from the adult's perspective. Conversely, caretakers need to guard against perceiving as "rituals" such highly desirable routines as teethbrushing, waiting for everyone to be seated at mealtime, or other behavioral expectations of adults. These are routines and need to be dealt with as such for their practical necessity rather than for any remnant of sacredness pertaining to ritual. Routines serve to accomplish required tasks smoothly with minimal energy and time investment, to achieve temporary order for each person involved. Rather, rituals introduce procedures which prolong or delay the business at hand and enliven the activity, establishing it as an event of consequence close to the realm of sanctity.

### Dependency Has to "Taste" Good

"Stay here — so that I can do it myself," a 3-year old pleaded with his parent. What this young child sensed correctly is a factor of development easily overlooked by adults: close attachment initiates freedom (Maier, 1982b). Children in residential care particularly are plagued by uncertainty and are often hampered by a severe lack of dependency upon dependable care givers. Children in residential care, as children anywhere, require secure dependence upon reliable caring adults in order to develop into dependable adults themselves. A child is, as Alfred Adler has been credited with saying, both the artist and the painting. If children in group care settings could verbalize their psychological state as freely as the 3-year old above, they would be apt to call out: "I want to count on your being with me so that I can comfortably risk doing without you!" Dependency begets independence (Maier, 1986d).

In human development, as recent research findings clearly highlight, a support of dependency and a nurturing of attachment leads to greater readiness to branch out and proceed on one's own. This apparent contradiction can be witnessed in the developmental progression of toddlers. Early in toddlers' development they hold on tightly. The more assured of a stable support, the more ready are these young children to venture on their own. Or, later in life, the more persons are certain of support the more they are ready to risk and to proceed on their own (Sroufe, 1978).

Studies on dependency formation, moreover, reveal that children with highly responsive parents are the ones who are the least fretful. Children securely supported in their dependency strivings are the ones who ultimately achieve secure independence in the very behaviors in which they clamored for support. (In essence these are children who have been pampered!) Our previous fears of spoiling children and succoring a prolonged state of dependence may not be justified. In fact, children who tend to be so adamant to perform on their own, as well as children who tend to tyrannize their child care staff with suffocating attention-demands, are predominantly youngsters who have suffered from too little attention and meaningful attachments (Segal & Yahraes, 1978). Findings in the past ten years strongly suggest that a lack of dependency support creates greater havoc in a child's development than prolonged dependency itself (Ainsworth, 1972; Ainsworth, Bell & Stayton, 1974; Brunner, 1970; National Institute, 1968; Schaffer, 1977).

In our work with children in group care, dependency support and nurturance are fundamental ingredients of care. They are respectable companions to the conventional basic three: food, shelter and clothing. Children and adolescents in group care setting, often having had scattered experience with having dependency needs met, have yet to experience fully that *being able to depend upon dependence feels good*. Group care programs have to be structured in such a way that child care workers have time, know-how, and above all, immediate support for dependency nurturance.

Dependency support and attachment-fostering efforts are typified by such activities as a child care worker helping a child with bed-making or doing it for the child. The worker may rightly consider it important to do such a task for or with the child, recognizing that the child needs to feel important and wanted. Moreover, bed-making becomes valued as an essential ingredient for comfortable living, and eventually the child will be able to do it independently. The child care workers attending to these child care chores may appear to superiors, peers, etc. to be slaves to the children; they are not. In fact, these workers deserve to be specifically recognized for their involvement and investment in their children's lives (Mehler, 1979). What they are doing is not too different from the common engagement of having a cup of tea prepared and poured or a small errand attended to by a close friend. All these small acts of attention feel good and enriching, even when they could readily have been done by oneself. To feel accepted and to savor such an experience of being attended to is not only pleasant, it is also normal, adaptive, and basic for satisfactory development (Dupont, 1978; Maccoby & Masters, 1970; Sroufe, 1978). (One feels so much freer and less alone, and paradoxically, one can then do much more by oneself.)

Acts of nurturing support and opportunities for added worker-child enmeshment occur throughout the day, often occurring through minute worker-child interplay. They most frequently take place by means of actions rather than words — for instance the worker stopping what he or she is doing while a child is sharing some observation or complaint. Dependency supports also include extra (requested or not) squeezes, pats, or, roughing up a child. (One must, however, be certain that "roughing up" communicates unmistakenly for both child and worker: "I like to be with you and care for you.")

Verbal communication can also be utilized toward this end. Workers sharing with children that they thought of them during a separation, or a worker spontaneously expressing good feelings toward a child, communicates caring, of "being with" the child. For example, 15-year-old Carolyn leaves for school after three days of suspension for fighting, and her worker was heard to comment: "Carolyn, I'll take a deep breath around nine o'clock this morning, the time you return to your class. Let me know what happens and what you thought and felt. I am sure that you will have some tough moments. Tell me how you managed." This writer is sure that this kind of interaction and involvement in Carolyn's conflict-prone life has more promise than well meant but distancing remarks like: "Be good!" "Stay out of trouble!" Children, like human beings anywhere, need to experience that someone is fully with them even when they are alone. In Urie Bronfenbrenner's cogent words: "Every child needs at least one person who is really crazy about him (or her)" (Bronfenbrenner, 1977, p. 5).

### Attachment and Attachment Behavior

The preceding reference to attachment formation is based upon formulations in which a distinction is made between *attachment* and *attachment behaviors*.

Attachment denotes the affective bonding experience — the feeling of mutual dependence — known or felt by an individual but not necessarily behaviorally expressed. Attachment specifies an experience of interpersonal intimacy and closeness where support has the promise of reaching beyond the present. In a sense, attachment formation is another way of conceptualizing what is generally called: "developing a relationship." Attachment emerges when a relationship moves beyond a beginning phase. It is a common event in early child development during the second half of a baby's first year. It is then, at this particular point of development, that stable hierarchies of preferences (attachment) develop. It is also the time when a good deal of trouble starts, such as the child's preference for one parent over the other, or demands for a parent's presence over a previously acceptable babysitter. These manifestations are promising signals that the individual is well on the way in his or her maturing process. These child developmental incidents are matched by similar occurrences in the selective attachments to different workers by the children in group care settings and by evidence of fluctuating feelings as work shifts change or substitute care workers are introduced. Attachments occur and are needed at any point in a person's life (Bowlby, 1969; Bronfenbrenner, 1976; Sroufe & Waters, 1977). After all, one of the signs of maturity is to have the capacity to choose on whom one will depend and to maintain such an attachment over time.[6]

*Attachment behaviors*, as the words already imply, represent efforts of striving towards attachment but in no way constitute attachment as such. Attachment behaviors signal that the individual's self-management capacity is experienced as unsteady. Attachment behaviors can be described by such proximity-seeking efforts as clinging, staying close, or repeatedly posing self-evident questions (e.g., "What time is it?" "When do we eat?") which actually are a cry to be noticed and included. It is useful in practice to be aware of this differentiation and to recognize attachment. Appropriate actions have to be directed toward the process of attachment formation rather than the attachment behaviors themselves. Attachment behaviors, moreover, are intrinsic and natural human reactions and are not merely peculiarities of children in group care settings. Studies of securely attached children bring out that in moments of stress, such as at points of separation, they seek the proximity of the care giver. After reciprocal response of inclusion by the care giver, these children can subsequently handle the separation more competently. In contrast, children with uncertainties in their attachments will either avoid falling back upon their primary care givers or will have added difficulties in facing the changed situation (Kagan, 1978; Sroufe, 1978, p. 56).

Applied to group care this means that such daily care events in attachment strivings should be dealt with as attachment seeking ventures rather than as behavioral expression per se. Frequently, when a child screams about other children's behavior with such penetrating volume that it can be heard in the farthest corner, this call is a cry of loneliness and a sense of desertion rather than a mere act of disruptive behavior. Workers may want to conceive of these cries as reminders that the particular youngster needs much active assurance of being included by the worker, possibly right at that critical moment or perhaps later on. The child's loud screams, i.e., the attachment behavior, is not the point to be addressed. Thus, the tempting reaction of shouting back: "Stop your screaming!" would need to be swallowed in preference to a caring response which has significance to the youngster.

### Theoretical Crossroads

The foregoing concern, whether to focus upon the child's specific ongoing behavior or the individual's assumed basic requirements, is actually a question of theoretical grounding. The previously cited illustrations may serve as an opportunity to highlight the differences and consequences between operating from a behavioral or an interpersonal perspective.

One can delineate the behavioral modification stance in the following: ignoring the child's cry is used as a technique for extinguishing an undesired response, concomitant to this is the reinforcing behaviors (showing attention) when the child is peacefully engaged. While within an interactional perspective in the preceding case example, workers are lauded for their response to the child's cry for assistance and human compassion in a moment of lonely despair. The piercing screams are not conceived of as the central issue but are automatically extinguished once the child feels a stronger sense of attachment. Both perspectives present as the desired end the elimination of undesirable responses and the strengthening of more effective behavioral capabilities. Yet the difference in the value orientation and actual practice activities and potential outcomes are in stark contrast. Within a behavioral perspective the emphasis is upon behavioral modification, as the name of the approach clearly signifies. Within an interactional perspective, the inter-relationship of people, the fostering of attachment and the reliance upon developmental process, move to the center. Behaviors, in contrast, are envisaged as instrumental rather than as the essence of human existence (Mordock, 1979). In the illustrative example above, workers in this context are expected to relate when needed to the total child rather than to the child's behaviors. Behavioral thinking, in contrast, conceives of the child's behavior as a manifestation of the child as he or she is.

The behavioral approach in one way is most inviting for its clarity in purpose and apparently simple application in complex situations (Browning & Stover, 1971). Also, a good range of research findings have heralded behavioral management approaches for their proven efficacy. True, behavioral modification is effective as long as specific behavioral changes are conceived as the immediate and ultimate target. The interactional approach has a stronger appeal to persons and institutions with a humanistic orientation. For them, their source of information and verification comes from research on child development within the context of a child's everyday developmental life experiences. Their basic concern centers in providing children with everyday sustenance. The interpersonal approach would maintain that providing a child with the needed support must occur when the child needs it rather than when particular behaviors are acceptable. Strong differences in belief and value systems come to the foreground with this last statement.

Which orientation shall prevail? Both find application within this volume — and more so, both points of view (and frequently a combination of them) are continuously applied in the many practice settings. This writer obviously relies upon an interactional perspective. This perspective is akin to his belief system, and belief systems ultimately determine every person's theoretical bias. Moreover, this position can also be well supported by recent research findings in child development. Findings point out that the *quality* of rootedness in interpersonal attachment determines the nature of behavioral expression and change rather than the behavioral output as determinant of the basic development of human relationship (Brazelton, Koslowski, & Main, 1974; Dupont, 1978; Kirigin, Braukman, Atwater, & Wolf, 1979; Maier, 1978b; Schaffer, 1977; Segal & Yahraes, 1978). In spite of wide usage of both orientations, there is a decisive difference between them. A behavioral point of view conceives human beings as basically a behavioral apparatus responding to environmental stimulations and reinforcements. An interactional perspective requires one to conceive of human beings as multidimensional, as feeling, thinking, as well as behaving persons — acting and responding all in one (Maier, 1976). To put it another way, the essential differences between these two basic alternate conceptions rest between linear, inductive thinking (basic to learning theory formulations) and nonlinear, cyclical, deductive thinking (underpinning system theory and an interactional conceptualization).

### Attention-Seeking/Human Contact-Needing

Let us examine more closely the phenomenon of attention-getting demands, for the previous brief paragraphs on attachment and attachment behaviors have not really addressed the common fear of feeding into attention-getting behaviors. Attention-getting behaviors are part and parcel of children's everyday lives. However, children uprooted from their original living arrangements tend to exhibit such behavioral expressions even more strongly. It is not that they require more attention than other children; rather, as a group they have experienced, thus far, less dependable attention. Attention-getting efforts are actually attachment behaviors, involving strong individual intrusive thrusts directed toward winning fuller inclusion. Thus, the child clinging to the worker, overwhelming as that can be, may be better understood in the light of the child's quest for inclusion rather than as undesirable "hogging" for exclusive attention.

Wanting attention is basically very human. Who doesn't want, need, and deserve it? In our work with children or youth the salient issue is not the fact that an individual wants attention, although this reasoning is frequently used to explain and by-pass a child's behavior. Instead, a child's desire for attention has to be understood and addressed as a legitimate expression. To reach out for approval and companionship, to turn toward others when in distress — these are all natural desires and requirements. The writer trusts that these human qualities are also valued by child care staff and their institutional programs (Chess & Hassibi, 1978).

The issue we must concern ourselves with is establishing more secure anchorage for these children and helping them move toward more effective inclusive behaviors. For child care practice the task is thus threefold: (1) Child care workers demonstrating an open attitude toward the children's desire for inclusion. Children are to be welcomed as vital and full partners in the unit's daily life and into society in general. (2) Workers responding sensitively to the children's urgent appeals for immediate satisfying contacts and clearly acknowledging the stress the child is undergoing. (3) Workers preparing to overlook at the moment the children's unsatisfactory behavior. Suitable behavioral expressions are taught when appropriate for the child's learning. Sometimes teaching takes place at the critical incident and sometimes later on.

The range of appropriate child care givers' interventions is vast. It may suffice to envision as model a mother's everyday response to the piercing screams of a child whose tower of blocks has unexpectedly caved in. A sensitive parent will respond to the child's frustration rather than to her inconvenience at being called away from her task at hand. She will respond to the child's experience of disappointment rather than to the unpleasantness of the screams. Above all, she will encourage the child to try again, possibly assuring him or her that there is no need to scream so vehemently. Even better, she may not comment at all the child's vocal outburst of despair (in contrast to trying to extinguish the screams lest the youngster become a screamer). Recent research points clearly to the fact that it is not the children's future behavior, but their future trust in others and consequent sense of independence that are at stake (Kagan, 1978; Sable, 1979; Segal & Yahraes, 1978).

### Bodily Comfort Speaketh the Loudest

"Try out these soft floor pillows," says a group care worker while handing cushions to a number of 15-year-old girls sprawled out on the floor for an evening of television watching. "I turned up the heat in the bathroom, so it will be good and warm when you get out of the shower," remarked another care worker. Concerns for bodily comfort, like straightening out children's blankets at bedtime in order to make them more comfortable for the night or sitting down with a child on the floor so that the youngster can afford a more relaxed bodily posture and eye contact, are common child care activities. But however spontaneous or mundane, this quality of caring is vital and should not be overlooked. Throughout life a sense of well-being and caring is closely related to the degree of bodily security and comfort a person experiences. Moreover, as an individual's bodily comforts are met, so does the person feel welcomed and wanted and more receptive to risk experience beyond his or her immediate bodily demands. Physical sustenance and comfort are thus essential measures of care.[7]

Care giving in many ways is anchored in the personal involvement aspect of the physical care rendered by the care giver. It is the care giver's personal investment which converts physical care into "caring care." A worker taking the time to tuck a child into bed, to offer suitable clothing, fix a girl's braids, or rub a youngster's cold hands — these actions deal with transmitting personal physical care and constitute some of the most fundamental components of child care (Maier, 1979, pp. 161-64).

Because the rendering of personal care of children is so closely associated with the provision of the necessities of life, it is common for child care services to theoretically justify the assignment of both homemaker tasks and child care to the same staff. Actually, budgetary considerations are frequently the basis for this dual assignment. It becomes then questionable what priority is given to the task of relating to the children per se.

Theoretically and practically speaking a group care setting is *not* a home. It is true that both family and group care settings are primary group systems. The primary processes are inherent in each, but group care programs are not comparable to family life existence. In order to draw a meaningful line between physical care and physical management functions, it is essential to classify all household functions as management functions; from ordering provisions to seeing that the toothpaste tubes are capped; from washing to the issuing of clothing; from cooking to the serving of meals; from scrubbing to achieving an orderly unit. These management functions need to be carried out by household *maintenance* personnel who can carry them out more efficiently.

With more flexible time at hand and a clearer assignment to assist the children with their most urgent everyday requirements care staff can pursue more readily their primary roles. Staff can then focus on training children in the tasks which must be mastered in order to live effectively as members of a household. Workers and residents together will appropriately take some responsibility for the maintenance of clothing, for joint sharing in some of the preparation and serving of their meals, and for a creative investment in personal care of their place. Maintenance staff just like the administrative staff for each program have to be selected equally for its specifically required capabilities *and* its readiness to be concerned with children's requirements. A cook, bookkeeper, gardener, agency director, or general maintenance person is a vital partner of the total care program. Each one is needed for his or her specialized competency. Each adds his or her vital contribution by which he or she brings to bear in the overall planning and in the interactions with children and staff whatever is essential in the care of children as persons in their own right. In short, the cook, child care worker, executive or janitor is always a person with his or her task speciality *and* a full member of the extended child care team.

Awareness of the physical comfort as a prelude for care can be expanded to the way we deal with an individual's personal space, personal belongings, and spatial orientation in general. The child's private place, or drawer, or his or her personal piece of clothing needs to be honored as part of the individual's special realm, even if the person is not present to claim it (Bakker & Bakker-Rabdau, 1973). We all can envisage instances when household pets have private spaces which are respected. Do we similarly grant to children in our group programs such rights and respect? Do children and adolescents in residential group settings also have a chance to establish territory which is genuinely their own?

Such spaces — private "corners," beds or other "mine only" places — have to be indisputably theirs as part of their inalienable rights within their child care arena. It is important to affirm such spaces as duty free regardless of acceptability. Youngsters need to find evidence of their right to exist in difficult as well as in good moments. We are reminded of instances when one child feels hurt that another has taken his or her favored seat although other chairs are "just as good." These are not mere nuisance occurrences. For the child it is an event of personal consequence. Studies of animal and human uses of space clearly suggest to us that invasion of private space is felt sharply as a direct assault to one's body (Bakker & Bakker-Rabdau, 1973; Freedman, 1975). There is a saying: "Good fences make good neighbors." This assertion might also apply to children. They too want their territory known and respected. (The concern for private space in the midst of much shared territory in our childcaring institutions and group homes will be more fully reviewed in the next section of this chapter.)

## *Transitional Objects*

As a corollary to the above, it is also significant that when children move from one setting to another, they require assistance in making the unfamiliar familiar. Transitional objects — a much loved blanket, cushion, stuffed beast, toy, photo or trinket — serve as linkage transforming a strange place into more familiar surroundings (Winnicott, 1965).[8] The children's treasured possessions, usually a meaningless old tattered object to a casual onlooker, can be vital sustenance for its owner.

It is inherent in the contemporary scene that each child care worker serves also as a personalized transition worker — a person facilitating children's transitions from one life situation to another. Children and youth need assistance with entering, coping and moving forward into a new situation. It follows then, that we need to guard against stripping individuals of their transitional objects as they enter new group living situations. Also, continuing contacts with previously supportive persons provide not only a helping bridge but are essential as transitional contacts for the child.

### Behavioral Training

The reader may have been puzzled while traveling over the preceding pages that little reference has been made to the training connected with self-management and the maintenance of discipline. These aspects of care are important features of child care. In fact they are so essential that they should be attended to when they have the fullest possible impact.

Children learn most readily from those who have vital meaning for them. They learn from persons like their child care workers whom they recognize as persons to be counted on. They copy those whom they perceive to be on their side, tending to follow those people whose ways of dealing with life issues are most akin to their own. The persons most meaningful for their power, as well as closest to the children's own life situations, have the best chance for influencing the children's behavior and training. In addition to the primary caring persons, very frequently it is the slightly older siblings and peers or the heroes in stories and on television, a few steps ahead in development, who represent models and idols. They may be almost of equal importance to the central caring figures as well (Bronfenbrenner, 1970; Kessen, 1975; Schaffer, 1977).

Social capability rests upon personal attachment. It is essential to keep in mind that the most potent behavioral training goes hand in hand with a sense of reciprocal closeness and attachment. Effective acquisition of behavioral standards is a consequence of the combination of accepting dependency and wanting to incorporate significant adults' behaviors as one's own (Maier, 1978b, chapter 3). When child caring adults have a sense of close attachment, effective child training starts and more complicated socialization efforts can take their course. While socialization proceeds, children or youth will periodically dip into emotional dependence upon their care givers. These linkages will be both fundamental and freeing. In other words, the fostering of self-management and of enriching children's behavioral repertoires are intimately linked with the formation of close attachment with the care givers (Maier, 1982b).

The preceding pages have essentially taken up the more immediate environment of personal care which has to be provided to children and adolescents anywhere — especially to those in residential group care. The points discussed thus far could well be enumerated as the "core of care," the essential ingredients for the development of children and youth at home and away from home (Maier, 1979).

## III. THE LANGUAGE OF SPACE — PHYSICAL ARRANGEMENTS

### Spatial Arrangements and How They Influence Daily Experience

"We shape our buildings — and they shape us." This sage comment attributed to Winston Churchill (Proshansky, Ittelson, & Rivlin, 1970, p. 18), also applies to the physical arrangements of residential group care settings. Spatial patterns have the possibility of enhancing or inhibiting activities. The use of residential territory is as much a reflection of the space available as of the quality of interaction between residents and staff (Wax, 1977, p. 51). Only by unusual coincidence will our readers be involved with the design or with the complete rebuilding of a residential setting. Most of us are confronted with the inimitable challenge: in which way can the present setting be adapted within its unalterable limits in order for spatial arrangements to shape service activities in the desired direction?

For the moment let us look in at the age-old phenomenon of children pushing each other as they enter the dining area. This tumbling and shoving is in part a function of age and it is not unusual for a child to thrust forward as if he or she is the only one to find a place at the table, even when customary places are assured. But in part, these scrambles are frequently a matter of the kind of space and timing we offer that take into account sufficient room for children's awkward body movements manifested in moments of hurry and excitement. True, these jostlings can possibly be controlled by continuous supervision and much child care effort. However, the same change in behavior can be potentially achieved with an alteration in the physical and timing arrangements. A wider "freeway" at the entrance and between tables is apt to cut down on the pushing and shoving. Such physical alterations can likewise conserve child care staff's energy and avoid an atmosphere of admonishment preceding mealtime gatherings.

### Chart of the Spatial Residential Arrangements

Ever present in the dialectic dilemma is the assurance of ample common space while guaranteeing each individual unhampered pursuit of personal interest and associations. Moreover, there is the clear need for continuous proximity of staff while simultaneously assuring the resident a sense of intimacy and private experimentation.

In order to make immediate use of ideas and questions reviewed within this section of the chapter, readers are urged to chart for themselves the physical realities of the residential service program with which they are concerned. On a large sheet of notepaper sketch roughly the groundplan of the residential building(s) and outdoor space of one child care unit. If the unit is housed on more than one floor, make a diagram for each floor level. Draw in existing walls, steps, doors, windows, built-in closets, major equipment (e.g., refrigerator and plumbing) as well as large pieces of furniture (beds, chests, tables, chairs, couches, television, sewing machine, etc.).

In a study of this diagram of the physical group living environment it becomes important to discern what the spatial set-up allows and encourages, and what it tends to hinder or negate. In which ways do spatial factors impact privacy, supervision, the flow and speed of interactions, spontaneous groupings, access to child care staff as well as contacts with the outside? In such a review, do the findings dovetail with the objectives of the service program? These questions are based upon the understanding that every spatial constellation implicity allows and hampers actions. Indeed, space controls behavior (Proshansky, Ittelson, & Rivlin, 1970; Sommer, 1969).

Wherever space supports the work endeavored, the question remains: in which way can spatial factors be altered to even further accentuate this process? Sometimes small spatial alterations bring about substantial changes in the flow of behavioral interactions. For example, care workers frequently maintain an open door while engaged with paperwork in their child care offices. The workers' availability or degree of concentration upon their office tasks can be signaled by the arrangement of their work space as well as their seating position. By arranging their workspace at the far end of the room rather than adjacent to the entrance, their position conveys clearly: "I am away and at work!" If residents want to establish contact, they are required to come fully into the room while separating themselves from their own peers' sphere of life.

When spatial arrangements are actually impeding or complicating the program, the challenge exists to alter these physical factors. This need becomes particularly urgent when existing arrangements are justified because they have been like that for years! Readers will quickly be reminded of settings (hopefully places of the past) where children are forbidden to run lest plantstands or other cherished mementoes get knocked down. One more illustration: in some programs where the doors of the children's room open to the inside, children are apt to barricade themselves in their rooms when severely agitated and in special need for adult contacts. A small carpentry alteration in the frame and a rehanging of the door may offer possibilities for additional and more promising avenues of intervention. Readers are challenged to review their diagrams and ponder about the residential unit's physical arrangements. Change space, and advance program!

### Private Space

Territory defines the person. A person's power position and value to an organization can invariably be estimated by the relative space granted as *private* (personal) working domain. Compare the size of the executive's office with those of other offices, the social workers' offices with those of the child care staff. Secretaries frequently protect their desk tops; janitors are intensely possessive about their supply closets; while child care workers guard closely the space alloted for purses, notebooks or other personal belongings. It is not surprising that persons without an office of their own jealously guard that vestige of private territory they *can* claim (Stea, 1970). In applying these observations to work with children and adolescents, we see quickly the importance for children to stake out their territory and the necessity for recognizing their private spaces as personal turf (Bettelheim, 1974). Private space is not only urgently required for a verification of self; private space is also essential for each person as a refuge for contemplation and revitalization of energy (Mehrabian, 1976).

What actually constitutes private space? It is an area recognized by the occupant *and* others as the claimant's full and rightful possession. It represents an area which the occupant can use, arrange and rearrange, or even disregard according to his or her liking. Most important, it is a place where persons have full control over themselves and their immediate environment. The occupant has the sole right to invite or exclude others within this safe place (Bakker & Bakker-Rabdau, 1973). It is a spot where intermittently the individual can be an island to him or herself. In the absence of any such assured sanctuaries, people tend to create their own "private spaces" by such behaviors as placing themselves behind a newspaper while travelling. Harassed parents may retreat to the bathtub as their sanctum. Children lacking private space of their own tend to seek out the privacy of a swing, toilet, etc.

The wish to be periodically alone and to have space of one's own is not merely a whim of children or adults, it is a human requirement. The latter becomes even more urgent for persons living or working in close proximity with others. (Freedman, 1975). Moreover, at moments of personal tensions and social change, individuals require added privacy and the assurance of ample space of their own.⁹ We are reminded of instances of crises when children seek out the assurance and solace of their rooms or wander off the institutional grounds or even run away. Similarly, we witness that when children are tense they require more space between themselves and others, even for instance as they watch television together. Conversely, conditions of sudden overcrowding can bring on intense anxiety, panic behaviors of either fight or flight, or even a suicide (Wax, 1977, pp. 51-52). The necessity to maintain more space in moments of stress is not necessarily a manifestation of peoples' irritability but rather their very human requirements for larger buffer zones (Horowitz, Duff, & Stratton, 1970). It is an established fact that persons in a schizophrenic state maintain a greater distance from people around them and are in need of more private space for themselves in order to function at all (Bettelheim, 1974, pp. 136-37; Sivadon, 1970).

### What Constitutes Privacy in the Fish Bowl of Group Living?

At this point it might be advisable to pursue further the diagrammed layout of the residential unit. Draw in with contrasting color or picture mentally for yourself the *private* space granted to child care staff.

This little exercise is apt to reveal quickly whether child care staff have such essential space actually accessible to them. Provision for space is a necessary privilege automatically assured to other professionals in their respective offices. If by chance other professional space is also inadequate, this still does not negate the need for such a refuge at the child care level.

As the next step, shade into the diagram (or visualize for yourself) the *private* space granted each child. Delineate in the children's rooms only those areas as private territory which are distinctly private. Also add in acknowledged "private space" within the larger residential setting and its neighborhood.

Children require private corners for their *personal* belongings and for solitary times. It should be noted that protection of personal possessions is primarily an issue of privacy and only secondarily a mechanism for keeping order in the unit. If the concern for order and safekeeping of a child's belongings is a justifiable issue, then some of the belongings may have to be stored selectively in order to safeguard personal possessions and to maintain basic clothing and equipment. To reiterate, a box, a drawer, or a shelf is a must in group care. Moreover, children and youth require territory in their own rooms and in other areas of their group living environment where they can be comfortable and on their own to brood or to gloat, to loaf or to concentrate, to be privately with friends or to indulge in solitary play. Private space also assures the freedom to leave one's project undisturbed for an eventual return.

The sleeping quarters, bed and room, in almost all cultures tend to carry a most personal connotation. For young and displaced people it seems to take on added significance as a vestige for anchorage when their course is unclear. Changes, especially arbitrary or frequent room or bed changes connote a sense of impermanence and casual disregard for the residents' place within the group care setting. The fundamental concern that we may want to bear in mind is that the residents' sleeping quarters are bedrooms belonging to the *residents* as their temporary home base. This principle may contrast to some settings where the rooms *per se* are conceived as belonging to the institutional service rather than an integral arm of the service itself. Special effort has to be directed toward establishing that the children's beds and rooms are not only attractive, comfortable, and practical, but that they symbolize almost more than any segment of the residence the message: "We care!" (Bettelheim, 1974, p. 153). Staff needs continuously to search out whether attention given to furniture, room arrangements, and decorations are really in the best interest of the children or whether these concerns reflect an adult conception of a spick and span and respectable place. A sense of *private* space and personal investment is not fortified by the imposition of adult standards. The reverse seems to be the case: a sense of personal investment and ownership leads to a greater openness to adult suggestions.[10]

The assurance of private space depends much upon marking off respective boundaries. Ownership has to be acknowledged by all parties involved (Bakker & Bakker-Rabdau, 1973). Putting up name plates on doors or posting of signs as "private," "stay out," or roping off an area, are effective means of reaffirming established personal space. Such notices are commonly employed by children in their own homes; and readers themselves will recall placards reading "no entry," "knock before entering," etc., which were loftily posted on doors. The same holds true for the creation of temporary private spheres within the public life of a group living environment in order that solitary or special sub-group activities can occur legitimately and without interruption. Similarly, children and staff need to map out permissible areas for practicing music, physical exercises, for taking a walk, or other recourses verifying the natural desire to be temporarily isolated.

### Public Space

Every home, as well as each group living situation, has extensive areas which serve as *public* territory. Public territory is the space which can be indisputably used by any one constituent member of the group. During the length of the time a person occupies the particular area it is that individual's "personal space." A seat at the kitchen table, provision for privacy in a common washroom, stretching out temporarily on the livingroom couch, are a few examples which assure people of sole occupancy as long as they maintain possession or hold onto the spot by proxy.

But let us go back for a moment to some basic issues. In a group living setting a decision first has to be made about who is to be included in the definition of public. Does public mean the general public? The public of the total organization? Or is public more limited, to mean those associated with a particular group living unit?

Usually space in front of a private home or a children's institution is considered common public space. Anyone has a right to it. But the decision to grant an open range of entry or to permit entrance selectively really rests upon a major policy decision. Are the children's residential units conceived as custodial or service programs? The custodial program can be readily defined and justified as within the community's domain and as everybody's territory. Such a conception fits more into a program which does little more than to warehouse troubled children and is out of step with contemporary thinking (Whittaker, 1979, p. 5). In contrast, if we accept the premise in a service program that the group living environment belongs to the residents and the staff specifically associated with the residents' *daily* lives, it follows that others—whether concerned citizens, friendly neighbors, policy makers, or management and other staff participants—only achieve access by knocking and being invited to enter. (Note: invited by the occupants—children and staff—and not by the management or the administration in general.) Although it can be argued that office staff, field-workers, repair specialists, and especially the executive director, are intimately involved in the services rendered to the residents, they would also appropriately get specific permission for entry. (In some instances, when staff persons have become much intertwined with the children's and staff's lives, they may secure spontaneous entry rights for their unique ongoing relationship with the unit's population.)

What about the children's *public* space? If space is public, then there must be access for all. Areas within and outside of the residential unit which are conceived as the children's territory necessarily must be set up as such for the residents' free use. Private claims can only last for the duration of a person's occupancy unless such space has by consensus become an individual's private space. Frequently, individuals will become attached to and are granted specific places as their accustomed spots within public territory. The latter is reminiscent of most homes where a particular place is reserved by "squatters rights" to a family member or sometimes household pets.

Again, it might be instructive to turn to the previously drawn-up diagram and reflect on the mental picture of a group living setting. Are the areas which thus far have not been marked off as private space actually the children's and staff's *public* territory? Space might be allocated for particular periods of the day (e.g., outdoor area for daylight activities only) or for special ranges of activities (e.g., music corner, fix-it shop or study room). Are these special limitations for public use clearly defined and understood by the residents and staff? It is not unusual that after taking notice of all clearly established public space, there remain areas that lack clear definition. These are the twilight zones, areas of uncertainty and potential conflict with regard to utilization. Frequently the kitchen, workshops, storage rooms, or porch make up these uncertain and conflict-prone territories. Difficulties can be decisively reduced by clearly establishing claims to the area: staff, children with staff, or open to all.

### Isolation Rooms as a Special "Service" Space

Some child care programs include as essential for their program the maintenance of an isolation room. Staff finds it necessary to confine children to a special bare lock-up room either to enforce policy of time-out,[11] or such a room may be desperately employed as a recourse when care givers are at a loss (possibly along with the whole treatment field) as to how to deal with a severely troubled child who is completely out of control.

Special caution is necessary here in labeling and using this kind of space. Isolation rooms are frequently euphemistically dubbed "quiet rooms" when they are in fact punitive and dehumanizing cells. If isolation actually is to serve its intended purpose to separate and calm a distraught child from ongoing agitation, then in most situations the child's own room—a quiet, familiar, and confidence inspiring refuge—is the logical isolation place. Moreover, in the latter setting the child would be encouraged to subsequently use his or her room in moments of severe tension as a safe harbor for finding a personal sense of balance. Children, as well as adolescents and adults, need people at times of distress; they need people nearby in a place which inspires comfort and that is welcoming. Rarely are isolation chambers conducive for bringing people together. Instead, their naked walls and cold emptiness further arouse a sense of personal negation, social insulation, and individual despair. Isolation rooms have also been justified as a place for children or adolescents to think, to reflect and to come up with a resolve for new ways of handling problematic situations. Since when is being locked up, seated on the floor or on a bare bedstead in an empty room, conducive to thinking? All of us require comfortable settings that transmit encouragement rather than drabness when we feel at odds with the world. Isolation rooms, if used at all, need to convey both personal reassurance and social inclusion for the time the child is temporarily apart from the group.

## *Let Space Speak*

On the preceding pages the focus has been upon the interplay between physical environment and care and treatment objectives, and upon ways that spatial arrangements can be used by care givers and care receivers for more effective group living. The same perspective can be applied to specific problem situations by evaluating the impact of variables in space that augment or deter human interaction (Goffman, 1971). For instance, the recurrent spilling of trash may easily be a function of space if the trash bin is a long distance from the clean-up place. Without this kind of spatial evaluation, one might easily point to such behavior factors as a child's clumsiness or personal disregard for people and place.

The message of this section can be summed up with the heading of Fritz Redl and David Wineman's chapter on "Structure and Strategy of a Treatment Home" in their classic book, *The Aggressive Child* (1957). According to them, residential group care requires "a home that smiles, props which invite, space which allows" (Redl and Wineman, 1957, p. 6), and continuous spatial adaptations which enhance the desired care and treatment.

## IV. GROUP LIVING AS AN EVERYDAY MILIEU EXPERIENCE

### *Three Different Perspectives of Residential Group Care*

The day-to-day periods of work or play, the association with others, the enjoying of one's own company, the dawdling and day-dreaming time, the pursuing of routine tasks; all comprise the minutiae of daily life and are the central components of our primary life experience whether adult or child. These encounters typify life in our respective homes, residential or otherwise. It is within the minutiae of life and not in the big events that one's personal pursuits and direction are determined. For instance, on awakening, the way a person feels about his or her companions, the expectations he or she has for the day ahead, or the impact of events that occur immediately upon awakening all strongly influence the beginning of a person's day.

With such a proposition before us, it is no longer a managerial but a basic care and treatment issue as to whether children in group care should be awakened by a bell, by impersonal calls, or by brief personal attention by the worker. Sensitive decisions need to be made whether messages conveyed to children upon awakening are to be perfunctory greetings, reminders or admonishments about the tasks ahead, or whether messages are to be genuine attempts to connect with children personally, communicating a hopeful vision of the day ahead. Into what kind of space are children awakened — are they surrounded by decorations of by-gone residents, or do they wake up to their own meaningful mementoes?

With this view too, it becomes important to handle with care the minute crises which occur in round-the-clock living — from the onset of the day to falling asleep and beyond. It is important how the worker encounters the youngster who crawls deeper under the blanket when reminded to get up. It is important how one reacts to the small crisis of a teenager missing one of his shoes.

In the last momentary crisis of the missing shoe, we could point to programs which absorb such events as common and of no special relevance. The concerns of such settings would stem from a practical managerial focus. Where is clothing located in readiness for the next morning? Did this boy finally locate his shoe, and did he get off for school in time? In other settings the focus would specifically be upon the staff's handling of this particular situation to forestall future crises of this type. The concern would be primarily with the *behavioral management and maintenance of an overall system* for meeting and overcoming such eventualities. In a third large segment of group care settings, attention would be drawn to the interaction between the staff and the youngster, with major emphasis upon *helping this particular individual in learning to hurdle a problematic daily dilemma.* Each of these three alternative approaches mirrors decisively different views of group care. Let us examine the characteristics and ramifications of each. At this point there can be little doubt about the writer's own strong leaning toward the developmental interaction approach.

The acknowledgement of the writer's predisposition is partially an effort to clarify communication with the reader, but is also an attempt to help the reader identify his or her own perspective. The challenge here is for each of us (and for each group care program) to articulate our own orientation, and our ultimate objectives based on that orientation. Pronouncement of a service's theoretical preference and organizational goals clarifies and gives direction to program development and frees staff for creative and accountable efforts. The alternative is to establish a service's policy by relying on a prescribed set of procedural goals (Seidl, 1977). Procedural accounts do provide staff, especially beginning workers, with direction and security but basically stultify organizational intent, ultimately limiting the care givers' personal investment.

A *managerial program perspective*, which is probably the most common emphasis in our contemporary group care field, requires a clear outline of the major daily program features. In general, this kind of program assures residents of a stable and orderly life experience to which they are expected to adapt. The uncomplicated structure of the service, limited program resources, unsophisticated demands upon residents, and the small staff required render these programs appealing to the public (Burmeister, 1960). The programs' emphases on the children's or youth's adaptation, i.e., fitting into the service, represent the strengths and limitations of this perspective. The structure makes uncomplicated demands at a time when life tends to be most complicated for the child. These services tend to be clear about expectations. However, there is no guarantee that the children's effective adaptation to institutional life will be transferable or applicable to effective living beyond the confines of the program (Durkin & Durkin, 1975).

A *behavioral perspective* and its token economy derivative (Kazdin, 1977), the second previously cited theoretic conception, has attracted interest in recent years, particularly in the United States, and especially in programs associated with correctional endeavors (Phillips, Fixsen & Wolf 1973; Whittaker, 1979, pp. 88-98). A behavioral perspective places the accent upon achieving specific accountable changes in children's or youth's ongoing behaviors in order that they can fulfill the expectations of their immediate social environment. Early accounts of behavioral approaches have shown astonishing results (Browning & Stover, 1971; Fixsen, Phillips & Wolf, 1973; Phillips, Phillips, Fixsen & Wolf, 1973). Subsequent experience with identical techniques, including an adherence to a token economy, has brought out that the results have not been as readily duplicated and the results are possibly attributable to factors other than the inherent reinforcement techniques. It seems to this author (Maier, 1975) and others (Kirigin, Braukman, Atwater & Wolf, 1978; Phillips et al., 1973; Whittaker, 1979, p. 59; as well as Wolf, Phillips & Fixsen, 1974) that the behavioral approach is valid for its quality to teach *behavioral* training. When the impact is reviewed for its overall effect, however, change seems to have been achieved through the counseling person's powerful continued involvement with the care receivers. The care workers' continued review and negotiations *with* their care receivers about behavior and about the points earned seem to be a central factor in effecting change, rather than the award or the denial per se. Psychologists instrumental in setting up these programs observed that an honest give-and-take and warm relationship is an essential component of every treatment program (Phillips et al., 1973). In short, effective change can be attributed to a combination of the care persons' involvement and the children's actual learning of more acceptable behaviors along with an increased experience of efficacy. In addition, and most essential, effective change has been an outgrowth of a new power alignment. That is to say that care personnel and the children are actually in charge of their own daily life situation as they dispense together the points, tokens, or other rewards. A segment of power has come home into the living unit (Maier, 1975, pp. 417-19).

The preceding observations have been introduced to raise questions about group living programs which primarily rely upon a token economy or other forms of purely behavior modification techniques for their utilitarian appeal. Such programs may create for their residents an artificial system with a heavy stress upon compliance and a barter existence in human relationships. Such an outcome may not be the actual objective of the service, and the service may not provide a style of life which is desirable or advantageous once a person is back in regular community life.

A third variation among basic group care approaches is group living as an *interactional experience.* Learning to live and living to learn could describe its central theme (Maier, 1975). The term "interactional" in the labelling of this approach implies that it places heavy reliance upon *process* rather than outcome per se. This approach also builds upon a developmental perspective. The group living experience, with its continued process of daily interactions focuses on the learning opportunities rather than on problem diffusion. In sharp contrast to the previous two approaches, problems are not avoided but exploited. Difficulties are not seen as obstacles but as sources for learning. Stress is placed upon learning to live within the residence and thus upon acquiring life skills for functioning beyond the confines of institutional services.

## Residential Group Care as an Arena for Everyday Life Experience

Children or youth in group living require life experiences within their immediate environment which assist them to feel comfortable but which also challenge and stimulate them. The manner in which such experiences are utilized within the residential community serves to foster continuous development and readiness for life within an ordinary family. Two illustrations might be in order here.

Let us first picture a table of five adolescent girls eating their attractive evening meal. They are rather happy if not boisterous. Such a tension free mealtime is possibly quite an achievement for the girls and the staff of the unit; but it also can be conceived of as the mere beginning, rather than an outcome, in the staff's and the residents' experience. Staff is challenged to assist the girls to expand their conversation, to have fun together when fun is not easily come by, or to be serious when a wisecrack too quickly glosses over worries and personal tensions.

At another time group care staff is confronted with three girls screaming at each other, one being accused of wearing a belt, slip and makeup belonging to another girl and used without permission. The accused girl charges that the other two are "always doing that" with her belongings. Undoubtedly the girls' unit has an understanding (a policy) with regard to borrowing personal belongings. It can also be readily assumed that such a policy, however well contrived, does not prevent alternate practices. The worker is faced with helping the girls straighten out this violation of their understanding about respecting each other's belongings. The managing of this phase of an everyday problem is merely a tangential problem in comparison with the worker's more pertinent task. That task hinges on two principles: (1) What can each one do with her own resources to find pleasure in dressing and makeup? (2) What ways can be examined to facilitate the graceful sharing of wanted items? The latter includes dealing with their mutual feelings about each other, as well as developing the capacity to ask effectively for an item which may or may not be withheld. The emphasis in both of these practice illustrations is that everyday life events within the group serve to enliven and enrich the youngsters. Such events do not, of course, rule out trouble within this system. Troubles are, after all, the grist for growing.

## The Developmental Aspect of an Interactional Perspective

An interactional approach in group care, as outlined in the previous paragraphs, builds upon a developmental conception of human beings. The developmental progression of children and adolescents, as well as those with variations in their developmental (designated as "pathological" in other frames of reference) is seen as a continuous cyclic pattern of growth and change, a progression that is relativistic rather than linear. Life is conceived as a process in which the human being is in a continuous search for stimulation, variation, and new experience rather than a homeostatic balanced, stimuli-free existence (Kuhn, 1970; Maier, 1978a, 1986d). Most important, a nonhomeostatic conception challenges us to value people for their capacity to reach out and to develop more fully rather than for their low risk striking for balance (Maier, 1974). With this perspective our work with children or adolescents focuses on what to do in the midst of trouble rather than on how to get the kids settled down. Managerial and behavioral approaches are concerned with problemavoidance or removal, as if the road of life were free of difficulty. In contrast, group care within a developmental perspective challenges the program to search for content, for forms of interaction which can provide the residents with continued stimulation and learning opportunities. Difficulties are a built-in ingredient and are "par for the course."

### The Normalization Principle

"Normalization" of life experience, a powerful notion originating in the Scandinavian countries and introduced as an ideal in the United States in the early 1970s, endeavors to utilize styles by which children or youth can live as typically (culturally normative) an existence as possible in order to establish personal behaviors and life events which are as culturally conventional (normative) as possible (Horejsi, 1979, pp. 44-45). Normalization does not mean being "normal"; rather it connotes that each individual's life ought to be as close as possible to the essence of the life experience of his or her contemporaries. This concept seems to simple and obvious; yet experience has shown that the application of the principles may be a threat to the status quo of any setting (Horejsi, 1979, p. 45). Normalization might mean the establishment of a "normal" rhythm for the year. For instance: vacations break into routines; seasonal changes bring with them a variety of cultural activities, foods, and alterations in routines. A rhythm for the week underlines a variation between school or work days and rest or leisure days. A rhythm for routines requires a progression where routines do not dominate but are interspersed in a day full of other activities. Clearing the table for instance, is as much a function of anticipating a subsequent activity as of the necessity to get the dishes washed.

The notion of normalization challenges staff, for example, to have a child make purchases at the nearby store even if the desired item (e.g., candy) could be obtained more quickly and economically and with less problem potential right within the premises. Group care units require petty cash not merely for emergencies but for providing the youngsters with expanded learning experiences of attending to errands for everyday items. Toothpaste purchased at a store counter, a mere "normal" acquisition, has greater meaning to a child than a tube from the supply closet!

### Rehearsive Practice

Let us turn to another avenue for enriching the life and treatment aspect of residential group life. The author postulates that a proactive stance is preferable to a reactive posture. To put it in another way, it is more useful actively to pursue creative avenues for change than to attempt to modify procedures in an effort to facilitate smoother outcomes. In fact, as long as much of the work focus is upon overcoming difficulties, a lot of energy goes into impacting children's behaviors at a moment when they are less open to change. A child who is upset about missing belongings, for example, has little interest at that moment in learning how to safeguard and take better care of those belongings. Our attempts to do intensive work for change at such a moment is apt to be singularly ineffective.

The notion of rehearsive practice places the emphasis upon learning when learning has a chance. Rehearsal of new and different ways of managing specific events can be addressed at moments of little stress, in a context of fun and interest-awakening procedures, and above all, in a situation where residents and staff can become fully engaged with each other. During such a period of practice the group care situation becomes the arena where children or adolescents learn not only to do the "what" of the moment, but the "how" of the future.

For example, in an institution for adjudicated teenagers some youngsters are on a go-it-yourself schedule. They are asked to man age their own timing for getting up, leaving for school or work, being on hand for meals, etc. Self-management is not a reward for previous good behavior, but it is rehearsed and learned for life's demands beyond the residential protectory. In this unique practice situation, focus is less upon what these residents can manage and more on what they can eventually learn. In addition, staff may practice with them in spare moments how to deal with such problematic situations as "arriving breathless but late at work." Learning occurs with actual rehearsing potential alternatives to such an undesirable but everyday event. It is important to note that more effective behavior is secured not by talking about these problematic situations but by concretely practicing them.

One more illustration: leave-taking and preparation for adapting to a new environment is a factor inherent in the life of each youngster in residential group care (Bale, 1979). Preparations for leavetaking and the actual departure can be faced with a child soon to return home as a real event, and used with the others as an opportunity to rehearse for the eventual day of their departure.

Earlier in this chapter we witnessed the group care counselor practicing with Ray and two of his unit mates how the former could discourage teasing by disregarding provoking comments. Ray had to practice these behaviors. Rehearsal practice in a period of, and as part of, an interesting experience made it more possible for Ray to engage himself and to learn. Special situations creating simulated life occurrences are for fun but also for keeps; new ways are practiced toward successfully facing previously problematic situations.

A rehearsive approach can also provide workers with a handle for dealing with acquisition of behavior that ordinarily would not be possible in the "hothouse" culture of institutional life. It is important to consider the *portability* of the behaviors;[12] in other words, inventing ways of doing things which children can effectively employ once returned to regular community living.

Children in residential care possibly need, even more than other children, to develop and rehearse their power to hold their own at home or at school, as well as within the environments of their group care program. Since institutional programs tend to diminish rather than enhance the residents' power, special rehearsive situations may have to be created in which the residents can practice using their power to hold onto their turf and to impact their own life situations. In a group home in the United States, as illustration, residents agreed to help Carl insist upon his rights whenever he felt slighted. They challenged him to stand up for his rights even if this meant disagreement and the necessity for others, including staff, to alter their own immediate preferences.

Conflict behavior is another feature which may require special attention by means of the rehearsive approach. In general, in everyday life at home or in group living situations, conflicts tend to be avoided or at best reduced, and to be set aside as quickly as possible. Often this is done with a shift of concern away from the person's intense response to apparent difficulties, diminishing the individuals' opportunity to learn new skills in handling conflict and to work further on the aspects which stirred him. Conflict situations may have to be specially and persistently exploited to assist the youngsters (as well as staff) in developing new ways of dealing with conflict (Maier, 1975, pp. 412-13).

## *Learning to Care for Others*

Finally, parallel to learning to deal with conflict, children require assistance in learning to demonstrate caring (Kobak, 1979). Children in group care, as probably their contemporaries anywhere, not only need love and affection, but also want and need to love others. Learning to care for others is acquired first by experiencing this care oneself; secondly by having caregiving modelled by esteemed persons; and ultimately by opportunities for providing some care for others. As so much of the residential program is geared toward the provision of care, residential settings have to be vigilant in seizing opportunities where children or youth minister to others. Special opportunities have to be created, such as an individual child fixing a mug of cocoa for him- or herself *and* a friend; sharing the concern of an unhappy roommate by trying to do something for the other — not necessarily to elicit a change in mood but as an expression of compassion.

Learning to care is also fostered by having opportunities for personal enmeshment in the care of dolls, stuffed toys, plants, and pets,[13] and by volunteering for attending to others in distress in and away from the institution. It is amazing how children, severely in want of attachment themselves, can get absorbed by the plight of children in heart-rending distress in distant places. Caring as an expression of love for others (humans, pets, or objects) has to be anchored in individual desires to do something and delivery of the care themselves. In learning to care, the caring process is the central issue. A child becoming concerned over another child in the home community, a frequent occurrence with many young residents, deserves a worker's follow-up. A call, visit, or note by the child to this real or assumed friend, regardless of whether the child's message can effectively offer comfort, is an important opportunity to experience reaching out to another human being. Some children are apt to express their affection to peers, others to younger children, and not surprisingly, many can share with their elders the very kind of care for which they themselves long. All require their respective opportunities (Wrenn, 1972).

### Programming and Freedom, Play and Productive Work

Play and work, programming, and spontaneity — the many components within one segment of this chapter may seem perplexing. It may help to clarify if we conceptualize that programming deals with the effort of guaranteeing the residents a sound diet of everyday life experience which will hopefully enrich development. The essence of programming is not the scheduling of special events but envisaging and planning a day which promises to satisfy: with adults to support and to guide, with routines which serve to relax, where old ways of doing things are tolerated and new ways are possible, and above all, where life can proceed for fun and for keeps.

Work or play for children, adolescents, and hopefully for adults, involves strong personal investment and opportunities for self-realization. It is essential for children to have ample opportunities for work, activities where they can invest themselves and see the outcome (productivity) of their efforts as useful (marketable) to others. In one program the adolescents are asked to contribute four hours a week of work. Work projects are recommended and posted by the youngsters and staff. Once a resident signs up for a task, a commitment has been established. These teenagers work and frequently they work more than required. Their work assignments are a challenge to them and have value in their own eyes and the eyes of their community. Among some of their tasks are painting, genuine repair work, errands with the maintenance person, and fixing things for elderly neighbors, or cleaning up the sports field after a public event. Such tasks are extra; different from the daily chores of cleaning up their quarters, washing dishes, or emptying trash containers which are routines. The routines are necessary and time consuming, but they do not constitute challenging work experience.

Parallel to work, play is children's major avenue for learning, for exploring, for verifying themselves and, above all, for interacting meaningfully with others and environmental events in general. "Play is active, energetic, creative and imaginative. . . . It is a vehicle by which youngsters learn of their world, of its construction and how they fit into the scheme of things" (Wilson, 1977, p. 249). In play children not only deal with their difficulties; play is foremost a vital resource for learning by trial and error, to risk and to do for fun what is either too scary for real or what is better not done or not done yet. It is human to dare oneself and others in play; it is also human to do in play, "just for fun," all the things which are taboo or at least not quite proper in ordinary life. In play we can win or lose without permanent repercussions; in play one can hurry or dally. In play, moreover, persons can practice and experience essential behaviors which can scarcely be tried out otherwise. Where else but in play can children or adults effectively practice at being outstanding or at playing unashamedly: the fool, to wait and to take turns while on the edge, to outwit, to cheat or to steal within permissible bounds without being caught, to co-operate, to hold back or to give for the greater good. Many forms of play have as a major ingredient a sampling of these: to bluff, to cheat, to steal, to annihilate as well as to share, to team up, or to save the day for all. Consequently, to play "high court" or Star Wars, Bionic Woman, or Treasure Island can provide a rich give-and-take in fun and learning.

In no way in the light of our contemporary knowledge can this writer reconcile the notion that play serves as a reward for or as reinforcer of good behavior. On the contrary, play is learning itself. Play provides sustenance for life, including good new problematic behaviors for further learning. The more disturbed or distressed children are, the less able they are to fall back on play as a help-rendering process. In other words, when play is needed most it is least at hand. With such an understanding, play often must be encouraged or induced as an essential ingredient of a child's daily life.

Program planning includes the creation of opportunities for children to do things together, to work, to play, and to fulfill the necessities of daily living (routines) in such a way that the customary procedures do not become high points of the day. Instead, each day's activities stand out for their challenge and adventure, with routines built in as a matter of fact. Program planning serves also the purpose of assuring each child ample private life in the inherent fishbowl existence of group living. Simultaneously frequent joint activities will link together the residents of each unit; periodically the unit will be linked with other units of the program, and whenever possible connections will be made with people beyond the institutional barriers.

Provision of activities for children and youth in group care is such a vital area of concern that special attention needs to be called to additional comprehensive resources for this aspect of group care services. Readers may find the following publications helpful. Although some of these resources date back more than a decade, their content is still pertinent: DeNoon, 1965; Nicholson, 1975; Plank, 1973; Redl and Wineman, 1957, pp. 318-94; Whittaker, 1969; and Wilson, 1977, among others.

### . . . And When the Expected Is Not Done

What should be our response when clearly enunciated expectations are not fulfilled? Such a question will likely bring forth a flood of answers or at least personal tension. Some readers may respond with the thought: "Stand firm and make them!" Others may protest vehemently: "It should not happen!" while many readers may be inclined to respond that "There must be discipline!"

Perhaps the real concern should be with the fact that our expectations are important. We value what we expect of a child. In other words, the focus should be on the expectation rather than the violation. Focus on the violation ultimately comes to revolve around authority issues and a power struggle over who runs the place (Polsky, 1962); while continued concern with expectations maintains the original concern with what we value to be important.

Let us imagine a group of adolescents who return later than mutually agreed upon from an activity, or who "forget" to pick up clothing strewn about their rooms. These kinds of situations are in conflict with a set of general expectations. Basic to this conflict is the clarity and degree of importance of these expectations rather than the implied disregard for the adults associated with these expectations. The care workers of the adolescents would have to explicitly convey again that they count on the youngsters' adherence to basic expectations. The expectations still stand regardless of being late or neglecting to straighten out belongings. Most noteworthy, non-compliance does not necessarily alter standards or become an issue of disobedience, rather non-compliance requires a persistence to find ways of meeting these expectations. The focus has to remain upon assisting children *to learn* to do as requested rather than struggling with them over who sets the rules and necessitating the establishment of a way of proving that expectations have been carried out. This latter approach shifts the issue from concern with standards to a power struggle over "who is on top" (Ebner, 1979).

Let us imagine the rather common occurrence of an adolescent storing her clothing in helter-skelter fashion on the bottom of her open closet in the face of her care worker's explicit demand to straighten out the disorder. The worker is now faced with many alternatives for dealing with this training situation — namely, the care of clothing. Among other alternatives, a worker could take up techniques with this resident demonstrating how she can get it done. A worker could do the job *with* the adolescent to convey the importance of the task. The worker could insist upon priority for this task before time could be given to other activities, or the worker could reiterate her *personal* dismay and with it, her personal concern. The latter would leave the youngster to wrestle with her own conscience over the matter. Incidentally, in the case of a worker with a close attachment with the youngster, more persistent learning would typically occur with the last approach. The youngster's value acquisition would be most intimately challenged by the worker's strong personal appeal; by the worker's identification with her requirements, and in turn, by the girl's identification. We note in this example that the worker does not doubt her authority or power position. In each of the techniques employed, the focus has been on attending to the task.

In the foregoing paragraphs we tried to deal with the ever-present concern for discipline. Emphasis has to be upon assisting a child or youth to fulfill expectations in terms of their actual appropriateness. No direct consideration has been given in the face of non-compliance to what should be done or when and how children should be punished. Concern centers around the critical incident, critical for the child's or youth's learning, rather than the worker's self-esteem and survival (Beker, 1972).[14] The question then shifts from the kind of punishment each piece of violation requires, to what can be done toward the individual's mastery. It is assumed that children and adolescents learn in many different ways. Every possible medium for learning is to be utilized (Whittaker, 1979, p. 38) as children and their care givers struggle together. Ways need to be found for learning to live together while living to learn, and for adding new styles continuously to meet and to fulfill tasks yet undone.

## RESIDENTIAL LIFE AS PRELUDE
## AND EXTENSION
## OF A CHILD'S HOME LIFE

### Concurrent Work With Family and Child in Group Care

Residential care is conceived in general as a temporary measure, even if placement sometimes promises to be for a considerable part of an individual's childhood. A child is placed, assigned, or committed—however the technical language denotes it—as a "client" of the group care service. The child never *moves* there. Basically, children conceive of their family setting as their home and their home community. Such awareness requires that linkages with the previous home, friends, and other basic community contacts remain part of the child's life while in placement. Moreover, these continuous contacts evolve into participant roles and possibly even recipient roles of agency service in helping facilitate the child's successful return to his or her regular community.

As already implied, children do not lay aside their previous attachments and associations by a mere placement to a new care setting. Old relationships continue; they impact the quality of new ones, especially if these previous associations have been touched by uncertainty and *conflictual* alignment. The notion of a sense of having a past with continuity is essential for the children. Their care giving service needs to work with the children's past alignments and community affiliations as an integral aspect of the children's lives. The same position could be justified on a humanitarian basis; it is their right. Those people who have been intertwined in the child's life have a continuous stake, interest, and commitment; parents, friends, and others cannot be locked out by the altering of a child's care arrangements.

In these days of rapid communication contacts can be maintained by phone, exchange of letters, and face-to-face encounters either by children returning to their home sites or by family and friends dropping in at the group care place. Many child care group settings set as part of their policy the return home of children on weekends or for other regular periods. By means of these contacts child and parent are able to see each other and honor their attachments, however smooth or difficult, so that all can be actively assisted in acquiring skills for dealing with one another. These continued child-parent contacts require active assistance and planning by the group care service. Both parties, separately and together, need to be helped with the progression of their relationship. Counseling by social workers (Magnus, 1974), family therapy for all parties involved (Letulle, 1979), child management and human relationship skill training by the child care workers (Webster, Somjen, Shoman, Bradley, Mooney & Mack, 1979), and any or all of these three inter-ventive approaches may be applicable.

Most important in the approach suggested here, there is a shift away from conceiving placement in a linear model. Instead group care and home life are viewed as meaningful and interweaving components. In this framework, when the child returns home for a short or long stay the group care worker's interest, concern, and active involvement will go along. Conversely, while a child is in group care the parent (or parents) wants to know, should know, and is entitled to know of the child's life in the institution.

To facilitate contacts between the children in group care and their families, special thought needs to be directed toward providing an environment which furthers spontaneity and natural give-and-take. Among other factors, these encounters can be enlivened within the group care setting by a comfortable and inviting meeting place. Fur-niture has to be practical and adaptable for rearrangement to suit the situation. Preferably such a place should also include facilities where people can prepare food right on the spot for eating together. Eating assists with linking people. Often a parent wants to provide and is missed for his or her "special" cooking. Child care workers might also on occasion join these gatherings. Indeed child, par-ent(s), and care workers are full partners in residential group care. Parents and care workers need not be competitive as alternate care givers; they are really co-care givers and are actually "co-parent-ing" (Berkman, 1979).

## *"Visiting" Home*

In preceding paragraphs the author purposely avoided referring to parent's or children's visits. The author has been made aware of the inappropriateness of our use of this term at a time when parents are challenged to become more engaged in long range planning for their children (White, 1979). What do we convey when we urge parents *to visit their children* and schedule children *to visit their homes*?

## Incorporation of Parents' and Others' Active Assistance Into the Group Care Program

In addition to continuous and meaningful contacts between child and parent, group care services may also want to search out ways in which the parents and other relevant home community contacts can be interwoven into the group care's service program. Involvement of parents, etc., in special events as spectators or participants or even as co-sponsors, are all possibilities. On other occasions, some parents, former teachers or friends, can be involved in helping with the painting of a room, a big cookie bake, a canning spree, a fix-the-bicycle day, spring gardening, or an ordinary house cleaning splash. These extra hands undoubtedly will provide a boost, and more important, parents and service become partners. Children and parents can also see and experience each other in different ways while being involved in a joint enterprise. At such work parties it might be even more advantageous when parents and their own children are not working together. Parents can then relate more easily to other children and perhaps a child could learn more easily about his parent's capabilities and contributions through the eyes of other children. Still more natural is the solicitation of family involvement when there can be ordinary give-and-take, such as stopping by spontaneously, thereby encouraging participation and exchange of information by an orderly but basically open-door policy. Parent(s)' and others' participation in parents' groups, advisory councils, service projects, or special task groups of the service, provide other avenues for sharing in the provision and hopefully the direction of the group care service (Whittaker, 197°, p. 7 and ch. 6).

## Partnership in Care and Treatment

The essential nature of a continuous partnership of the child, the group care agency, and the client's family or other relevant parties in devising the best care and treatment within the group setting can be well buttressed by recent research. These studies find a positive relationship between parental involvement and effective planning and successful outcome following foster (Fanshel, 1975) and group care (Durkin and Durkin, 1975). Moreover, much effort in residential care work is typically directed to overcoming the residents' unusual susceptibility to undue peer pressure. Such peer pressure is lessened in the face of stronger parental ties (Bronfenbrenner, 1970).

It is important also to point out that a good range of research findings over the past two decades have concluded that the effectiveness of residential treatment is more highly correlated with the amount of help children receive with their post-institutional problems of living than with the nature of their residential experience as such (Allerhand, Weber and Haug, 1966; Taylor and Alpert, 1973). Post-institutional follow-up work logically requires the joint work of the persons involved in the actual group and home care: the child care workers (Maier, 1975, p. 414), family members, social workers, and possibly other key persons (siblings, grandparents, neighbors, teachers, etc.).

A host of questions can be rightly raised whether this broadside approach is feasible at all. Ample case illustrations can be offered in which clients' families have either been perceived as unable or unwilling to cooperate and there will be situations where all efforts will be to no avail. In the majority of situations, however, the clients' families can be involved on some reasonable level, with range and degree of involvement varying greatly. This working partnership typically will not be smooth or complete; it will generally require an all out effort to move along in as active and synchronized a way as possible.

## The Group Care Service Environment

What has been outlined as a full partnership between clients' home and group service environments can be also repeated as a refrain for the mutual involvement of the group care setting and its peripheral social and physical environment. Regardless of whether it is located in a densely inhabited area or in an isolated country spot, every group care setting has neighbors, a community, institutions, local events, and notable landmarks within its vicinity which make up its living environment.

The group care service, residents as well as all staff members, are in turn actually neighbors, community members, and a decisive service addition to their particular community. The group care service has a host of rich program opportunities in the utilization of neighbors (which in rural settings include the chickens, cows, horses, or pigs). Program is also enhanced by the mere fact of being a constituent part of the community — on a social, economic, and political level, the service has an intrinsic identity as one contributing institution among many others (schools, post office, churches, service clubs, businesses, and so forth). These aspects open up to residential children multi-resources for varied contacts and potential new footholds for a sense of belonging. To cite one illustration: a child writing or dictating a note to someone on the "outside" requires the purchase of a stamp at the post office. Thereafter, the note has to be mailed. The course of that piece of mail from post office to delivery offers the possibility of establishing a sense of one's place in a regular continuity of the world beyond the child care center. (Youngsters who have absolutely no ordinary contacts back home to write to still have their present or former social service workers, old teachers, policemen, or others they may recall.)

The environment of the group care setting provides the immediate social realities for program. As such these realities should be utilized and ultimate utilization depends much on the staff's own sense of anchorage in the community. Consequently a service has to expend considerable ingenuity and resource in assisting staff to be and to feel part of the community. This means seeing to it that staff members first feel fully a part of the agency itself, secondly that they have time and resources to become acquainted with the community as part of their work expectations, and lastly that staff members are continuously dealt with not only as constituents of the service but also as members of a joint community.

## CONCLUDING SUMMARY

Looking back over this chapter we have been drawing an ever widening circle of environments; the rings expand like the rings of a pebble thrown into a pond. With every expansion each ring has become more inclusive, while the center has become a fuller part of the whole. We started out with an everyday scene of group care. The difficulty of a single child intrinsically drew in other children and their child care workers. In reviewing a number of ordinary struggles which children face in their everyday growing up process, particularly when they have to deal with multi-primary attachment experience, we have been alerted to the pivotal role of the nurturing person. These primary life experiences that we have witnessed are strongly impacted by the spatial arrangements and accessibility to resources. As Bettelheim once wisely proclaimed, "Love is not enough" (1950).[15] We paraphrase him, "neither love nor space are enough." We have learned that even the most caring workers within the most promising setting must be knowledgeable about human development and the application of such knowledge to the everyday care of children.

Curiously enough, much of residential work deals with the contradiction of differentiating and uniting. The moment the child leaves his or her home efforts have to be directed toward his or her return. New associations in the residence must not obliterate past and future ties. Ultimately then, group care extends beyond mere alternate care. It demands joint participation and the caring efforts of all parties in the child's life constellation.

Finally, in our visualization of this full partnership of child (or youth), his or her famiy and kin, and group care service program, we have briefly acknowledged that the group care service has its own neighborhood as a vital resource for clientele and staff — and a rallying ground for temporary anchorage. If we place a high value on the child as a full part of this network, we note that the group care service has to ensure that staff themselves experience anchorage and ready entry into active community participation. Assured of these prerequisites, group care staff can venture in similar direction with the children or youth under their care.

## NOTES

1. In earlier literature such counseling sessions have been defined as "marginal interview." They occurred "marginally" to the ongoing casework or psychotherapy (Wineman, 1959). Presently, such counseling is more realistically conceived as part and parcel of the group care and treatment processes.

2. Feeding, clothing, and attending lovingly to a child's needs are essential parenting features. However, the care worker becomes essentially "the professional caring parent" when ordinary parenting does not sustain a child's regular development.

3. See Morris F. Mayer's dictum that an effective intervention has to meet the dual criteria, "It has to be logical and it has to be psychologically correct" (Mayer, 1958, p. 140).

4. "Buffer zone" refers to the personal spatial distance each person requires for his or her sense of personal privacy. These requirements are both idiosyncratically and culturally determined (Horowitz, Duff, & Stratton, 1970).

5. One may wonder whether an old bust has a place in the livingroom of a residential treatment unit. In this instance, the eleven 13-year-old boys had incorporated this "built in" piece of sculpture of the founder of the place as a useful feature of their living space.

6. Credit for this cogent observation goes to a colleague, Monte Berke, Mercer Island Youth Service, Mercer Island, Washington.

7. Conversely, the negation of physical comfort is a vehement message of nonacceptance. Consider the studies of penal settings, punitive expressions and the accounts of concentration camps. In each of these accounts a restraining or denial of bodily requirements signify the one-down positions, disdain and isolation these captives had to endure.

8. The Peanuts cartoon of Linus with his blanket is a classic illustration of the human significance of a transitional object.

9. We need merely to envisage the young people of the 1970s as they wrapped themselves in corners, front entrances, or passages, detached from life around them, as well as these young people's insistence upon "doing their own thing" amidst the close life of their communal living arrangements.

10. In fact, children or adolescents rarely destroy things which they conceive as fully their own and they themselves enjoy. It is the author's experience that children at moments of severe anger, including temper tantrums, destroy many valuable items. However, somehow their radio, picture of a genuine friend and cherished pieces of clothing, etc. survive their seemingly blind path of destruction.

11. See Jon R. Conte's searching cogent monograph on time-out procedures (Conte, 1978).

12. Appreciation to Ted Teather for introducing me to this descriptive term.

13. This necessity for caring opportunities suggests that pets, plants, pretty things and pseudo-art objects, brief service projects, etc. are apt to be more than marginal features of a residential treatment program.

14. Beker (1972) is an excellent reader and teaching tool on the manifold individual and group crises which occur in the run of a day, week and month in a residential group care setting.

15. It is the title of Bruno Bettelheim's first and most impactful publication: *Love is Not Enough* (1950).

Chapter III

# How Children and Adolescents Conceive Their World Beyond the Group Care Setting

## INTRODUCTION

The place where children actually spend their daily lives and where their everyday requirements are met, whether this be in their own homes or in alternative group settings, constitutes the *center* of the children's world. As children grow older, not only the people within their particular abode, but also those next door and beyond are included in their intimate environment — the children's personal world. The progression of this widening childhood perspective is pertinent to the following pages.

In social terms, as well as in the professional literature, we tend to differentiate between the lives of children growing up in their own home and those who "live away from home" (Whittaker & Trieschman, 1972). This designation may be descriptively correct; yet, at the same time it reveals our own ambiguity about these children's status; we can only describe their major life experience as where they are *not*: "away from home." This designation challenges us to scrutinize the living experiences of these children, where they are, in order to comprehend more fully how they, and we, perceive their mode of existence. Their socially engineered *group* or *residential* mode of living, is in the words of Arieli, Kashti, and Shlasky an " . . . organized separation of varying degrees, both from their original community and from the social environment [their residential living arrangements] (Arieli, Kashti & Shlasky, 1983, p. 11).

This article also appears in Kashti, Y. and Arieli, M. (Eds.) (1987). Residential Settings and the Community: Congruence and Conflict. London: Freund. Reprinted by permission of Freund Publishing House, Chesham House, 150 Regent Street, London, England.

This chapter focuses specifically upon the children's conception of their lives "away from home" while they are in residential settings. We are interested in these children's notions about "family life," "home," "neighbors," "community," and "society." This kind of focus reflects an effort to augment, in particular, earlier publications about residential institutions which have been unwittingly engaged in context stripping (Bronfenbrenner, 1979), as if residential living occurred independent and apart from the residents' family roots and community associations as well as the institution's organizational auspice. In place of a sole focus upon micro issues, the intertwining of micro and macro forces is central to this kind of scrutiny.[1]

We ourselves are conscious of the continuous interplay between personal and communal perspectives of life. We note the interweaving of individual (primary) and societal (secondary) group demands; or technically speaking, the interactions of micro- and macro-system forces which make up the patterns of daily life. In fact, we acknowledge that in this interplay forces of the macro-system decisively determine and define micro-systems, including an individual's life course (Capelle, 1979; Monane, 1967). We are cognizant of the fact that *the context creates the index*[2] and the range of life experience which is possible at a given time. At the same time, individuals tend to vary in their capacity and readiness to understand and to define their macro-systems' relevance (Piaget, 1975). Throughout this chapter we have to ask ourselves: to what extent are children conscious of their personal and communal situation? And in which way can we assist them to deal with communal, with contextual issues when these contextual factors are beyond their intellectual grasp? Consequently, as backdrop for looking at children's conception of their world around them, we shall deal with three major contextual factors. First, we are interested in children's *context boundaries*; we want to discern what constitutes the children's actual active world within the course of their development from childhood to the emergence of early adulthood.

Secondly, in everyday life, when societal forces are particularly powerful, these forces tend to be experienced and seen as personal phenomena. However close a societal reality impinges, *the personal reality is always more apparent and imminent* (Maier, 1978b, p. 21). We are faced throughout this chapter with the sensitive question: How can child/youth workers, administrators, or policy planners effectively deal with societal issues, recognizing that they are experienced as personal factors by the residents.

Third, and basic to this deliberation, is the recognition that the family and the non-familial contextual living arrangements are conceived differentially, depending on the *developmental status* of the children or youth. It is the residents' appraisal and comprehension of the various systems' demands rather than the demands per se which ultimately shape their behaviors, feelings and thinking. It follows then that we have continuously to inquire in each child care situation: What is the child's/youth's actual level of comprehension about his or her current living situation *and* what are the contextual forces determining the residential program. To illustrate, it seems that children and other family members "interact" with one another in familial ways as long as they live at home. When they live in a group residence, parent and child "visit" with one another at the residence or at home. Note our contradictions in the use of these terms in our practice. Children *visit in their own home*. Similarly, parents *visit* with their own children! We must face our confusions about the status of these inherent relationship systems. Another example would be when children go to nearby friends' homes outside of confines of their institution. It is designated as going to see friends *"in the community."* Is it not also true that the residential setting and the children therein are also part of the community? "The questionable assumption here is," to quote Leon Fulcher, "that residential institutions are . . . *not* in the community, resulting in the naive view that institutional care is bad and community care is good" (Fulcher, 1983, p. 63).

## TO WHAT EXTENT ARE SOCIETAL REALITIES CONSTANT "REALITIES" FOR ADULTS?

It might be assumed that adults view their daily life experiences and societal events from a consistent adult perspective which can be readily equated with "reality." By further inspection we come to note, however, that adult reality tends to vary. Nearby events or intimate experiences are apt to be viewed for their qualitative impact upon a person, and in contrast, events personally more removed tend to be viewed more for their societal relevance (Maier, 1978b). As an illustration, a residential staff member may contemplate that s/he has an extra day off, as staff, unlike parents, are entitled to time-off for having worked on a holiday authorized by society. When a staff member needs personally a day off, this day due becomes a personal requirement and a personally earned free day rather than merely time due as part of the work arrangements.

The differentiation between personal (primary) and societal (secondary) experience, is of particular importance for policies and practices affecting human relations work. A policy shift in organizational or communal arrangements may be readily understood by the community-at-large as a new societal approach to service delivery. (An example of this would be establishing active parental participation in the service program.) The parents and children, however, who would be directly involved, very likely would see this new policy in terms of the immediate personal impact for them and far from the "reality," stemming from a new innovation or reform by society.

We know, furthermore, that in moments of stress or in crisis situations, societal measures are perceived by the individual as very personal events. The mechanical red light traffic signals, for instance, may personally frustrate a person in a hurry. An automatic dismissal from school for continuous non-attendance as a general policy matter, is apt to be seen as "being kicked-out of school" by the youth discharged. It is this *personal* experience which requires attention first, before the individual involved can eventually relate him or herself to the wider societal issue.

### What Then are the Contextual Realities of the Family, Peer, Group, Community, Service Organization, and Society-Systems for Children or Youth?

Foremost, is the necessity that each of these diverse systems be understood as conceptual constructs with no particular individual or "*I*" as its center. These systems exist and function primarily in response to societal not personal requirements. They are conceived as basic frameworks for human existence within a social context. Interestingly, even when systems are fully understood for their social reality, they become anthropomorphized to assume a personal quality. Highly technical and complex factors become charming, touchable, and animated characters: e.g., "Uncle Sam" for the U.S. government; "Good Neighbor Efforts" for a welfare drive; "Boystown" for a socially-engineered service delivery program, etc.

For the average *adult*, society is "out there." The adult also perceives that "out there" phenomena do belong to the objective world and are accepted as such. "The apparent agreement between outside [societal] and inside [personal] generates in people's minds the experience of truth, fact, and obviousness" (Furth, 1980, p. 5). In adult thinking, contextual systems exist a priori as "ominous" situational realities — as supra-systems; the adult thinks of interpersonal events as sub-system occurrences. Tokens of exchange (money, budgets), boundary maintenance (charters, information exchange, licenses, etc.), and role acquisitions (occupations, ranks, etc.) represent some of the major commodities of exchange of contextual systems; while attachments and personal support, power, values, and prestige (status) are the attributes which are of major personal significance within the course of interpersonal interactions.

For *children and youth*, regardless whether in day, residential, or immediate family care, these matters assume quite different "realities." Societal or personal experience, i.e., contextual or immediate physical experience, are blurred. Distant, contextual influences are either non-apparent to young children or they have to be anthropomorphically cast into immediately physical explainable everyday phenomena to be recognized at all. For instance, socio-cultural values for neatness and order are represented by smiling, personally-awarded stickers. Children's interactions with the physical environment are more readily comprehended by them than influences from their social world. A severe cut in the budget, a political priority decision of the responsible societal body, is explained by the children in concrete terms affecting the institutional life. An example would be: we no longer get money to buy ice cream for snacks. "Societal events as *societal* events are only captured as a developing child's thinking gradually approximates adult thinking" (Furth, 1980, p. 4). Our explorations of children's understanding of their social world opens up a rather unexplored domain of socio-psychological knowledge (Forbes, 1978, p. 133).

## THE "OUTSIDE" AS VIEWED
## FROM THE "INSIDE"
## WITHIN A DEVELOPMENTAL PROGRESSION

Residential careworkers with a range of experience would confirm that the announcement: "Someone is here to see you!" evokes quite different spontaneous expectations, depending upon the children's developmental age. A preschool-age child is apt to visualize his/her parent as the announced visitor regardless whether this is possible or not. Older teenagers, in contrast, will typically weigh whether the prospective visitor is a family member, a peer, or possibly a representative of one of those welfare establishments. (After all, representatives of various establishments are, for them, everpresent.) Children do conceive and expect varying encounters with the world beyond their immediate daily life experience, depending upon the level of their developmental progress. Within each age phase, contextual factors are decisively and differentially indexed (Damon, 1977, 1978; Datan & Ginsberg, 1975; Maier, 1978b, Ch. 1; Piaget, 1975).

### Preschool-Age Children

Basically, for children below school age contextual events are seen as *undifferentiated personal* events. Personal and societal roles and functions are seen as one. Usually, children under six tend to adapt readily to adult requests when the adult is a person close to them. In contrast, young children shy away from strangers, from persons outside of their experience regardless of the nature of the requests or the roles assumed by these adults (Forbes, 1978, pp. 124-130).[3] As in fairytales, events *just happen.* They are conceived in terms of the individual's own immediate perception (Furth, 1980, pp. 6-7). Whatever belongs to the moment, constitutes the total system. What adults may readily interpret as "outside" events, the child (or crisis-struck person) experiences solely as an on-the-spot happening. It is akin to the old adage: Heads off for the bearers of ill tidings! In residential care life, a depended-upon care worker's departure is experienced as a worker who *left* the children. The children cannot conceive of this person as one who had to return to further his or her own education or to fulfill other commitments.

The foregoing summation of the restrictive conception of a wider world — that life proceeds entirely within a personal and personalized world — points to the necessity to think through and to utilize a personal frame of action in residential work. For instance, communal requirements for vaccination, to infants or young children are not a preventive health practice; it means for them a person painfully pricking their skins. It requires intimate caregivers to physically hold the children supportively in order to validate and counteract the unpleasant act rather than merely seeing the activity as one of salient service provision. The same approach is involved in the transfer of a preschool-age child to a new day care group or living arrangements. Regardless of how logically, child-oriented, and organizationally necessary the rearrangements are, so long as the children view them as purely personal, planning must be dealt with as such. For instance, to a four-year-old girl, it is meaningless to learn that she will be placed in a new day care program because the state has closed her previous program. Rather, she has to experience her parent taking her to the new one with the explanation: "I am taking you to a new center. *I* would like you to be there." In early childhood years, young children either proceed by their own momentary conceptions or the ones posed by their adult caregivers. The adults' society is their society; adults are "authorities about society" (Youniss, 1980, p. 28).

The personal perspective of children in this age group also readily explains their actions, and conceptions of their actions when they overlook well-established societal practices instead of recognizing a contractual transaction (Furth, 1980, p. 7). Similarly, roles stem from the activity rather than belonging to the context. It is very logical, for example, for a young child to see her or himself as a caregiver while passing out the cookies at dessert time. Or, a child will experience a wait at a street crossing as a personal affront, even when the traffic sign indiscriminately turned red for everyone at the curb.

### Children of Early School Age

With added life experiences, children, roughly in the early grade school years, slowly develop some notion of context; they discover an "outside" world. They learn that events occur beyond and apart from them. They eventually understand and are able to generalize what specific persons do and are supposed to do and also can register an awareness that many happenings occurring around them are beyond their comprehension (Maier, 1978b, pp. 45-46). Most important, in the understanding of cognitive development, particularly for persons testing or working intimately with young chldren, is the notion that there are two decisive, separate developmental steps: (1) *information gathering*, and (2) *information processing*. Children progressively learn to observe, to hold on to, to order and to classify what they learn of the world around them. They gather a wealth of information. It takes, however, their added experience and continuous cognitive development to *process* such understanding, making it fully comprehendible (Maier, 1978b, p. 29). Such overall knowledge is important for all forms of work with children; the practitioner should be aware that knowing something can remain several steps away from making use of such knowledge.

Indigenous to this growing-up process is the child's increased capability to conceive role differentiation bound in a personal realm, while the individual's societal relevance is still unrecognized. (The same holds true in general crisis situations for us all. A policeman stopping a speeding driver, for example, is apt to be appraised in terms of the officer's degree of personal interactions . . . friendly, polite, or strict . . . , rather than for his or her law and order functions.) Within this maturing phase, children note the existence and regulatory power of rules, societal edicts, and customs. However, the child tends to personalize the "guardian" of rules as the creator and owner of the very rules he or she advocates. Basically, policy makers, that is, government and councils, are still outside of their daily life experience; they are merely conceived via the *persons* connected with these bodies (Furth, 1980, p. 43). Nevertheless these bodies, in a general sense do exist. The children recognize that there are rules, forces, and establishments beyond their own personal action spheres.

In the realm of residential work, children can separate care, education and other forms of human relations work which are for pay from the corresponding "natural" activities such as parenting or neighborliness. They see a precise difference between socially engineered, that is employed, and "natural" caregiving. Beyond an awareness of these two forms of child-tending, they give not a second thought to the caregivers' linkages with their sponsoring agency's systems. They conceive that the societally-sponsored caregivers are performing their caring tasks in a certain way as a matter of personal choice (Furth, 1980, pp. 31-34).

Even while the children of this developmental age effectively relate to their caregiving adults primarily for their personal rather than their organizational relationships to them, they more and more become cognitively intrigued with existing hierarchical arrangements, variations from the rules as they see them, and the actual operation of the world around them. Their observations tend to be shrewd but primitive because their comprehension is still without any substantial awareness of contextual circumstances. They may miss the important contextual cues while sporting much of the raw reality. At this stage, they are the ones who will be fascinated with the Emperor, because he *is* in his underwear ("The Emperor's New Clothes")! In another instance, children quickly conclude that a diligent cleaning of the institution's kitchen equipment forebodes a visit from the Sanitation Department inspector. They tend to see it in terms of a visit of "that man" rather than as a check by a representative of a licensing agency. Correspondingly, behavior expectations in school or in the community in general are readily conceived by the children as generalized rules but they are even more impressed by the persons enunciating them. Children begin to see clearly the parts of any immediate system *or* the whole; however, parts and whole are not yet for them a congruent totality (Maier, 1978b, p. 47).

This differentiation has direct implications for residential work. In either case, organizational directives are understood and typically responded to for their personal rather than their logical, universal dimension and the actual ownership of authority. Residential childcare workers need to transmit in words, by example, and personal conviction what form of behavior is expected *by them* rather than as a matter of organizational arrangements and agency policy.

Significantly we must keep in mind that it is often in this phase (roughly in the first and second or third years in elementary school), that children are considered for placement in residential settings such as school, camp, and children's institutions. Most children understand why they are at a boarding school or a residential program. Almost all boarding school children uphold the belief that it is a special, beneficial arrangement for them. Their confidence rests with the optimistic belief of their original caregivers. Boarding school placement reflects parental support and a shared belief by parents, society and, consequently, also the pupils that there is something to be gained from the experience. In contrast, when they are placed in residential settings, their parents, staff, and society-in-general are seldom convinced that such an institution is primarily for the children's "salvation" and even less so that their future after placement is assured (Clough, 1982, p. 10). In short, placements in boarding schools and in residential institutions, may establish from the outset different sets of expectations, because children are capable of "reading" their family's and society's set of expectations and values assigned to each.

Typically, children at this age will note differences: individual differentiation of standards, and conflicting values. Life issues will be primarily seen as "good" or "bad," as "lawful" or "evil," "fair or unfair" (just as in the Star War films or TV shows at home). It is at this point that their *personal* anchoring point, i.e., their immediate caregivers, have to help them to see these "worlds" for what they are. Above all, care workers need to puzzle out the incongruencies with the children from the *children's* perspectives rather than as the defenders of an imperfect agency, community, or society. The workers' readiness to do so depends much upon the welfare system's and the employing agency's concrete preparedness to grant their staff the time and support to fulfill these difficult tasks (Fulcher, 1983).

## The Vulnerable Age Period

Research findings within the past ten years have brought out that the early school years are not as carefree as thus far assumed. A particular vulnerability seems to be evidenced for children who experience a *personal* social dislocation such as drastic cultural neighborhood and school changes during the approximate ages of six through nine. Children who experience cultural transitions, especially those shifted into the cultural settings (schools) which are of different ethnicity than those of their family, do not do as well in school, in their educational career, and type of early work commitment as their contemporaries who do not have to endure such a change. Significantly, the siblings of these children in transition who are either in an older or younger age phase do not evidence such undesirable effects although they have to face apparently identical circumstances (Inbar, 1976; Inbar & Adler, 1977).

If these and correspondingly other findings are correct (Maier, 1986e) it seems that these moments of difficulties are associated with the children's point in development when they migrate from a life purely engulfed in primary (micro) life experience to one in which they also have to pursue their lives in the streams of secondary (macro) life. Moreover, this phenomenon occurs at a time when they start to conceive their life experience for both micro and selected macro events. It is a point in children's development when they *transit* into the spheres of their secondary worlds. We note that strain with subsequent impact tends to occur when the children are faced with "strange" macro-systems of which their own primary system (family) is not yet a part (Inbar & Adler, 1977). These observations remind us that children of ethnic minority groups in the United States frequently encounter learning (or is it: teaching?) difficulties within the second or third grades of their schooling (Maier, 1986e). Could there be operating in these circumstances a "cultural migrant syndrome" (Runstein, 1983)? There is the possibility that these findings may have special relevance for residential settings where in some countries a good number of the residents are members of minority groups; in particular, where these children have to undergo a migration to new secondary settings with a different cultural context than their family of origin. It is not only a question as to who will care for the children, how will they be fed, clothed, and sheltered. It will be of equal importance to ascertain where they will be housed and schooled, and in which way will their new environment provide a sense of continuity for the children, their families, and their familial reference systems (Maier, 1986e). After all, residential care is not an alternate to but a supplement of family living (Davis, 1981, pp. 87-101; Whittaker & Garbarino, 1983, p. 185).

## Later Childhood Years

Roughly around the ages of 9 to 11-12 years of age (or an equivalent developmental period) children tend to comprehend that there are organizational, communal, and societal spheres. Primarily, they see the societal systems for their parts, for the scatter of systems with which they are here and there in contact. A comprehension of the interconnectedness of the various parts and the overall systems is yet to come.

It is useful for us to know that "outside" worlds are primarily seen for their qualities, as acting *part*-systems, but not yet quantatively belonging to an integrative network of a societal matrix (Furth, 1980, p. 49). The children give little thought to the circumstances or consequences surrounding these *sources* of power (Furth, 1980, p. 44). The auspices of the program with which the residents are personally associated, for instance, are perceived as rule giver, primary source of funds and regulators of events beyond their grasp. Life is still very much as if it were put together like film strips, a series of action sequences experienced as unconnected events. For instance, with a situational perspective a child will be at odds with adults' normative outlook. From the adult view, an example might be: a bed *has* to be made after sleeping in it. However, it seems picayunish to a ten-year old to make his or her bed, because there are so many more important things to do. The bed will get messed up again anyhow. At the same time, *situational* factors, the events within this figurative filmstrip, are recognized as more and more a force in determining outcome. In other words, situational events as contextual experiences represent early glimmers of societal manifestos (Forbes, 1978, p. 131).

Children at this developmental stage are at a point where their energy is invested toward discovering and absorbing system operations beyond the bounds of family life. They are curious and inclined "to case out" the school beyond the classroom, the shops beyond the neighborhood store, the neighborhood beyond their own street, and in residential care group to explore life beyond their own unit and frequently beyond the residential setting (Maier, 1986e). These explorations require the full supportive attention of their immediate caregivers. They represent forays into new territories and experiences with *other* social systems and different systems of their adult worlds and the worlds of peers. It is a period when children discover how to deal with peers — to experiment with new adult contacts and specifically form agemate friendships. They derive new definitions of self, of other persons, and of differential relationship systems (Youniss, 1980, p. 29).

Also importantly, the youngsters are able to form conceptual constructs beyond their observed experience, even while their thinking is apt to be confused and contradictory (Furth, 1980, p. 158). They can describe and designate proper role functions, and in particular, can associate people with the various societal units. They quickly size up the formal and particularly the informal power functions of the institutional staff network. They spot who actually has power among all of the residential power brokers. Children in this age group look at them with a very personal perspective as they (along with their elders) evaluate their social systems. Their neighborhoods or selected welfare systems are seen and related to, for the impact these have upon them personally. When, for example, a residential organization conceives its community as a totality, offering service commitments, the children are apt to view it for its recreational resources, possibly its delinquent exploitation opportunities, or other qualities or lacks rather than utilizing the adults' value measures. The newly discovered secondary worlds are "conquered" for situational expedient rather than societal yields. In other words, even when community, welfare systems, and society become social realities for children, it is in no way certain that the children will understand, classify, and value the same opportunities and indigenous dangers as their adult counterparts. These observations have particular implications for the selection and training of community people as *indigenous* linkages for the residential program and as potential "guideposts" for the children's development of "proper" societal reference systems.

### Pre-Adolescent Years

Pre-adolescence is a period known for its transitional wanderings between childhood and adolescence, and represents a time of transitional hurdles such as transfer from grade schools to junior high or formerly the 11 + exams. In almost all educational programs, a shift occurs from being taught an array of subjects in one classroom by one teacher, to an exposure to many teachers and a daily migration from classroom to classroom. These wanderings amidst a variety of places, subjects, and people, appropriately mirror pre-adolescents' readiness to relate to a multi-systemic world of home/institution, community, social welfare system, and society-at-large. Preadolescent thinking begins to approximate adult perspectives. At this stage, pre-adolescents now knowingly conceive societal phenomena and employ appropriately the terminology used by their world of grownups. They witness societal institutions as real, active, and as powerful; but cognitively, they can not yet fully conceive societal systems as distinct conceptual entities (Furth, 1980, pp. 198-200).

Agency, social welfare delivery system, and government units are understood for their specific functions and services. Children readily comprehend lines of communication and hierarchical relationships; they recognize that these systems are privately or publically funded by donations or taxes. Their comprehension, however, is quickly thrown off track when hierarchical lines become detoured by intervening circumstances or when the support and payment systems become complicated by other budgetary considerations (Furth, 1980, p. 45). Organizations and governmental units are understood for their service functions, but less for their *reciprocal* relations to societal requirements. In other words, organizations, to pre-adolescent way of thinking, are there to serve, to do, and to be responded to, but not because the systems depend upon or are served by larger requirements. For these older children, an

> . . . understanding of the political system and governmental functions is still quite vague and their thinking about the general needs of a societal community, its traditions, and cultural

symbols is concrete and therefore unsystemic and principally on an affective-emotional level. (Furth, 1980, p. 50)

In many ways, these children are in the twilight zone of being simultaneously children of families as well as residents of a care institution and budding citizens of an organization, school, and community.

In the everyday life of these children, societal understanding beyond personalized experiences comes about through continuous and repeated active experience with their secondary world's institutions. These include such activities as going shopping, handling the exchange of money and goods, the use of public transportation and communication systems, interactions with officials like postal clerks or police officers, school principals or custodians. Also helpful is the utilization of information services on the phone, at a shopping center, or library. Above all, the children can be challenged to encounter a vast array of societal roles in variant roles themselves: as information seeker and giver, as a personal inquirer and as an inquirer on behalf of others, as rule violator, as seeker of a clarification, or as advocate for a change of rules. Each of these interactions furnishes experience with environmental factors — and move the youngster along his or her ladder of learning social skills. We cannot stress enough the importance of such experiences and the fact that they have to be salient features of residential programming (Hedin, 1982). During these activities, children may learn from their caregivers, most likely for the first time, how to become members themselves of a caring community.

The fact that children in their pre-adolescent ages and beyond are keenly aware of communal forces beyond their primary group experience, provides these youngsters also with opportunities to choose their preferred societal alliances. Children in residence, as children anywhere, do not necessarily choose their elders' societal reference groups, but gravitate to those of their own preferences. Children with special ethnic or racial identification are apt to see the community not necessarily along geographic divisions, but on the basis of ethnic demarcations. Some youngsters may gravitate to other subsystems such as a delinquent culture, religious sect, a gay community, a counter-culture segment, or other possibilities. Consequently, nurturing the children's growth towards total community enmeshment, necessitates that residential staff, and their supporting organizational systems spread their capabilities and readiness for dealing with added and (at times for staff) undesirable systems. Nevertheless, it is at these critical points that the organization, its sponsors, and the staff in charge are the ones faced with the challenge to be open to bi-cultural, multi-ethnic, and differing forms of behavior and value systems (Green, 1982, pp. 53-54).

### Adolescence

As we follow children's developmental progression, we notice that their range of activities from childhood to adolescence can be summarized as doing more, with more people, in more places, with a wider range of systems, to an ever-enlarging societal context. With growing experience, adolescents gradually come to, and become competent in relating to, societal issues as such. They also will be able to tease out personal considerations as separate from organizational and communal matters. In fact, the teenagers

> . . . normally are capable of remarkably sophisticated reasoning about the social relations and regulations of their social world. . . . [They] take into account a multiplicity of important considerations and reconcile these considerations to suit the needs of specific situations; in constructing solutions to social problems they show both coherence and flexibility. (Damon, 1977, p. 335)

Conceptually, childhood ways are typified by *doing* because it seems natural and adolescent/adult ways as *processing* selectively. This budding adolescents' capacity to generalize brings with it also the young persons' tendency to assume that their conception of order is applicable everywhere (Youniss, 1980, p. 30).

We can readily picture a teenage girl in a group home impatiently asking her worker: "When *are* you getting word about our clothing allowance? I must have a new warm jacket, my old one is all shreds and outgrown!" We note that this adolescent no longer envisages the careworker as her provider with money for the purchase of her coat. She fully comprehends that her trip to the store, however urgent and personally justifiable, is grounded in the personal *and* organizational commitments of *her* careworker. She also is cognizant that much depends upon the agency's backing of the worker and the *agency's* capability to secure the proper funding from the child welfare service network. (In actuality, that projected budget depends upon priority determinations of its "society" — that is, the respective communal supra-systems, a combination of socially involved, established, and politically elected citizenry.) The adolescent, however, tends to see her caregivers and the immediate institutional systems as the determinants. Attitudes about people and institutions are formed at this level and grounded in these specific and personally significant experiences.

Adolescents increasingly do discover and comprehend the complexity of contemporary life. In fact, much of their repeated concerns with social and organizational issues is directly associated with this new social learning. The teenager's daily life experience in school, at work, in recreation, peer experience, and hopefully in meaningful community activities (e.g., selected volunteer tasks) brings them face-to-face with contemporary living in a multisociety. What in pre-adolescent years involved a recognition and experience of reciprocity becomes now more and more an engagement in reciprocity. Reciprocity is practiced, valued, and incorporated as an instrumentality of living. *Social* life comes into full force as reciprocity finds its ethical extension in *social responsibility* and its contextual counterpart of a *caring community*. An adolescent's induction into a caring community will vary with both the degree of social responsibility valued by the young person's immediate and larger society, and the extent such an individual is able to comprehend the *reciprocal* dimensions of his or her communal experience (Maas, 1979, p. 6).

Adolescents' newly developed grasp for *societal* issues illustrates a common human developmental fact: "what is learned is used." Adolescents will quickly spot the "realities" of life, including the ones which reveal new conflicting dimensions of life to them. These new discoveries, especially the awareness of stark inconsistencies in the adults' world of "realities," will get much of their attention affirming that their adult counterparts are also subject to improvement! They will discover the powerful *informal* networks which counteract or obscure the formal systems. They are particularly apt to spot processes which can serve their immediate personal advantage. Corruptive or criminal informal systems are quickly identified (Polsky, 1962). Moreover, adolescent development brings an intimate preoccupation with identity formation; ethnic, racial, and other socio-cultural variables are important to them. Identification occurs with those segments of society which represent the adolescent's aspired allegiances, and not necessarily the ones favored by their residential setting. Black youth, for instance, will be particularly conscious and critical of the racial climate within the institution, practices of the welfare system, and will likely align with their own ethnic groups, cross-cutting the system networks which are basic to organizational existence. Other adolescents may align with counter-culture groups because they seem to respond to their queries and interests. Eventually, adolescents' attraction to contemporary musical groups, sports teams, activist causes, and regional fads, titillates them toward regional, national, and international endeavors and thereby locating their own loyalties apart from those cherished by their elders. In short, adolescents do deal with contextual variables, but not necessarily the ones in the foreground for their respective adult worlds.

In residential work, it is the adolescents' preoccupation with organizational issues of their own *and* beyond their immediate living spheres which continuously require the residential worker's attention. At this point, it is no longer the necessity to supply added community experience in general. Instead it means offering community experience utilizing continuous and consistent encounters with people. This includes persons of their own age *and* other age groups, persons with similar and with different perspectives. In other words, it calls for opportunities for full participation in formal and especially informal, community activities, similar to their age-mates living at home. Accompanying all of these encounters, there is the necessity for continuous reflection about these experiences. The latter requires lots of "rapping." Such unending talking serves as a means for thinking, sorting out, ordering, and eventually conceptualizing the invisible, but very real contextual world. It is in these moments, in rap session or an informal chat, where residential workers prove their mettle, (their real professional relevance) for their occasional input, questions, and frequently, for their symbolic silent presence as representatives of a joint complex world.

## SYSTEM INTERACTIONS INFER
## AN INHERENT STRAIN

Thus far, we have presented a simplistic model as if *personal* and *societal* concerns were two opposing parts of a scale to be balanced. It seems that in the earlier years of life, the personal scale carries the heaviest load. While with incremental development, the societal scale is tipped until in adolescence, and especially in adulthood the weight is heaviest on the societal scale. In moments of crisis, however, for adults adolescents, and children personal needs tip the balance once again until the individual's ordinary living patterns are re-established. Such a figurative model is valid if we view human development solely for its socio-cognitive progression. A more complicated model and conception are essential, however, if we look at human interactions within the context of primary and secondary, i.e., individual and organizational, systems. In such an undertaking, we become interested in the interactions of the systems involved — the focus of our conference.

In this chapter, we have been looking at personal and societal events *as if* they were separate entities on one continuum. Actually, there is an intimate linkage of systems involved. A personal context constitutes a micro-system enmeshment, while the corresponding societal dimensions demand macro-system entanglement. Micro- and macro-systems, to follow Talcott Parsons' formulations (1964), require distinct separate and essentially contradictory processes of functioning even while constituting a solid whole.

We need to recognize that assuming a *societal* (macro-system) perspective of residential work also requires adopting the management and accountability values inherent in an organizational perspective. In many ways, this then, counteracts or at least somewhat balances the requirements of micro-systems and their strong emphasis upon individual-oriented, personalized values.

As children, and in particular teenagers, acquire greater cognitive "maturity," that is, perceive adult social "reality," they also become less clear about what is supposed to be ultimately "right." Following micro-systems demands within the context of a macro-system perspective creates inherent strains to choose continuously and to compromise with two apparently unreconcilable alternatives (Parsons, 1964). As adolescents mature further they become increasingly cognizant of their multi-worlds. They move from primary (family, peer, and other close personal) associations to increased organizational system commitments (e.g., school, work, community, business, government). In this developmental progression, children and adolescents need to gradually become acquainted with these variant systems and particularly with the resulting inherent conflicting demands.

Just a few highlights to examine the importance of handling these counterdemands of individual and organizational system requirements. Primary life experience in the family, in friendships, and particularly in therapeutic encounters, demands individualization and personalized care. In organizational life however, unless the organization is to succumb to chaos, uniformity and impersonal objectivity are the landmark of effective organizational operation. Micro- or primary-systems tend to serve manifold interests with a thrust toward the individual members' life experiences. Macro- or secondary-organizational-systems tend to concentrate upon specific interests in well-defined areas in order to accomplish efficiency in those tasks for which they are organized to undertake (Resnick, 1980). With these formulations in mind, the strain is evident how residential workers as well as teachers and other human relation workers must experience being engaged in micro-system work while employed in macro societal welfare system services. (A discussion of the tension inherent in being caught between primary and secondary systems demands is fully explored in chapter IX.) For the present, we merely want to raise these factors as valid gravitating pulls for the workers' role performance. It is also an essential factor in children's and youth's learning; they must comprehend and deal with system demands as well. As we align ourselves with the perplexity of *macro*-system demands for *primary* care settings, this inherent strain needs to be recognized for its inherent interactive force.

## CONCLUDING OBSERVATIONS

Our deliberations have dealt with a relatively uncharted area of study: contextual factors influencing the planning, operation, and evaluation of residential settings. While our focus may be upon macro-systems as the supra-system, we must be mindful that our actual concern is with the *connections* between these macro-systems and their respective micro-systems.

In this meshing, it is clear that residential settings find themselves in a curious dilemma. In one way, they are conceived as small, child- and family-oriented care and educational programs, regardless of whether we think of them as we once did, as alternates to family-care, or whether we align ourselves with recently emerging conceptual models of residential settings as family extensions (Whittaker & Garbarino, 1983) or family supplements (Davis, 1981, p. 92). Within each formulation, residential settings are valued for their *primary* care, teaching or treatment functions. The residential setting is envisaged as a component of the residents' *familial* network. Simultaneously, however, these same settings are also conceived as *society's* community responses toward certain children and youth. The residential settings by this latter perspective become service organizations and are ordered into the welfare or educational network of communal services. We note that at one and at the same time residential programs carry out primary and secondary (micro- and macro-) system functions.

Moreover, the representatives of organizational or community programs in their interactions with residential settings, as they are personally involved, will deal more likely on a primary level, with the personal aspects, however starkly apparent are the societal aspects. Persons further removed are more apt and inclined to deal with these macro thrusts as organizational issues. However realistic and "obviously clear" these factors might be in our scientific accounts, they still remain personal events for the individuals involved, regardless of whether they are enmeshed in the micro, mezzo, macro, or literally in all of them. The personal and societal dimensions must consequently remain before us as ever present.

Finally, developmental psychology as well as our own work with children have made us aware that children, youth, and adults experience and conceive the worlds around them differentially, depending upon their developmental and age progression and at times, their momentary personal requirements. We know well that in the course of a child's life history, the act of receiving a gift assumes different dimensions. For the very young child, a gift is just there. In early childhood, a gift is known to be brought by Santa Claus or an integral part of the Chanukah observation. Later a gift comes from Santa or from the parent as Santa's helper. And a year or so later, gifts are seen as part of a special occasion, and eventually as a personal/societal "program" event related to a significant occasion. Children's conceptions of their daily life experience take on new wrinkles and dimensions with the enhancement of their understanding of people and contextual circumstances. Cognitive development assists the individual to progress from a personal to a societal perspective. Consequently, in our work, we want to see how residential life is actually embedded in the various complex societal service networks and to be aware of the interconnectedness of these factors with the human care efforts. At the same time, it is important to keep in mind to what extent are these factors *comprehensible* to the children and youth about whom we are concerned.

# NOTES

1. In most previous studies, with few exceptions (e.g., Polsky & Claster, 1968; Wolins & Wozner, 1982; and most recently Whittaker & Garbarino, 1983), the social context has been treated as backdrop rather than as an independent variable.

2. Indexes are an orderly arrangement of content, based on a projection about which items are anticipated to be of special interest to outsiders. Contextual concerns determine what an index will highlight within its microsphere.

3. These findings have direct bearing on the staffing of day care and 24-hour care settings for very young children.

Chapter IV

# The Core of Care:
# Essential Ingredients
# for the Development of Children
# at Home and Away From Home

In the following pages I shall bring together some recent studies about child development with a number of critical issues in child care. I shall try to interweave these two spheres of learning, child development and child care. Usually child development and child care interests are pursued as separate concerns in disconnected research and teaching in departments far apart from each other in our universities and in our fields of practice, and more often than not by persons unknown to each other. In actuality, a solid background knowledge in child development offers basic directions for the care of children. In turn, the everyday care activities provide rich data for the study of child development.

In order for you, the reader, to become personally immersed in the ideas to be presented, pause and think of an incident where you experienced nurturing care. This would be a moment in your life when you had the sense of being the one, and only one, who counted at that particular moment.

In reviewing such recollections of experiences of personal care, the following components become apparent: (1) a sense of physical comfort; (2) a certainty that whatever care was experienced would continue or be repeated beyond that instance of care; and (3) most likely an involvement with a familiar and close caring person. In

This article originally appeared in *Child Care Quarterly*, 8(3), 1979, 161-173. Reprinted by permission of Human Sciences Press, Inc., 72 Fifth Avenue, New York, NY 10011.

short, at that moment there was as sense of specialness, a sense of being worthwhile, being fussed over and taken care of. These are our "whispered moments of glory, our Camelots."[1]

These personal experiences of being nurtured reflect then some of the core components of care. Although these components appear to be very simple, they are more subtle and complicated when we try to implement them in the everyday care of children and adolescents at home and away from home. These basic care considerations apply in our work with children at all ages, regardless of whether care is rendered in their own family or a foster home, in day care, temporary shelter, group, or residential care programs.

I would like to consider seven components of care. Each component is based upon a compilation of long established child care wisdom. The most recent findings in child development research shed light on the meaning these ingredients have for child care. I have tried to scan our knowledge of child development as if to search for the "proper chemistry of care." Each component is presented separately as a facet of care, but must always be viewed and utilized in combination with the other six components. In totality, these seven components constitute the core of care.

## COMPONENT 1:
## BODILY COMFORT

Bodily comfort as well as physical orientation, is basic to personal care. This first component entails the kind of activities which we almost take for granted. These actions are nevertheless, vital caring events. Consider the caring act of straightening out a child's bed sheets in order that the child can sleep in greater comfort, or sitting down on the floor with the child in order to afford him or her a more relaxed bodily posture and more convenient eye levels. One might say, as a child's bodily comforts are met, so does he or she feel actually treated with care. Throughout life a sense of well-being and care is experienced when one's body is secure and free of somatic stress. With a sense of physical well-being a person becomes more receptive and is, in fact, eager for experiences beyond the immediate bodily demands. Physical sustenance and comfort are basic for life and constitute one important measure of care.

In line with Component 1, physical comfort is strenghtened by the involvement of another person. It is this personal involvement, the investment of personal energy which converts physical care into "caring care." The infant has to be cradled into physical comfort. Newcomers to home, office, or a social gathering need someone's personal presence in order to find a sense of physical welcome and well-being. The same holds true in our everyday public life. For example, the bus conductor's friendly overtures can render the automatically opened door an easy and gratifying entry. In our child care practice, it occurs to me that when I want to convey a "welcome" to an individual, my words or smile might be less important than the energy I invest in the bodily welcome I provide by means of a nod, touch, and comfortable physical arrangements for the newcomers. Conversely, the negation of welcome, we know, is readily accomplished by denial or restraining of "bodily rights." Consider the studies of penal settings or concentration camps where extended periods of standing, sitting, and sleeping in uncomfortable, or crowded conditions quickly give the residents the understanding that they are unwelcome, worthless, and isolated (Freedman, 1975; Helmreich & Collin, 1967; Radloff & Helmreich, 1968).

### Physical Orientation

We have established then that concern for physical comfort is a prelude for care. This concern is further conveyed in the way we deal with the individuals' personal space in their presence as well as in their absence (Bakker & Bakker-Rabdau, 1973).

In our everyday lives, household pets have their private spaces which are duly respected. Do our children and adolescents also have the chance to establish territory which is genuinely their own? In their rooms for daily activities, and in their spaces for their belongings, for personal rest, retreat, and sleep, this is especially true. Such private space has to be theirs "tax free." In other words, this private space is theirs regardless of whether their behavior has been acceptable or not. Their personal (private) corner, bed, or other "mine only" place is undisputedly theirs as part of their inalienable rights within the child care arena. Youngsters need to find this evidence of the right to exist in difficult as well as in good moments. I am reminded of instances when one child feels hurt that another has taken his favored seat although other chairs are available and which appear to the casual onlooker to be equally desirable. Studies of animal and human uses of space clearly suggest to us that invasion of private space is felt as sharply as a direct assault to the body

(Bakker & Bakker-Rabdau, 1973; Freedman, 1975). Robert Frost said it well in his poem: "Good fences make good neighbors." This assertion might also apply to children. They too want their territory known and respected.

Parenthetically, it is also significant that when children move from one setting to another, from home to a residential setting or vice versa, that is, from a familiar territory to a strange one, children require assistance in order to make the unfamiliar familiar. Transitional objects — a much-loved blanket, cushion, stuffed beast, toy, photo, or trinket — serve as a linkage transforming a strange place into a more familiar surrounding (Winnicott, 1965).

It is inherent in the contemporary scene that each child care worker or other helping person serves also as a transition worker — as a person facilitating clients' transitions from one life situation to another. Clients need assistance with entering, coping, and moving forward into their new situations. It follows then that we need to guard against stripping individuals of their transitional objects as they enter a hospital, correctional institution, day care center, or other residential settings; continuous contacts with a previously supportive person are not only a helping bridge, but are essential for the child as transitional contacts.

## COMPONENT 2:
## DIFFERENTIATIONS

Individual differences inherently produce different interactions. A number of recent challenging longitudinal studies suggest that from birth children are quite different in temperament. These differences bring about distinctly varying patterns of interactions with as well as by their caretakers (Escalona, 1968; Thomas, Chess & Birch, 1968; Thomas & Chess, 1977). Such findings suggest that efforts to establish standardized expectations of behavior and "consistent" handling within a group of children is questionable. I submit here that it is essential for caring persons to differentiate in the way they respond to various children, even those with similar behaviors. To be "consistent" is not necessarily a virtuous position. On the contrary, it is neither an acceptable nor a desirable quality. To align our responses in terms of the individual child is far more effective and natural and in no way a deficient response.

If children do vary in temperament, then they logically secure for themselves different life experiences from their caregivers (Brazelton, 1977; Lewis & Rosenblum, 1974). More precisely, children and caring adults discover each other as units of care and establish their mutual mode of interaction. Most important, children's daily interactions are more likely to vary on the basis of the childrens' native temperament than on the basis of their differences in personal history, sex, and social class (Thomas & Chess, 1977).

There are some children who seem to absorb rapidly what is going on around them. They appear as if they were living radars. Although they strike us as rather "inactive," they are in fact very active "stimulus-scanners." They can deal with input over an extended time while maintaining spatial distance from the events at hand. Thus they relate most efficiently when they can interact with a predominantly visual situation. In contrast we observe that other children require continuous physical contact and bodily experience in order to feel involved. These children tend to have manifold experiences within a short time. For them one interaction leads to another. They are the "stimulus-bound" children—as if they were in perpetual motion. Let us discuss the latter ones first, the more bodily active youngsters. These "go-go" children are apt to enter immediately into whatever is happening within their reach. Almost any stimuli becomes for them a "call for action." Their own activities bring them continuously to new and novel experiences.

When these "go-go" children were observed with their caregivers (Escalona, 1968; Thomas, Chess & Birch, 1968; Schaffer & Emerson, 1964) a unique process was observed. Spontaneously, caregivers tended to channel as well as to limit their input. For example, while reading a story, the caregiver might read with attention-stimulating manner, while at the same time holding her arm around the child to reduce his/her bodily activities.

It is the child's temperament in interacting with his/her environment, as we learned in the previously cited studies of Escalona, as well as of Thomas and his associates, which shapes the quality of interaction, while it is the caregivers' culture which defines the style of interaction.[2] The caregiver, for instance, makes the cultural choice between sponge or tub bath, cold or warm water, but the nature of interaction within these boundaries is found jointly. Readers may recall instances from their own contacts with babies where quickly stimulated infants tend to be offered fewer toys because each additional toy seems to detract from the previous one. Such children also have a tendency to keep the caring adult on the scene of the child's actions. They constantly involve themselves with the caregivers.

In contrast, in each of these studies we note that another large group of children are active in another style. They are active "scanners."[3] They tend to "case out" a situation and maintain deliberate distance from others. Their caregivers in turn provide them with bodily space or a buffer zone between child and adult. Simultaneously, the caregiver recognizes the necessity to bring extra stimulation into the child's activity. In infancy these children's cribs are filled with objects. During feeding, bathing, and other forms of daily handling, caregivers tend to introduce distinct stimulations by means of speech, touch, and visual stimuli in order to evoke a mutual engagement (Escalona, 1968).

In child care settings we witness similar differences and handle them according to variations in temperament. Some children come dashing to the dinner table. They reach for the food while inquiring: "What's there to eat?" The natural adult response then might be to focus on one thing at a time: "Sit down!" "Sit!" "SIT DOWN!" while a pair of hands might be actively facilitating this anchoring process. In contrast, in the instances of the "living radars," we would find such boys and girls approaching the dinner table by giving it a complete survey first. Typically they would focus on one item at a time, while still at some distance from the table. They may call out: "She has my cup!" The spontaneous adult reseponse then might include offering several alternatives in order to get the child fully into the scene. "Come sit down." "Here is another cup just like the other one." "See here, your soup is served." "Here is a place for you. Sit down!" All these introductions of added stimuli occur from a distance, while the caregivers' eyes, words, and perhaps their gestures are brought into play as intervening anchoring mechanisms.

From longitudinal research we learn that both the "living radars" children operating over distance, as well as their more intrusive counterparts, the "go-go getters," develop satisfactorily. It seems that child and caregivers tend to educate and find each other, to create, so to speak, the proper fit. We learn from these studies that practical caring is neither an activity to be delivered nor one to be developed out of manuals or house rules. Rather, caring is a reciprocal interactive process of mutual adaptation which requires time and experience — and training for the care of special children. Training will enable the caring person to discern which children require immediate body contacts as part of close and intense personal interactions, and which children can better achieve "closer" personal contact over distance with a reliance upon eye and marginal body contacts. In short, "different strokes for different blokes."

What does all this mean for the core of child caring? It suggests that the care given and received requires frequent and undisturbed extended periods of time together in order to find a mutual fit. Parenthetically, this does not mean that parents must stay at home at all times nor that the same child care personnel should be continuously on their job. We know that children of working parents do as well as children with the parent at home so long as the caring parents, in either situation, feel relatively free and are fully involved with their children in the times spent together (Robinson, Robinson & Wolins, 1976). For child care settings it might imply that it is most important to devise a program which allows the child caring person full personal involvement when actually with the children.

## COMPONENT 3:
## RHYTHMIC INTERACTIONS

Rhythmicity is a vital feature of all human development. It is a salient underlying force: the syncronization of child and caring adults. They must somehow find their joint rhythm. (Brazelton, 1977; Byers, 1972; Condon, 1975; Lewis & Rosenblum, 1974; Maier, 1978a; Schaffer, 1977, p. 63.) Recent research findings hint at the possibility that basic units of rhythmic interactions make up the "molecules of human behavior" (Byers, 1972; Condon, 1975). These "molecules of human behavior" require the enmeshment,[4] the blending of an individual's internal rhythms with environmental rhythmic demands. It is this subtle rhythmic involvement which determines the quality and possibly the direction of interaction.

Rhythmic experiences, such as rattling a rattle or repeatedly stroking one's hair or beard, playing patty-cake or the shaking of hands, are all essential ingredients of the experience of finding indicators of continuity. We note that rhythmicity is the hallmark of baby toys[5] as well as of real "togetherness" in later life events, such as in group singing and dance, play or sexual activity.

*Rituals* are a social counterpart to psychological rhythmicity. They represent a confirmation of sound cultural practice. People experience a full sense of togetherness in the carrying out of these practices.[6] In work with children rituals assume special significance. By this I mean rituals of significance to the child rather than routines which are neither rituals nor training but purely for the purpose of achieving temporary order.

What does rhythmicity actually accomplish? Rhythmic activities seem to secure for the individual the experience of repetition and continuity of repetition. The actual experience of lasting repetition fosters a perception of permanency. Rhythmic action contains the experience of repetition with the promise of further repetition and hence the opportunity for experiencing predictability (Maier, 1978b, Ch. 1).

When people get together, they attempt to locate joint rhythms in movements such as the nodding of assent, or walking, laughing, or even crying together. They create a type of mutual sympathetic rhythm. In this connection, I hypothesize that in play rhythmicity is one of the salient features which renders it a vital life experience. Notice for instance the rhythmic component in playing ball, table tennis, or playing tag. These playful experiences provide the possibility for becoming enmeshed in rhythmic encounters.

How is rhythmicity applicable to the core of caring? I propose it is essential that children have ample opportunities for both experiencing rhythmicity in their own activities and in their interactions with caring adults. When we observe children engaged in repetitive, that is, rhythmic play such as "aimlessly" bouncing or tossing of a ball, tapping out some rhythm on the table, children chasing each other or bantering insults, etc., we must recognize that all these are far from time-wasting activities. Moreover, when adults while caring for children can become part of the joint rhythm, they have the possibility of finding themselves momentarily fully "in tune" with the children. Children and adults share moments of moving ahead together.[7]

## COMPONENT 4:
## THE ELEMENT OF PREDICTABILITY

The capacity to predict is a measure of knowing and an essential ingredient of effective learning. In other words, to know which things will happen in the immediate future lends a sense of order and power. It becomes a major breakthrough for a youngster to discover that she/he can predict the outcome of her/his action. He or she can make things happen.[8]

Child care activities must therefore offer continuous work with children in such a way that they truly experience and cherish the meaning of their own activities. It will be significant then for the caring person to mirror his/her experience of the happening for the effectiveness of the behavior rather than as a gauge of approval. The caring person might say, in sharing the events of the child who performs somersaults as a guest arrives, "You got my full attention all the way with that one. You really did it!"

Actually, we tend to use such an approval quite easily with very young children. With older children, however, we are less prone to do so. With this latter age group we are apt to shift our involvements away from the doing and learning directly; we tend to engage ourselves instead in regulating or evaluating. With older children it is of equal importance to be constantly involved with a boy's or girl's actions and mastery. For instance, the youngster accomplishing a new task requires recognition for the mastery rather than an evaluation in terms of "good," "brave," or "industrious." Children require feedback on their competence acquisition rather than another checkoff on adults' list of approved conduct.

## COMPONENT 5:
## DEPENDABILITY

A sense of predictability heralds a sense of dependence (Maier, 1978b). The sense of prediction assures an individual a sense of certainty. A sense of certainty gives a person an assured feeling of dependence. As children come to know and to predict their experiences with others, so will they depend upon these persons. Moreover, these very experiences become significant encounters in their own right. To be able to depend upon dependence feels good! It assures the child that she/he is not alone and that she/he can depend or rely upon support. The feeling of dependence creates attachment and having attachments feels good, too (Brazelton, Koslowski & Main, 1974; Bronfenbrenner, 1977; Maier, 1986d). The caregiver in turn also wants to be depended upon. Dependence feels good and is good for both of them.

Dependency then, is natural and desirable — and basic to child care. The continuous and very personal involvement in the caring process fosters a dependence to the point that child and adult deeply care for each other. After all, little people need big people, and big people also have the need for others, both big and small ones. In

Bronfenbrenner's terms, every child needs at least one person who is really crazy about him or her (Bronfenbrenner, 1977, p. 3). When a child feels that someone really believes in him (her) the child then feels good about him/herself and eventually about other people. Curiously enough, when persons experience secure dependence upon one another, they can in fact function more independently as they feel assured of mutual attachment (Maier, 1986d). Secure dependence breeds clear independence and ultimately the freedom for new dependence in new and more complex relationship systems (Maier, 1986d).[9] Recent studies on attachment development have made us aware that a lack of dependent experience creates greater havoc in a child's development than prolonged dependence itself (Brunner, 1970; Maier, 1986d; National Institute, 1968).

## COMPONENT 6:
## PERSONALIZED BEHAVIORAL TRAINING

Social capability rests upon personal attachment. The reader may have noted that thus far there has been neither a reference to the maintenance of discipline nor the training in self-management and manners. The reader could easily wonder whether the writer cares at all about children's behavior. (I do! In fact, I care so much that I want the behavioral training to have the fullest possible impact.)

Children learn most readily from those who have vital meaning for them. They turn to the persons they have experienced as the ones to be counted on, namely those whom the children perceive as on their side (Bronfenbrenner, 1970; Kessen, 1975; Schaffer, 1977, p. 100). Children are most likely to follow the persons whose ways of dealing with life issues are most akin to their own. The persons most meaningful for their power, as well as the persons closest to the children's own life situations, have the best chance for influencing the children's behavior. (In addition to the primary caring persons, very frequently it is the slightly older siblings and peers or the heroes in stories and TV, a few steps ahead in their development, who represent the models and idols; and they may be almost of equal importance to the central caring figures.)

Concern with social training has been purposely introduced late in the sequence of the seven components. It is essential to keep in mind that the most potent behavioral training goes hand in hand with a sense of reciprocal closeness and attachment. Effective acquisition of behavioral standards is a consequence of dependability. When children and caring adults are in a close relationship, effective child training really starts and the more complicated socialization efforts can now take place.

It is important to recognize however, that both child and caring adult must eventually go far beyond their mutual attachment to other spheres of life, where children will be more and more independent of their caregivers within new spheres of dependencies (Maier, 1977). In child care settings, the children's continuous involvement with their larger community and with their own family or future foster or group home setting is of utmost importance.

The core of care in and away from home has to be experienced in a series of meaningful activities as children mature. While engaged with their caring adults, children will periodically dip into emotional dependence upon these caring persons, and this linkage will be both fundamental and freeing. In other words, fostering self-management and enriching children's behavioral repertoires are intimately linked with the formation of close relationship with the caregivers.

## COMPONENT 7:
## CARE FOR THE CAREGIVERS

Component 7, care for the caregiver as the final ingredient, is fundamental to the previous six. Care can only be received to the extent that the caregivers are personally prepared and ready to engage in these interactions. It is inherent that the caretakers be nurtured themselves and experience sustained caring support in order to transmit this quality of care to others.

Caregivers are enriched or limited as agents of care according to the care they receive. Are their activities in their role as givers supported by their own personal caregivers, their primary groups, and their wider social institutions? Are caregivers assured of their own physical comfort and ample personal privacy in space and time, and are they provided chances for secure support from others when the caregiving becomes rough? Do they have access to resources for doing what has to be done? In short, is there ample care for the caring?

## CONCLUDING COMMENT

The essential message can probably best be summarized in the greeting which nowadays is frequently heard among young adults. On leave-taking, they often exchange two simple but powerful words: "Take care!" This phrase seems to encapsulate a theme: true caring largely reflects the mutuality of care received and care rendered. All of us, adults and children, need this exquisite blend of affirmation.

## NOTES

1. A line from the song on the life and dreams of King Arthur — "Camelot."

2. Stimulus (S) and Response (R) become interchangeable. One person's S is simultaneously the other person's R, while the other person's R becomes also the very same person's S.

3. Schaffer called them the "non-cuddlers" in his Glasgow research project (Schaffer and Emerson, 1964).

4. The descriptive term "enmeshment" is adapted from Schaffer's term "social enmeshing" (Schaffer, 1977, pp. 64-66).

5. For instance, rattles, tops, music boxes with repetitious tunes, lullabies, or action toys with built-in rhythmic actions.

6. For example, the shaking of hands among some people, repeated bowing, or the rhythmic ritual of kissing on both cheeks in some parts of the world.

7. Mike A. West, a social worker in Seattle, Washington, called to the author's attention the fact that, at different developmental levels, children, adolescents, and adults are more "in tune" with specific relevant musical rhythms. For adolescents, regardless if it is within the jitterbug, twist, or hard rock area, the rhythm remains alike for each variation of "contemporary" music.

8. Professor Resnick, of the University of Washington, phrased such discovery aptly: "a shift from random to randomless behavior"; that is, a move toward controlled existence in an orderly world.

9. For a full discussion of the author's formulation of dependence/independence oscillation, the reader may want to turn to his essay on "Dependence and Independence Development throughout the Human Life Span: Implications for the Helping Professions" (Maier, 1986d).

# Chapter V

# To Be Attached and Free

In this decade the children we honored in 1979, the "International Year of the Child," will grow into adulthood, eventually to become parents of the next generation. What precisely have we learned that our once and future children can utilize as part of their generation's knowledge and practice?

As an aid to answering this question, research findings on reciprocal care-receiving and care-giving interactions are reported. Particular attention is directed toward the issue of how we can ensure children a developmental path in which dependence is experienced and yet, at the same time, individual identities are sustained and nurtured. In short, how to help children be attached and free.

## THE FOCUS OF CONTEMPORARY RESEARCH IN CHILD CARE

Within the past decade the view that child caring and parenting are activities directed toward children has changed to a view of caring as a process of reciprocal, continuous interaction between parent and child (Rutter, 1979, p. 286). Indeed, child-parent interaction has emerged as a vital focus of child development research (Brazelton, 1977; Brazelton, Koslowski & Main, 1974; Chess & Hassibi, 1978; Lewis & Rosenblum, 1974; Rutter, 1979).

## DEPENDENCE SUPPORT IS BASIC

Interaction implies a mutual dependence, and this reciprocity is the major process by which parent-child relationships develop. De-

This article originally appeared in *Child Welfare, 61*(2), 1982, 67-76. Reprinted by permission of The Child Welfare League of America, Inc.

pendence support is essential in all beginning relationships. Sensitive and effective response to the child's particular requirements in the initial phase of a relationship enhances the child's capacity for functioning. The caregiver, in turn, finds pleasure in the child's response, which validates the caregiver's competence in predicting the care required. The interactive process of the child's dependence and the caregiver's sense of power and satisfaction serve to strengthen their bonds. Caregiver and care receiver become dependent upon and interconnected with one another (Bronfenbrenner, 1976; Maccoby & Masters, 1979; Sroufe, 1978; Waters, 1978).

Recent research indicates that active nurturance of dependence leads to a child's readiness to independently engage in activities for which he or she may previously have demanded dependence support. For instance, children continuously assured of their caregivers' dependable presence, followed by predictable absence and return, will eventually not require expressed assurance of the caregiver's return. But children who have experienced uncertainty require "props" as explicit reassurances of a caretaker's return (Ainsworth, 1972 and 1974; Ainsworth & Blehar, 1978; Rutter, 1979; Segal & Yahraes, 1978, pp. 76-80). It seems that previous fears of spoiling children with dependence nurturance or of encouraging a prolonged state of dependence may not be justified. In fact, a number of studies reveal that absence of dependence support creates greater havoc in a child's development than prolonged dependence (Ainsworth, 1972 and 1974). Furthermore, children who oppress their caregivers with severe demands for attention are often youngsters who have suffered from too little individualized attention and dependence support (Segal & Yahraes, 1978). These findings point to the necessity for altering our perspective on child caring and on social work intervention from a preoccupation with avoiding dependence to one of nurturing dependence.

## ATTACHMENT AS A VITAL COMPONENT OF DEVELOPMENT

Satisfaction in the process of seeking out another person and in finding a response fosters mutual attachment, which is a mode of relating preferentially to a particular person. One or both parties experience an attraction toward the other, creating an affective tie and a sense of certainty about each other. For an individual to anticipate being wanted by another person is both personally satisfying and productive. Such experiences are events of interpersonal intimacy and support, expanding beyond the present.

Attachment emerges as new relationships move beyond the beginning phase. One example in the child development context is the mobilization pattern that occurs during the second half of the first year, when stable hierarchies of preferences develop. It is also the time when a lot of "trouble" starts! The child may prefer one parent over the other, or may demand a parent's presence in lieu of a previously accepted babysitter. This "trouble" signals that the child is well on the way in his or her maturing process; after all, one of the signs of maturity is to have the capacity to choose on whom to depend.

### Attachment Behavior

A child's efforts to make attachments are generally described as attachment behaviors, which signal that the child's self-management capacity is in a state of flux. Typical manifestations are familiar: clinging, calling out to a parent figure, insisting on having the caregiver in sight, and other proximity-demanding behaviors.

These behaviors occur either when attachment is in the formative stage, or when the attachment process demands readjustment. It is useful for those in child welfare practice to note that the attachment, not the behavior, is at stake. Therefore, appropriate responses have to be directed to the process of attachment formation, rather than to the behaviors themselves. The three-year old's repeated requests for a drink of water, a blanket, a backrub, and so on, may require a firm assurance of the caregiver's continued proximity (e.g., an open door, a hallway light, or a strong verbal message of comfort), rather than a corrective admonishment for the attachment-seeking behaviors.

In studies of securely attached children, it is clear that in moments of stress, such as times of new experience or separation, they seek the proximity of their caregivers; however, after a response of inclusion by the caregivers, these children regain confidence and can subsequently handle the stress. In contrast, children with uncertain attachments may cling to their primary caregivers or may be most hesitant in facing the changed situation and may also protest separation (Kagan, 1978; Sroufe, 1978). It follows that in counseling with parents or alternate caregivers, one should encourage them to recognize accentuated attachment behaviors as loud appeals for close contact and a feeling of acceptance. If the behaviors alone are addressed, the child will be even more at a loss and will not only be denied opportunities for strengthening attachments, but also the confidence to risk novel experiences (Belsky & Steinberg, 1979; Chess & Hassibi, 1978; Sroufe, 1978). In Harlow's findings with Rhesus monkeys in experimental settings, for instance, monkeys that become familiar with new exploratory play repertoire will not employ these play behaviors in new environments until the strangeness has been dispelled. A close child-parent relationship frees children for growing and helps them incorporate their parents' values (Kenniston, 1968).

## MUTUALITY OF CAREGIVER
## AND CARE RECEIVER

To reiterate, attachment is a reciprocal interactive process. Children not only invite and provoke attachment behaviors from their caregivers, but the caregivers themselves initiate and solicit attachment behaviors on their own behalf (Bardwick, 1974, p. 43; Sroufe, 1978). The parent requires that his or her child be close, in part to affirm his or her parenthood. Caregivers frequently initiate and ask for physical contacts (e.g., "Give mother a hug") as if they needed a refresher in bonding behaviors — that is, immediate and reciprocal physical enmeshment. In animal bonding, for instance, immediately after birth, a mare and foal lick each other extensively before the mare noses her foal to get on its feet. This reciprocal licking process is repeated when the foal falters, and after intervals of separation (Scott, 1958). Caring activity is a prerequisite for effective growth. Brazelton, in his microanalysis of infant-parent interactions, describes these as a kind of "dance," in which caregiver and care receiver invest energy in getting into step with one another in a cyclical pattern (Brazelton, 1978, p. 3). In a process of mutual inclusion, each one searches for a way to establish and reestablish contact in a quest for joint rhythm.

The importance of the mutuality of bonding experience has been further highlighted by followup studies of newborn infants who were cared for by their mothers from the moment of their birth (Broussard, 1976; Hersh & Levin, 1978, pp. 3-5; Segal & Yahraes, 1978, pp. 80-85). These mothers found it easier to relate to their babies and had a harder time leaving their children with others than mothers who had had traditional hospital experiences. Currently, as seen in a number of 10-year followup studies, differences between the children of these two groups have continued: the "bonded children" seem to have adapted and progressed with less conflicting behaviors and personal complications. These data strongly suggest the importance of reviewing the neonatal conditions of mother/child hospital-care practices in order to foster early mother-child bonding processes.

Moreover, these and other findings are a challenge to reevaluate practices in the placement of children in day, foster family, and residential care. It is essential for child and caregiver to have both the time and the know-how to establish connectedness. Initial casual meetings with ample time to be together leisurely might be a vital prerequisite to placement in both group care and foster homes. Social workers, moreover, might appropriately turn from one-dimensional inquiries such as "How is the child progressing?" to questions reflecting attachment concerns, like "How are you two doing with one another?" Similarly, in counseling programs, workers might consider scheduling initial treatment sessions for extended time slots so that worker and client(s) can "find each other" rather than having the first three to four treatment sessions strung out into a series of aborted beginnings.

Again, it is important to emphasize that attachment experience must precede and then be integrated with behavioral expectations. Caregivers cannot merely be advised about what they should do with children or how they should anticipate behavioral expectations. Instead, caregivers have to learn to see themselves and the children as interactive units that "try each other out." Specification of behavioral modes, and ultimately behavioral training, have the promise of lasting effect only when the parent or alternate care person has affectual relevance for the child (Maier, 1978a). In social learning, including behavioral reinforcing, it is the power and personal relevance of the influential agent that makes the reenforcement effective. In short, it is the interaction of key figures within a social matrix, rather than any specific strategy as such, that helps a person adopt appropriate behaviors. Attachment experience linked with behavioral training contains the promise that the learner will not only emulate the desired behavior but will use it freely — and adopt it as his/her own.

## THE EFFECT OF DAY CARE

If attachment to primary caregivers indeed seems to facilitate young children's development, what are the effects of daily separation, such as day care? One research study after another has established that children with a history of years of day care do as well later on in life as home-cared children (Belsky, 1980; Belsky & Steinberg, 1979, p. 21; Kagan, 1977, p. 36; Kagan, 1978, pp. 74-100; Powell, 1978). However, concern must be directed to the caliber of day care services. Kagan emphasizes that most findings of the positive impact of day care on children's development were drawn from children in high-quality day care programs (Kagan, 1978; Rubenstein & Howe, 1979). Differences seem to be strongly correlated with the direct service staff-children ratio, as well as with the qualitative diversity of care facilities (Kagan, 1978; National Day, 1979). Kagan's observations can be linked with Mary D. Ainsworth's findings of more than 10 years ago: "Children who were given the opportunity to attach themselves to substitute care-taking figures . . . [confirm the postulation] that warm, enduring interaction with specific adults facilitates optimal growth" (Ainsworth, 1969). Most recently, in the National Daycare Study of over 150 centers, it was reported that for infant and toddler age, staff ratio is a paramount factor. For children above toddler age, group size has the most significant impact. The smaller the group size, the better the children's experience in day care (National Day, 1979). This latter point carries practice implications either for creating small day care centers, or for subdividing large ones into small separate units in which the children can find their intimate circle of attachment.

### Parents Are Still Primary

Day care seems neither to undermine nor to dilute a child's primary attachment to his or her parent. Contrary to common fears, children who spend most of their waking hours in day care centers turn to their parents for significant comfort and nurturance. These children, just as home-cared youngsters, want their parents when happy or bored, comfortable or apprehensive. If it is true for the day care youngsters that parents retain the primary role in nurturing needs, then we must identify ways for day care programs to facilitate attachment experiences between child and parent at crucial daily events, such as morning separation and when the parent returns (Powell, 1978).

## ATTACHMENT AND AUTONOMY
## FOR OLDER CHILDREN

With the development of greater attachment comes independence and greater freedom. The awakening notion of inclusion in a group — dependence upon a social network — while maintaining previous attachment support, is part of all autonomous independence striving (Bardwick, 1974, p. 51). With each acquisition of dependence, a new region of independence is also achieved. In turn, with each new step of independence, freedom is gained for the development of new attachments. New levels of dependence are in the making (Maier, 1986d).

Children's ability to separate and manage on their own is anchored in the degree of security of their attachments, combined with their acquired capacities to get to, and to do more with people, activities, and things that provoke their curiosity (Maier, 1978b, pp. 144-151; Segal & Yahraes, 1978; Sroufe, 1978). Consequently, one might say parents neither push nor cajole their children out of the nest — rather, they widen the nest. By allowing social space and encouraging children to expand their interactions on their own, parents support children's continuing efforts toward new mastery. Throughout life, growth requires that continuous support come from previous attachments, from peers, and from new attachments.

For school-age children, peer attachments serve as added resources and become vital freeing factors in the sequence of human development (Hartup, 1979). Peers, along with parents, make up school-age children's primary support systems, and it is largely through the child's attachment to peers that life's important attitudes and behaviors are shaped. Forms and degrees of school-age aggressive behavior, the overcoming of fears and anxieties, or establishing norms for doing with or without material items, represent distillation of peer interactions (Segal & Yahraes, 1978, pp. 237-242). Studying the manner in which school-age youngsters relate to their peers can give pertinent prognosticators of their developmental progress. Reports of a child's performance in school should therefore include an account of the scope and quality of the child's association with his or her peers.

## CONCLUSIONS

A primary assertion is that child and parent, or caregiver and care receiver, need each other reciprocally and need to find their mutual fit. In this country, children are rarely responsible for the economic maintenance of the family; now, they are needed for expressions of care. Parenthood and the child's natural maturing are becoming more of a search for self-fulfillment than an issue of either economic or socioreligious family survival (McDonald, 1978, p. 53). In this search is the inherent desire to maintain each other's love. Parent and child (as well as worker and child), need each other for their own validation and verification (Kagan, 1978, pp. 41-45). Maybe we have been recognizing not only the "Year of the Child" but also the year of the parent and child.

Recent research strongly indicates that children mature satisfactorily when they are assured a pattern of reliable dependence. It is through this assured dependence that they repeatedly find freedom to grow. Steps toward freedom must be underpinned by a sense of anchorage through dependence. "Have you hugged your kid today?" asks a bumper sticker and TV spot. The same question is embodied in Bronfenbrenner's poignant conclusion: "Every child needs at least one person who is really crazy about him or her" (Bronfenbrenner, 1977). Briefly, the issue of dependence and freedom can be summarized in the statement made by a 3-year old to his parent: "Stay here — so I can do it myself!" (Matthew Daniels, Seattle, Washington).

Chapter VI

# Learning to Live
# and Living to Learn
# in Residential Treatment

*"It is time to come in!,"* a phrase voiced almost daily by many
child care workers in residential or day care settings, exemplifies
the essence of child care. *"Come in"* conveys the personal request
of the worker who wishes to shift the living from outside to inside.
*"It is time"* denotes that life proceeds in an organized fashion within
this program.

Child caring within a group living context brings together two
interesting spheres of life: (1) the "primary life" sphere, *the interpersonal joint life of children and caring adults*, and (2) the "secondary life" sphere, the constituent partners as clientele and staff in
an organizational program. Within the first sphere, the interpersonal
interaction is central. The words "It is time" imply that there is or
needs to be agreement that "it *is* time" for both parties concerned —
and also that it is developmentally appropriate for the children who
are called in. Within the second sphere, the issues are intertwined
with those of the first, but different; they introduce the caring person's concern for status within an organization and the children's
concern for their turf within their group of peers. This paper ad-
dresses issues related to child care within group living situations.
The child care worker's continuous involvement with the children in
care is the conceptual focus, with emphasis upon interpersonal involvement rather than the traditional "problem solving." Figura-
tively, child care work and group living are analogous to the action
of a film rather than a slide show.

This article originally appeared in *Child Welfare*, 54(6), 1975, 406-420. Reprinted by
permission of The Child Welfare League of America, Inc.

## *PRIMARY LIFE IN GROUP CARE*

Let us consider children coming to treatment settings as children who want alternate modes of living rather than as children with problems for the caring persons to solve. These children require central persons in their lives who will nurture, support and guide them as they try to hurdle the problems of daily living. Vital everyday experiences provide the most promising opportunities for working effectively with these children. It is the child caring person's continuous interaction with the child that counts.

Human development is nourished by interpersonal experience (White, 1972). The worker's effectiveness seems to be directly correlated with the degree of personal struggle child and adult allow themselves to engage in with each other (Bettelheim, 1967; Craig, 1973; Dennison, 1970). In the example of "calling in the children" the degree of mutual involvement might have a more pervasive impact upon a child's (as well as the worker's) personal development than the behavior per se. I submit that children develop neither by conditioned behavior nor by their reflection and insight into their fears and anger; they develop by interpersonal engagements with each other and with adults. Some preliminary data support the view that it is neither the caring message nor the system of reward or punishment that constitutes the essence of child care work; rather, it is the experience of the caring person's involvement in the issues facing children and caring adults that really counts (Browning & Stover, 1971; Phillips, Phillips, Fixsen & Wolf, 1971).

This perspective places the stress on what worker and children do with each other, rather than on the outcome of each other's separate actions.[1] An accent upon the experience people have with each other also challenges a current trend toward the depersonalization of institutional life and bureaucratization of therapy.[2] The latter stands as a particularly stark factor where standardization and predictability are perceived as the measures of group care and living; in these situations the rules rule the practice. My stress upon interpersonal intervention is based upon the observation that a vast number of the children in our services of today experience an unresponsive rather than an overinvolved environment. They have encountered a faceless society, and long for experiences in which they come face to face with others (Maier, 1971b, pp. 123-126). They need involvement. Yet many of the traditional treatment approaches stress noninvolvement, objectivity, and keeping one's nose out.

To illustrate, John, while entering the living room, slams the door. Worker: "John, I don't like your slamming the door. It makes me jump each time." Note, the experience is between worker and child, which is quite different from such alternate approaches as: "Doors should be closed carefully," "You know the rules," or "Stay in the room for 5 minutes." These latter approaches, at times most appropriate interventive techniques, imply the pronouncement of a third party on being "good," being "bad," or "sticking to the rules." Conceptually, these approaches rely upon a homeostatic outlook, with an emphasis upon maintenance management, upholding order, tension reduction, and problem removal in order to bring an episode to a close. In contrast, the former approach, with the worker's more personal involvement, would more likely remain a link in the continuous chain of mutual encounters as the search goes on for finding ways of living together effectively. Such an approach is within the heterostatic perspective (Maier, 1971b, pp. 123-126) with an emphasis upon mastery of ongoing events as precursors and stimulations for the new experiences to come.

### Everyday Engagement in Group Living

Residential treatment or group care work has its critical strategic moments when child and worker are engaged with each other in everyday tasks. The group living situation serves as the arena of life. It is the arena for meeting and separating, for eating, for making decisions, dealing with social requirements, and so on. It is the arena where children and caring adults discover each other's ways of giving and taking. These joint experiences constitute the essence of development and of treatment. This interpersonal and developmental stance puts the emphasis on the minutiae of everyday life (Maier, 1971a, pp. 111-114; White, 1972). Child care work is in full force at such moments as when a child "merely" inquires, "What is on TV?" The issue is how shall a worker respond? That response is as critical as any intervention in other therapeutic encounters.

To illustrate further, at a treatment home for girls, at the end of dinner the worker comments casually to a resident: "Jane, it is your turn to clear the table this evening." No overt response from Jane. The worker, looking at Jane, says, "Jane, I checked it; it *is* your turn." Still no response, while several others are looking toward Jane and the worker, wondering what is to follow. What *is* to follow? More is involved than getting Jane to do her turn; the worker's own sense of survival depends on eliciting an effective response. It is here, in the daily interactions, where work, change or, in traditional language, "treatment" occurs. This holds true, whether facing each other in the morning or the last good night. The utilization of life events is the source of residential or group care work (Maier, 1963; Maier, 1971a; Nicholson, 1975).

There is another frontier of practice on the threshold of developing knowledge. The studies of Escalone (1968) and Thomas, Chess, and Birch (1964) suggest new perspectives for understanding and working with children. Their seperate researches show that infants' life experiences are as much influenced by personal temperament as by the environmental experiences, interpersonal and other, offered to them.

The studies indicate that "active infants" (bodily active) generate different and wider ranges of experience that result in maintaining a high rate of stimulation at the expense of holding onto a given experience for itself. Low-temperament, "inactive infants" (less active in gross body movements) explore tactilely their own body and immediate environment, while distant experiences are dealt with visually. These infants experience their environment through visual cues and tactile stimulations; their environment remains more limited in number and variations of experiences. Most important, the Escalona studies tend to establish that caring persons relate differentially on the basis of the child's variation in responsiveness to stimulation. Such findings, though inconclusive, suggest that some children may require a reduction in stimulation, while others may require an increase of stimulation in order that experiences become significant to their developmental progression. In other words, we may be able to stop torturing ourselves with maneuvers aimed at "motivating" a child, when the actual issue is: In what way can the child's repertoire be widened in order for him to enter differently into ongoing life experiences?

Take, for example, a treatment center with adolescents who tended to act out in whirlwind fashion. The residential workers discovered that they could be helpful to these youngsters when they themselves managed to focus on one immediate behavioral event, even though each attempt to focus brought about a dozen other disruptive incidents. Work had to be focused on one issue at a time, regardless of cost in energy and self-esteem to the workers (Nicholson, 1975).

### Behavioral Approaches in Group Living

It is possible to view group care from a behavioral perspective. Some recent studies on behavioral approaches (Browning & Stover, 1971; Phillips, Phillips, Fixsen & Wolf, 1971) suggest the importance of the interpersonal association within the context of a behavior-shaping process. At Achievement Place, a series of group homes in Kansas, a token economy proved instrumental in the adolescents' progress both during and after placement. Yet the same treatment system, duplicated in form but without the same degree of personal involvement, did not yield the same results (Phillips, Phillips, Fixsen & Wolf, 1971). I wonder if it is really the token economy, the reinforcement through a pronouncement of "good" or "bad," the giving or withholding of reward, that makes the difference. Perhaps it is the child's experience of the worker's pleasure or annoyance over his or her change (or lack thereof) that is the key factor. The comment of "good" or its equivalent is a powerful reinforcer, provided "good" is also experienced as a "good" by the child and the conveyor of the message of "good" is an important person to the child.

Behavioral thinking and training do add an important dimension. A behavioral perspective helps the worker focus his or her thinking upon the child's behavioral requirements and his or her own participation in the child's development. The worker achieves greater clarity and direction in his or her work, as well as in its evaluation. Each point earned by the children is also for the worker a token of success in behavior shaped and a promise of an easier life within the residential setting. Having a concrete program, as behavioral approaches demand, can enhance rather than mar the residential worker's involvement with the children. But what counts is the involvement, the person-to-person struggle, either over the fact that the worker cares what happens to each child or the worker's dogged insistence that he or she won't budge on the established point system. What's important is the worker's personal excitement, with the child, over his or her improved personal effectiveness or an increase in his or her score.

Followup studies on Achievement Place in Kansas (Phillips, Phillips, Fixsen & Wolf, 1971) show that the major difference between success and failure is that in the successful program the workers reviewed their scoring and accomplishments each evening with the residents. Such findings hint at the importance of each child and worker experiencing a sense of mastery, a sense of efficacy, in their daily lives.[3]

## THE REHEARSIVE APPROACH
## IN GROUP LIVING

While coping with daily experiences, children need guiding adults for the rehearsal of new and different ways of managing their lives. Group living becomes the arena where children learn not only the "what" of the moment, but the "how" of the future. For example, in one state institution for adjudicated teen-agers some youngsters are on a "go-it-yourself" schedule. They are asked to manage their own timing for getting up, leaving for school or work, being on hand for meals, etc. Self-management is not a reward for previous "good behavior," but is rehearsed and learned for life's demands beyond the residential protectory.

Institutional life is really a culture that by necessity is deviant and foreign. Group-life expectations have to be continuously appraised by the caring adults for their effectiveness inside institutions as well as for their linkages to potential life requirements on the "outside."

For example, a residential worker reports:

> Jim (age 14) is fun to have around the cottage as long as he is busy. He is able to stay with his work or other activities for long periods of time. He does get into trouble with the other kids the minute there is nothing for him to do. He can be easily distracted, if he is given something to do to take up his energy in either work or play.

With the help of a vigilant worker, Jim can live easily without getting into trouble. Yet, the issue is that Jim needs to learn to relate effectively to others. Special practice situations must be introduced in which Jim can experiment with making successful contacts with others. Jim and his peers can be drawn into devising, setting up and carrying out sessions for rehearsing new ways of relating to others, even if he gets into trouble while learning.

The rehearsive approach allows an emphasis upon learning. From time to time children need extra periods of practice in which their learning is "beefed up" by the introduction of specifically selected learning experiences. For instance, Mike, 12, tends to blow his top whenever something unpredictable happens, as when a worker other than the scheduled one appears for duty. At the time of his agitation he is not able to learn something new. Special situations must be created in play, simulated life situations, and the like, where he can rehearse facing and managing "the unpredictable."

A rehearsive approach can also provide workers with a handle for dealing with the acquisition of behavior that normally would not be possible in the "hothouse" culture of the institution. Problems arising from cultural differences and differential power alignments (Polsky, 1962; Polsky & Claster, 1968) might be managed with this context. Children in residential care need even more than other children to develop and to rehearse their power to hold their own at home, at school, in their own neighborhood, and just the same is true within the walls of the group care program.[4] Since institutional programs tend to diminish rather than enhance the residents' power, special rehearsive situations may have to be created in which the residents can practice using their power to hold onto their turf and to have impact on their own life situation. I am reminded of a group home situation where the young men agreed to have Carl insist upon his rights whenever he felt slighted. They challenged him to fight for his rights even if it meant disagreement and the necessity for others, including staff, to adapt their own immediate preferences.

Conflict behavior is another area that needs special attention within the rehearsive approach. In everyday life as well as in group living situations, conflicts tend to be avoided, or at best reduced and set aside as quickly as possible. The tendency is to bypass the conflict itself rather than to assist the individuals with their skills in handling conflict. As conflicts often require immediate resolution, conflict-handling skills should be developed by rehearsal. Special situations may have to be arranged repeatedly to assist residents with learning conflict-handling skills.

For instance, in a particular group living situation joint play led to group conflict. The moment the play activities became exciting and worthwhile, a participant tended to cheat, or was alleged to have cheated; in either event all hell broke loose. At this point, order had to be established through conflict elimination or avoidance. As an alternative, residents and staff developed the game "shit on cheating." Dealing with conflict after an assumed or real cheat became the game. The new venture was at times bloody, at other times hilarious, but most often conflict-laden and rich in learning how to deal with conflict.

## Planned Experiences in Group Living

A rehearsive approach accentuates an attempt to link experiences in group living with experiences the child may have to master "out" in life. Such linkage can be achieved through planned experiences — both rehearsive and real. An example of the latter is bumming around a segment of the inner city. Too often groups are taken to visit places — parks and pools with strong middle-class flavor — where many of the children will not venture again once back in their own community.

It is helpful if the worker can involve himself or herself in the home life of the child after discharge. He or she may even become the child's family worker[5] (Goocher, 1975; Hammond, 1975; Magnus, 1974; Taylor & Alpert, 1973). It is the parent and child care worker who deal with the nitty-gritty aspects of life,[6] and they probably can talk best with each other. The worker can then assist the child in his identification with his own culture. In such an approach the focus rather than the locus of the work becomes the basic determinant (Whittaker & Trieschman, 1972).

The foregoing stance is a decisive reversal of a previous practice stance in which the residential worker was protected from involvement with the child's family in order to make him more accessible to the child within the group living situation. A residential worker's involvement would add reality to the worker's concern for the child's progress in life beyond the temporary residential experiences.

In support of a shift in perception of child care workers' operating sphere, recent research findings suggest that the effectiveness of residential treatment is more highly correlated with the amount of help the child receives with his or her post-institutional problems of living than with the nature of his or her residential treatment experience (Allen, 1973; Allerhand, Weber & Haug, 1966; Browning & Stover, 1971; Taylor & Alpert, 1973). Having child care workers serve also as aftercare workers lends meaning and impact to their residential work. It also would allow continued work with a child at the time he or she returns home, when a replacement in worker would tax rather than relieve the situation.

There is also the possibility of rotating working spheres so that periodically the residential worker's major assignments would be child/family/community work while the child moves from group life to home life. Such periodic cycling of work assignments would also: (1) grant periodic leave for the worker from the exhausting demands of group care work; (2) overcome the worker's isolation from the child's everyday life; and (3) lessen the alienation between residential workers and the children's families.

## SECONDARY FORCES AND GROUP LIVING

In practice, the residential worker is always subject simultaneously to personal (primary) and organizational (secondary) forces. Caring efforts are shaped by the agency's policies, structures and resources.

It is the institution's policy and power structure that shapes group life as a mini-society. The norms of each particular organization specify how giving and receiving will proceed, who will be given first, second, last or never. But a worker's concern for a youngster's cleanliness can be as much a personal expression of care for the child as an organizational effort simply because "clean children validate an effective child care program." In other words, when, where, and how a child has to be clean are as much influenced by the worker's personal concern as by institutional standards. While administrative personnel are preoccupied with workers' standards of performance, residential workers have to influence policies in order to be able to carry out their work on a primary level. Consequently, organizational issues are an integral part of the residential worker's child care efforts.

Group living and organizational processes have to be reviewed for proper fit. To what extent are the objectives of each group living unit understood and given priority, and conversely, how are institutional objectives made operational in the life of each unit? In Wolins' studies of kibbutzim (Wolins & Gottesman, 1971), as well as in Polsky's research (Polsky, 1962; Polsky & Claster, 1968), the success of a program is specifically correlated to the clarity and determination of purpose in each unit and in the institution as a whole.

### Power Distribution

The distribution of power also deserves particular attention.[7] The power structure of the organization defines staff's and residents' access to resources. Residential staff must have power within the organization if they want to assure themselves the resources they need for their work (materials, repair, space, equipment) and the resources they need to tolerate the demands placed upon them as employees (better salaries, working conditions, private space, etc.).

Knowledge on power distribution can serve as the backdrop for the residential care work at hand. For instance, that children with higher status will get food more quickly than those with lower status suggests the degree of intervention necessary to assist a child not only in getting his or her due at the moment, but in helping him or her assert his or her power in the future. It also reminds the worker that the high-power residents who need the least assistance might be getting the most. Effectively assisting the ones with less power is likely to lead to unrest and a boisterous unity, whereas support of an ongoing power distribution might assure an orderly and quiet but less change-oriented program.

The distribution of power can be further assessed through a study of communication patterns in any one unit. Youngsters on top of the power structure receive the important messages first; those at the bottom tend to get information last. This holds true for communication between children, children and staff, and within staff. Staff is more likely to test out ideas, to share plans, directives and personal chitchat with high-power persons, while lower-power individuals — be it children or staff — receive news or inquiries in the more condensed form and considerably later. Unfortunately, they are the ones who have difficulty in making input in the first place. In other words, organizational development favors least the children who need help most.

Power alignments also define who can do what and who is most likely to be affected. Higher-status individuals have the chance to do more without censorship by peers than lower-status persons. A high-status person who spills a glass of milk might be seen as amusing and worth copying. A low-status person spilling milk is quickly seen as clumsy, triggering a reaction of ridicule.

The material on power is just as applicable to the staff system. Child care workers tend to find themselves anywhere between the low and the medium power position within the institutional structure. While low in organizational power, child care staff tend to be rated high in the power they are supposed to generate in order to fulfill their functional tasks. This discrepancy creates stress and strain not only for the workers involved, but for the total institution. What happens to this strain? It is passed on and "dumped" on individuals in a strikingly lower power position — the residents.

In the total power alignment, residential staff and high-power residents are likely to be in a similar power range. They are the ones most concerned about and affected by each other's power. Each one holds the key to the other's success. The high-power residents are the ones who are "to determine the extent to which the worker can succeed at his job" (Birnbaum, 1973).

## Workers' Power Status

The essential dilemma rests with the substantial power difference between the high-power administration and high-status professional staff and the low-power residential workers. Residential workers are too distant from the major power group, which results in deprivation in resources, information and valid communication. The residential workers' closeness in power alignment with the residents is essential as long as their work is built upon intimate interpersonal involvement, identification, and development of shared and differentiated values. The issue remains: Can the gap be narrowed between residential workers and those above them while child care workers continue their close power linkage with the residents?

Behavioral approaches in residential work have unwittingly introduced a significant elevation of the power position of the residential worker. Application of behavior-modification principles adds solidarity and clarity in objectives throughout the organization, with the tally being kept by the residential worker within the living unit. The case record, unseen but often referred to, somewhere in the social worker's office, has been replaced by the behavioral chart, points cards, or token banks plainly visible right in the residential worker's office. The worker now has free access to resources, as well as the power to dispense them — be they points, tokens, candy or material rewards. The residents have to turn to him or her.

The worker has acquired legitimate power, with "tokens" to apply it. It may be that the behavior-modification approaches will bring about a realignment of the power balance between residential care staff and the other more established professional staff forces.

Though the worker has gained power, there are still the power gaps between the residential workers and the residents, and the intensification of a double-standard mini-society. These children live within a reinforcement economy, with staff monopolizing the banks. In contrast, staff operates within an interpersonal relationship economy, subsidized by the residents' reinforcement economy.

If behavioral reinforcements constitute the lifeline to effective living for residents, then I hold that the same rationale is also applicable to the staff's world. Suppose residents passed out tokens or punch cards to staff, to reinforce staff's efforts in areas essential for the residents' life maintenance. I could readily see a token economy for staff in regard to their availability to a needy child, the keeping of promises, and above all, for the degree a staff member manages to "keep his cool."[8]

Behavioral techniques may be viewed as temporary levelers of power alignments between staff groups, or on the other hand, as the secondary strivings of the organizational world of efficiency and accountability, rather than as primary treatment objectives.

In essence, behavior modification focuses upon management within established standards, and upon finding satisfaction for being in step. Behavioral learning is important for many individuals in residential treatment. Yet the majority of children need help with their primary relationships, values and skills. They require something different, and in addition to societal adjustment skills for life within their secondary institutions (schools, clubs, churches and treatment institutions). They also have to acquire a capacity and a desire to effect change within their organizations. Consequently, development of this capacity can be as much a concern of child care as the ongoing interest in the children's capacity to adapt to their lives' demands.

This paper was introduced by the illustration of a worker calling in the residents of his unit. In this child care effort the worker is faced with primary and secondary group life issues regardless of the children's response. Shall the worker respond with the give and take of primary life requests whose rules are bendable? Or shall the worker support secondary demands, because a bending of a request at one point leads to further alterations at other points? Shall the worker see the request as a negotiation of alteration in the system or an attack on the system? Shall the worker see it in terms of the relationship of these children to each other and their relationship to him? Shall the worker perceive the children's response as a matter of behavioral response and their process of earning or losing points? Or, shall he deal with their coming in or the failure to do so as a personal encounter between the children and himself? The issues inherent in each of these alternative perspectives, I trust, have been pointed up in the foregoing pages.

## CONCLUSION

This paper has stressed the interpersonal and organizational underpinnings of group living and residential care, with group living perceived as an arena for practicing with life's demands. The theme has been that individual development and change proceed through interpersonal experience and the context in which they occur. In short, child and child care worker meet each other, and this meeting is structured by the organizational context.

My perspective has been an interpersonal one. I have tried to envisage behavior-modification efforts within a complex interaction perspective. Behavior modification, or any other mode of intervention, operationalized as one-dimensional creates havoc in a context that is by nature multidimensional. New or old interventive techniques, without interpersonal investment, are not sufficient for growth and change. As emphasized throughout the mutual investment in struggles and the periodic experience of resolving them competently foster a living and learning that make a difference.

## NOTES

1. Child care work is not like business transactions where the give and take are rung up on a cash register or can be computerized.

2. Bureaucratization of therapy refers to therapy either purely "by method" (theoretical orientation) or therapy "by measurability" (*only* on the basis of empirically established measures).

3. This experience is akin to that of Liza Doolittle and Henry Higgins in the "Rain in Spain" duet in "My Fair Lady," when Higgins sings, "I think she's got it." Child and worker search daily for life events that can confirm to each other the experience, "I did it!" (the latter is theoretically akin to Bandura's notion of "self-efficacy" [Bandura, 1977]).

4. My colleague, E. C. Teather, helped me with this notion of "linking" problematic behavior with rehearsive practice for fostering alternate behaviors.

5. This practice had been already established at the time of the writing of this essay in such programs as the Albany Home for Children, Albany, New York; the ARK, Seattle, Washington; Edgefield Lodge, Troutdale, Oregon; and the Walker School and Home, Needham, Massachusetts, among others.

6. Mary Resnick, Seattle, a child care nurse and daycare supervisor, made the pertinent observation that with such direct interactions between parent and worker(s), the sense of competitiveness would become more real than fantasy.

7. Special appreciation to my colleague Hy Resnick for many stimulating discussions on the variables of "power."

8. My concern is akin to the issues raised by Henry (1957) when he challenged the double standards in psychoanalytically-oriented residential programs, where children were challenged to express freely their emotions while staff held each other to curtailment of emotional expression. I am concerned when I see that residents gain or lose points for their capacity to stick to a prescribed task while staff more or less tend to relate to the children (their tasks) on the basis of their affect and power relationship.

# Chapter VII

# Influence Techniques

Parents, child care workers, teachers, counselors, babysitters or others spend much of their energy and thought trying to influence young people's behaviors. Much of the time these efforts proceed rather smoothly. There are, however, moments in every caregiver's daily work with children or adolescents when the adult in charge feels at a loss, or at her or his wit's end. And the adult is then uncertain in which way to influence a child's or a group of youngsters' behaviors. "What to do!" is frequently the frantic thought. At such moments, adults tend to fall back upon their standby influence "tools" such as verbal command, threat, or even in desperation, physical interference. Each one of these can be valid techniques; but usually not in a moment of crisis. These standard tools tend to be overused and not especially fitting for the moment.

In confronting difficult child care situations, one could apply the analogy of comparable decisions faced by a competent carpenter. A skillful carpenter uses more than a hammer and a screwdriver, especially when delicate work has to be done. A proficient carpenter chooses the fitting tool for each particular task at hand. The same holds true for child care work.

The following 40 techniques can be used to assist children or adolescents, thereby *influencing* behavior toward adherence to the adult's guiding directions — and hopefully toward eventual incorporation of such directions as their own.* The techniques, developed for child and youth care worker, are mostly self-explanatory and are amplified by a few descriptive sentences. Caregivers may want to

---

*The idea and term of "influence technique" included a good number of selected techniques originally developed by Fritz Redl and David Wineman (1957, pp. 395-487). Full credit and appreciation are due to these two creative clinicians and authors of the classic publication just cited.

expand their repertoire beyond these 40 selections and add their own techniques. A large and diversified repertoire of influence techniques will undoubtedly come in handy in tense and perplexing moments of child care. Try them!

## FORTY INFLUENCE TECHNIQUES

1. *Planned Ignoring*: Purposefully "not seeing" is used to provide children with an opportunity to release tension through active behavior within safe limits or "to let go." It is hoped that by letting the child proceed as he or she is, the next time the child will do all right. It actually entails a planful putting aside of one's influence.

2. *Acknowledged Ignoring*: Purposefully "not seeing or knowing" but with the tacit understanding between the child and the care giving adult that the latter is aware of the "oversight."

   It is helpful when a child (or children)** needs to have opportunities to err and such acknowledged "erring" helps him or her to become more aware of the undesirability of the manifested behavior.

3. *Signal Interference*: Conveying by means of gesture such as looks, facial expressions, motion by hand, tapping of foot, and other forms of signaling that the caring adult is aware what the child is about to do.

   It is used when it is thought that a reminder, especially an unobtrusive signal, can mobilize the child's memory or conscience to refrain from proceeding or to go ahead — whatever is intended to be "signaled."

4. *Proximity Control*: Moving within visual, hearing, or reaching contact of the child or children in order to be in *proximity* as a controlling force.

   It is used when the actual presence of the caring person within "proximity" is necessary, in order to assure the child with the needed sense of control and support to function effectively, or at least from refraining to function inappropriately.

---

**From now on, "child" is used although it may apply as well to several children or

5. *Touch Control*: It is one step further in direct involvement from "Proximity Control" (see #4). It involves conveying *proximity* by actual physical contact such as a "touch" with one's hand or fuller body involvement.

   It conveys, as in the case of "signal interference," the idea that the caring person is there to maintain control or to encourage a relaxation in controls—whatever is desirable to occur.

6. *Interest Relationship*: An attempt to involve child and worker in a joint activity or conversation which is of special interest to the child concerned and will ultimately involve them both.

   It is used when an absorption in an appealing joint experience with an adult can direct the child toward new and appropriate activities in place of the anticipated or ongoing inappropriate ones. Note—there is no reference to that which the child was about to do. The focus is upon finding something different and more appropriate to do.

7. *Humor*: To introduce humor to help child to relax and to influence her/him to find more appropriate activities or expressions.

   It is helpful when there is a need to reduce tension and child can share humor. (Note, most important! Sarcasm, cynicism, fun at the expense of others does *not* constitute humor).

8. *"Hypodermic" Affection*: Give special support and/or affection to convey to the child, "I am with you in spite of your feelings and behavior."

   It can be used when a child is provocative and most likely anxious. A child will calm down when the caring adult ignores the provocative behavior and gives support to the child's feelings about the situation.

9. *Hurdle Help*: To do with the child in the beginning what he or she is actually expected and capable to do on her/his own.

   It is appropriate when a task seems to the child too big or undesirable but s/he is capable of doing it. Actively doing with her (or him) will help to hurdle a sense of futility, loneliness, or powerlessness, and get her/him on the way.

10. *Labelling*: To specify a situation, to clarify—what it is all about in order to place it within the child's sense of comprehension.

It is helpful to specify a situation and bring it within the context (or vocabulary) of the child's understanding and experience.

11. *Interpretation*: To explain a situation by amplifying important points and what it means to the child.

It is used similar to "labelling" (see #10) as an effort in bringing the situation within the child's understanding. In interpretation the effort is directed toward changing behavior through a change of the child's cognition of the factors involved.

12. *Reminder*: To repeat a previous direction or understanding.

It is helpful if a mere recall of a previous understanding is sufficient to influence adherence to the cited expectation.

13. *Stated Permission*: To repeat a previous permission or understanding about an activity in order that the child can proceed on his/her own.

It is used to strengthen and to influence a child's sense of freedom with support in order to carry on what otherwise would cost the child some qualms or uncertainties.

14. *Joining In*: To join the child in the activities.

It is helpful to influence (to support) a child's activities and to encourage his/her following through with them — to emphasize the worthwhileness.

15. *Direct Appeal*: To make a request directly to the child and to rely on one's own (personal) authority.

It is used when the person "appealing" has more relevance than the desired change in behavior. It requires that there is a mutual relationship between the child and the caring person and the child desires to identify with such a caring adult.

16. *Restructuring*: To rearrange the situation (space-time-physical arrangements) in such a way that it will effect a child's behavior in the desired direction.

    It is to be used when the complications are seen as directly impacted by the contextual circumstances and a restructuring (contextual change) will make a difference and predictively change the interactive process or outcome.

17. *Regrouping*: To make a shift in the group or subgroup's composition.

    It is used if a different constellation in interpersonal relationships can bring about a change in behavior or prevent undesirable behavior.

18. *Environmental "Props"*: To set up special environmental factors which will help shape (influence) behavior.

    It is useful when proper use of furnishings, space and equipment can influence behavior (e.g., closing doors, numbered tools, removal of tempting gadgets, etc.).

19. *Appeal to Rules*: To remind a child of existing rules and/or agreements.

    It is used when a child has an awareness *and* comprehension of the meaning of rules as well as the capacity to hold him/herself to such rules.

20. *Change of Rules*: To adapt existing rules to situation or make exceptions of the rules.

    It is appropriate if a purposeful deviation from the rules will help a child to live eventually more successfully within them. In short, it makes the rule, rather than the child, expandable.

21. *Appeal to Higher Authority*: To refer a question, concern, or problem to the arbitration of a higher authority or, at least, a reminder that such a step could be undertaken.

    It is helpful when the judgment of a "higher authority" is considered more appropriate to influence the desired outcome *without* denying the authority of the caregiving person. This technique is pertinent when questions, concerns or problems fall outside of the jurisdiction of the caregiving person.

22. *Appeal to Intellect*: To challenge the child to think it through, to reason it out for her or himself.

    It is appropriate when a child has capacity to approach the behavior under consideration in a rational way *and* to control him/herself accordingly.

23. *Counseling—A Personal Marginal Interview*: To discuss the total situation with a child in a manner in which the focus is primarily upon helping the child to adapt to or to master a particular personal reaction to an ongoing or projected situation.

    It is helpful when a child needs to explore together with an adult his or her own *personal* affect, behavior and understanding of a situation.

24. *Rub in*: To point out repeatedly the undesirability or futility of any one particular behavior or the results of such behavior.

    It may be pertinent when a child's anxiety needs to be mobilized in order to become more "conscience stricken" or aware of the consequences of his/her behavior or situation.

25. *Scolding*: To blame a child for his/her behavior (or lack of appropriate behavior).

    It is useful if the child is aware of his behavior, the consequences of it *and* has the capacity to behave differently. Similar to #24, it appeals to his conscience and assumes that s/he has a desire and capacity both to do differently and to satisfy (to please) to some extent the person who is scolding.

26. *Heighten Anxiety*: To stress the implications of the behavior for the child and others.

    It is pertinent when a child needs to become aware of the consequences of his/her behavior and the impact upon him/her personally. Similar to #24 and #25, it is only appropriate when the child can and needs to be more conscience stricken.

27. *Personal Appeal*: To appeal to personal relationship between caregiving person and the child in order to rely upon the *personal* meaning the request has for the adult(s) asking for it.

It is significant when desired influence can apparently only be shaped through the relationship with the person. Desired behavior will be influenced to sustain or improve the personal relationship with little concern for behavioral change.

28. *Appeal to Honor*: To appeal to a child's sense of honor and self-esteem.

It is appropriate if child has the proper balance of a sense of fairness and can employ it appropriately in order to function effectively.

29. *Appeal to Group Goals*: To appeal to child's or children's identification with their group.

It is appropriate when a child has an identification with his/her group and desires continuous group membership, then an appeal can be instrumental to accomplish the desired change.

30. *Appeal to Group Pressures*: To appeal to the group to handle the particular situation as an internal group problem.

In order to rely appropriately upon "group pressure," two conditions have to exist: (1) identification with group, as indicated under #29 and, (2) the individual must have sufficient secure status in the group in order that such group pressure remains fair (without scapegoating) and helpful to her or him. Appeal to continued maintenance or enhancement of positive group relationships.

31. *Authoritative "Permission"*: To expressly permit a behavior to occur.

It is appropriate when open *permission* or sanction helps either behavior to go into the desired direction or such permission takes the edge off a need to defy, imitate or antagonize. "Permitting" something openly often can stop behavior which is meant to try out the adult or to express an attitude of rebellious defiance.

32. *Authoritative "Verbot"*: To declare precisely on the basis of one's authority what is and is not allowed ("verboten").

It is helpful if an authoritative statement that a certain "piece of behavior" is intolerable serves as a deterrent and circumstances do not favor any other influence technique.

33. *Teaching of Behavior*: To demonstrate the ways a "piece of behavior" can be carried out.

It is helpful when a child needs help in learning the *skills* of carrying out a behavior and if his eventual mastery of these skills will mean applying them.

34. *Replacing a Child's Action by One's Own*: To do for the child what s/he could and should do on his/her own.

It may be appropriate when doing an act on behalf of or for the child might help him/her do it at a later and appropriate occasion upon his/her own.

35. *Promise*: To promise a reward (reinforce) beyond the result of the desired behavior and compliance.

It may be helpful when the desired behavior may not be sufficient reason in itself to be carried out and when an increase in desire to do so is most important. It also includes the notion that the promised reward is instrumental at this time but will either be unnecessary in the future or always an intrinsic part of the desired behavior.

36. *Reward*: To connect a "piece of behavior" with a reward upon accomplishment.

It may be useful if the accomplishment of a behavior must be stressed far beyond the accomplishment itself (also, see #35).

37. *Isolation — (Time-Out: T.O.)*: To separate a child from the immediate ongoing peer associations and/or activities/events.

It is pertinent when a child has to be separated from ongoing events and/or associations because the ongoing environmental situation is not conducive to his or her functioning on a level he or she is capable. Note, it involves isolation from *ongoing* events and associations. It does not necessarily require isolation nor separation from caring persons. In most instances, isolation requires continued contact with the caregiving persons.

38. *Physical Restraint*: To control a child's movements when s/he lacks the necessary self-control.

It is helpful and, at times necessary, to hold a youngster physically either to keep him or her from doing physical harm to him/herself or others or to remove him/her from the scene of "dangerous" involvement. It must not be confused with "physical punishment." Physical restraint is used only in cases which constitute an emergency.

39. *"Antiseptic" Bouncing*: To take a child out of ongoing situation to prevent her or him from getting into greater complications for her or himself.

It is pertinent when caregiving person can predict serious subsequential behavioral events of which the child him/herself is not aware *and* which can be hopefully avoided by techniques such as isolation. (Also, see #37 and #38.)

40. *Threat*: To indicate forms of reprisals as a subsequent consequence of undesirable behavior.

It may be advisable to remind a child of unpleasant consequences of his or her behavior if the *thought* of such consequences will help him or her to control his/her behavior. A threat also must contain the ingredient that the person advancing or implying the threat is able and willing to carry out. (In many ways, a threat also implies a dare and a desire, or even the necessity, to make the threat come true.)

## IN SUMMARY

The foregoing 40 influence techniques, as has already been suggested, are introduced to expand adult caregivers' repertoire of interventive techniques. An expanded, readily available "stock" of facile means of intervention is essential in professional care and treatment work in order to mesh the interventive efforts with the care receivers' immediate personal requirements. The major step from spontaneous to professionally-oriented care work involves a worker's capacity to be *personally* involved with the care receivers while simultaneously sacrificing the worker's own favorite personal style of doing things. Redl and Wineman alerted us many decades ago that an effective therapeutic caregiver trades his or her favored private way for handling children or youth for practice strategies needed in each particular circumstance (Redl & Wineman, 1957, pp. 48-59).

This chapter is included in this publication as a mini-workbook. Reading its content may stimulate caregivers; it might possibly sharpen and specify the techniques already known and practiced by the reader. Rarely, however, does the mere reading or reflecting of a particular learning content lead to an acquisition of added skills. An intermediary step is necessary. The reading of new skills has to be bolstered by rehearsal and trial practice with them. Then, such skills have a chance to be adopted and with *added use* to become eventually part of a worker's interventive practice repertoire. It is hoped that those interested will strive for this mastery. A person with an ample repertoire of techniques will have a better chance for gaining more *effective* influence.

Chapter VIII

# The Space We Create Controls Us

"We shape our buildings — and they shape us!" A sage comment attributed to Winston Churchill (Proshansky, 1970, p. 18), can also be aptly applied to the spatial arrangements of our residential group care settings. The way we arrange the physical space of our service settings can strongly enhance or inhibit the program of care and treatment we provide.

Just two quick illustrations: the location of a superintendent's or unit supervisor's office has great effect on this person's accessibility to the residents, staff, and public, regardless of how available an administrator may wish to be. Similarly, the location of the television set in the resident's unit strongly influences ranges of activities in the unit, including the role of television in the daily lives of the children and youth.

People working in the residential care and treatment field rarely have an opportunity to design or rebuild their residential settings. Yet, the challenge is always there to alter the physical arrangements in order to effect service activities in a specific way. In short, *change space — and advance program!*

## TERRITORY DEFINES A PERSON

Each of us tends to value showing our personal territory to friends, family, or strangers, be it our home, study, garden, work-room, or private corner. We proudly show (and share) our private space, because it defines who we are. Private space spells "ME!"

In the world of work, a person's power position and value within

This article originally appeared in *Residential Group Care and Treatment*, 1(1), 1982, 51-59.

*153*

an organization can invariably be estimated by the relative space granted as *private* working domain. Compare the size of the executive's office, or the highly-guarded boardroom, with the size of other offices; or compare social workers' offices with those of child care staff. (The latter may, in fact, have no office space at all.) People without offices — secretaries, janitors, and frequently child care workers tend to guard carefully the little private territory they *can* claim (Stea, 1970). Private territory, in essence, stands for the ecological verification of self and serves as a tangible symbol of one's power base within an organization.

## PRIVATE SPACE

*Private* space is an area recognized by the occupant *and* others as that occupant's private domain. It is a place where one has full control over self, environment, and possessions — a space that can be arranged, rearranged, and above all, ordered or "messed-up" at will. Within this space a person has a sole right to invite or to exclude others (Bakker & Bakker-Rabdau, 1973).

Most important, private space is an area where a person can be an island to him- or herself. The wish to be alone periodically and to have space of one's own is a human requirement (Merabian, 1976) not merely a wish of children or adults in residential settings. In fact, in the absence of assured sanctuaries, people tend to create their own private spaces by such behaviors as placing themselves behind newspapers or retreating into themselves. A harassed parent may retreat to the bathtub. Children lacking private space of their own tend to seek out such retreats as faraway corners, swings, closets, or the guaranteed privacy of the toilet. The thrust for privacy becomes acute for persons living or working within close proximity of others (Epstein, 1981). At moments of personal tension and social change, individuals require added privacy and the assurance of ample space of their own. Children and adults living and working in situations with much personal stress and change demands need private spaces that are clearly demarcated in order to function and to grow.

What about *private spaces* for the superintendent and supervisory staff? Do they have places of their own in the crowded "market place" of institutional life? Does the superintendent's office represent the character of the present occupant, or is it merely representative of a former superintendent? Superintendents and supervisors need to have the freedom and the initiative to arrange their offices to their liking. As "one's home is one's castle," so one's office is one's sanctuary, a place one can use for assured or shared privacy. Superintendents need a guaranteed sanctum for moments of respite, for thinking, and for launching activities.

The essential human and professional need for private space holds just as true for child care staff as it does for administrative staff. Guaranteed private space is an essential resource for child care staff, a place free of demands while they work, are off-duty or taking momentary time-out. Do they have space which they can stake out, arrange, leave in any form of array, and store their things? Provision of such space is usually accepted as an essential privilege automatically assured to other professionals (social workers, psychologists, nurses, and others). Do child care staff have space which is recognized as their meeting, resting, and recreation place (R 'n' R retreat)?

And the residents? What constitutes privacy and private space for them in the fishbowl of group living (Wax, 1977, p. 51)? Children also require private corners for their *personal* belongings and for *solitary* times. It should be noted that protection of personal possessions is essentially an issue of privacy and is only secondarily a mechanism for keeping order in the unit. To reiterate, to have one's own private box, drawer, shelf, or hopefully, personal cupboard is a must in group care.

A sense of permanency is directly related to whether a person feels he or she has guaranteed private space. Moreover, children and youth require territory in their own rooms and in other areas of their group living environment where they can be comfortable and on their own to brood or gloat, to loaf or to concentrate, to be privately with friends, or to indulge in solitary play. Private space also assures the freedom to leave one's project undisturbed for an eventual return.

The sleeping quarters, bed and sleeping space, in almost all cultures tends to have highly personal significance. For young and displaced people this space seems to take on added importance as an anchoring place when their course is unclear. Changes, especially arbitrary or frequent bed or room changes, connote a sense of impermanence and casual disregard for a resident's place within the group care setting. We need to keep strongly in mind that the residents' sleeping quarters belong to the *residents* and function as their permanent-for-the-present home base. Special effort should be directed toward insuring that the children's beds and rooms are not only attractive, comfortable, and practical, but that they symbolize, almost more than any other segment of the residence, the message: "We respect your need for a comforting private space" (Bettelheim, 1974, p. 153).

Staff needs continuously to search out whether attention given to furniture, room arrangements, and decorations are really in the best interest of the children or whether these concerns reflect an adult conception of order. Any one person's sense of order may easily spell confusion to another. A sense of *private* space and personal investment in one's own room arrangements provides a secure place from which to branch out into the less secure and public world around one.

Private space, whether for superintendent, child care worker, or resident needs to have clearly-defined boundaries in order to serve its assuring function; territories have to be acknowledged by all parties involved (Bakker & Bakker-Rabdau, 1973). Nameplates on doors, the lofty posting of such signs as "keep out," "knock before entering," etc., practices commonly employed by children in their own homes, serve as effective means of reaffirming private space. Such space has to be clearly staked out and sanctioned in order to be an available refuge.

Emphasis in the previous pages has been on staking out private territory for supervisory and residential staff and residents. *People* (regardless of positions) require private space. The creation of private space for each person in a residential setting allows each to find a personal balance, because paradoxically, as one finds more time for oneself, one simultaneously becomes more available for others.

## PUBLIC SPACE

Homes, as well as other forms of group living, have definite areas which serve as *public* spaces. These territories can be used individually or jointly by any constituent member, and become personal space when in use. Sitting at the kitchen table, standing temporarily in a doorway, occupying a washroom or stretching out momentarily on the livingroom couch are all examples of sole occupancy of public space that is assured as long as the occupant maintains possession of the spot in person or "by proxy." Thus, "personal space" can be marshalled within any public space (Bakker & Bakker-Rabdau, 1973; Mehrabian, 1976).

*Public space* is most importantly an area which allows people to be together, to be in touch with and aware of each other, to engage in parallel or joint activities, and to include "outsiders" as "insiders." In a public space people can meet and come and go *without* violating anyone's private boundaries.

For example, in private homes some spaces such as the entrance hall, an area around the telephone, the livingroom, space in front of the refrigerator (particularly at parties), and the walkway to the garage, are public spaces. These are "neutral" spaces whose occupancy is in constant flux.

Where are these public spaces in our residential settings, and are these areas genuinely *public* places? Residential settings require at least two public arenas. The first is the public space of *the setting as a whole*; territory where staff and residents, as well as "outsiders," can plan to meet or spontaneously gather — a place where people can be together in various constellations and associations, and where "outsiders," visitors, family or work associates, friends or adversaries, business contacts, or transients can become temporary partners in the residential scene. The second public arena exists *within each living unit* (when the residential program comprises more than one subunit) — public space that allows the residents and staff of a unit to be with each other and with visitors. Public space of the larger institution and of the smaller living units serve as individual and joint play and work spaces.

A public place needs to be welcoming and inviting of equal access. Do the physical arrangements of our institutions allow such access and invite children, adolescents, and adults *to use* the space?

Public space in the residents' quarters ought to be free for use and to be unencumbered by objects such as privately (and possibly jealously) guarded large plants, fishtanks, or other features which hamper the full use of the space. Are public spaces, livingroom, hallways, front or backyard, genuinely *for use* by residents and staff? Are these places where children or staff can be themselves and be freely with others? Or, do the spaces demand highly controlled behavior and selective associations? When the latter is the case, public space ceases to be genuinely "public." Spatial arrangements and makeup may need to be reviewed in order that the space becomes an area which smiles, with props that invite, and space which allows (Redl & Wineman, 1957, p. 6).

If we accept the premise in our service programs that each group living unit *belongs* to the residents and staff of that unit, it follows that other people — whether they are concerned citizens, residents or staff of other units, administrative personnel, or board members of the program — should achieve access to the unit's indoor or outdoor public areas only by gaining permission from the occupants.

Whenever public space is temporarily used for activities such as music making, play, or school work, this "special purpose space" needs to be clearly marked off as a temporary "private" area. Lest such areas become "twilight zones" — areas of uncertainty and potential conflict due to inconsistent accessibility — boundaries and limitations have to be made clear. In this way, difficulties can be decisively reduced around such potential conflict-prone and less clearly defined territories as food serving areas, kitchen, storage rooms, and workshops.

As has been previously suggested, a private claim to public space, such as a seat in a common dining- or livingroom area, can last only for the duration of an individual's occupancy. Frequently, an individual will become attached to and is granted a specific place as an accustomed spot within public territory — by consensus the space becomes the person's private space. In private homes it is not unusual for a family member or a pet to have established "squatter rights." The same would hold true in group living settings.

Public space serves as the arena for people to be safely present and to become engaged with other people. A dual question and challenge exists here. First, to what extent does the public arena "smile," have furnishings which "invite," and space which "allows" and "encourages" give-and-take between the residents and their staff? Secondly, to what extent is the public arena fully used by residents, friends and family — neighbors by the superintendent, and other supervisory personnel. While the personal contacts that take place in the staff offices involve specialized, "private" encounters, more casual exchanges and group involvements need to be made possible through the use of public space.

The contacts between child care workers, administrators, social workers, other staff, and visitors within public spaces constitute more than casual and unimportant chance encounters. These are opportunities for *vital* interactions which enhance the children's or youth's residential living experience. One may then ask the question: In what way does the public space control potential contact? Does the spatial arrangement convey a sense of welcome and encourage comfortable visiting?

## SPATIAL ARRANGEMENTS CONTROL ACTIONS

Spatial arrangements *control* one's actions (Stea, 1970). It is common knowledge that the arrangement of furniture in one's livingroom controls the flow and quality of interactions. A small dining table that seats four to six enhances listening and discussion, while round or square tables minimize authority issues, rectangular ones accentuate authority positions. Tables seating more than six intensify engagements between neighbors but limit contacts beyond a person's immediate vicinity. In short, interactions are often impacted more by spatial arrangements than by personal characteristics of the people involved (Wax, 1977, p. 51). Thus, the space we create controls our actions.

We can apply such knowledge from research and other writings (Freedman, 1975; Mehrabian, 1976; Proshansky, Ittelson & Rivlin, 1970; Seaburg, 1971; Sommer, 1969; Stea, 1970; Wax, 1977) to our own experiences with controlling interactions through spatial arrangements. For example, how does the furniture arrangement in residential waiting or visiting rooms effect interaction? Is the furniture lined-up along the walls, spaced apart from each other in such a way that people are forced to sit separately — staring into the room or hiding behind a magazine or a coke for privacy? Is the spacing representative of the classic but anti-social schemes of waiting rooms and yesterday's parlors? Or, is the furniture arranged in close clusters that encourages small groupings and intimacy?

In multioccupant bedrooms, particularly in dormitories, we need to look at sleeping arrangements. Are the beds lined up in orderly barrack fashion, as if to warehouse troubled children (Whittaker, 1979, p. 5)? The latter constitutes spatial arrangement for strict control and the enforcement of egalitarian standards. Or, are the beds arranged in clusters that accentuate closeness within each subgroup. Such spatial arrangement leads to greater individualization and forces caregivers to individualize — to place human concerns over managerial ones.

As mentioned earlier, individuals require added privacy and an assurance of ample space of their own at moments of tension and social change (Horowitz, Duff & Stratton, 1970). Repeatedly we experience that children who are tense require more space between themselves and others, even for such absorbing group activities as eating or watching television. The necessity for more space in moments of stress is not necessarily a manifestation of a person's irritability but rather a response to a "crowding experience." Namely, recent studies have revealed that crowded conditions cause people to become tense and antisocial as if people within their immediate proximity were their adversaries (Friedman, 1975). We are reminded of instances of crises when children or adolescents dash off to faraway corners, actually run away, or in intense moments of "crowding panic," engage in fighting or other flight behaviors — and even in suicide (Wax, 1977, pp. 51-52).

We are familiar with these tense times. Some occur almost daily at such unavoidable moments as waiting for mealtimes, the school bus, or one's turn in an involving event. Others, such as sharing unwelcomed news, occur less often. A restructuring of space for these anticipated crisis events that assures ample buffer zones and action space for the individual (Horowitz, Duff & Stratton, 1970), will render such crises more manageable for child and staff. The added space created permits the child or youth wider range of behavioral expression.

## SUMMARY

The theme of this paper can be wrapped up in a single sentence: *Space speaks loudly*. Spatial arrangements serve us all as resources for expressing individuality, for enhancing personal privacy, for finding human connectiveness, and for developing socialization skills. The strong human strivings for individuality and sociability are central concerns of child care and treatment. We, therefore, need to assure that spatial arrangements further, rather than hinder, our work. Most important, these are factors which we *can* control. And surprisingly (and what welcome news) most of these steps require little or no budgetary consideration.

# Chapter IX

# Child Care Within
# an Organizational Context:
# The Inherent Strain

## INTRODUCTION

The ever present struggle of reconciling *primary* care requirements of children[1] living in group care facilities with the programs
*secondary* organizational demands, finds its expression and potential balance in the daily work of the child care staff. Actually, workers seem to be serving two masters. The following account of a staff
meeting at a prestigious child care agency serving forty severely
disturbed elementary and high-school age youngsters has all the
symptoms of the aforementioned strain. I submit that the underlying
themes[2] are inherent in staff deliberations almost anywhere.

Let us look in on a typical one-and-a-half-hour staff meeting.
Forty minutes have been taken up with general announcements, en-
quiries, administrative admonitions, and "success proclamations."
Finally, the main topic of the particular staff session was raised: In
which ways can we strengthen the group care components of the
residential program? This topic was introduced and interpreted by
the group life supervisor expressing the need for more precisely
tailored individual approaches to the residents' therapeutic requirements. One worker immediately elaborated on her idea that she
could do more for the children if she were to work solely on week-
days. It seemed that the children with whom she was the most involved tended to be away on weekends. Additionally, she pointed

---

This article originally appeared in Fulcher, L. C. and Ainsworth, F. (Eds.). (1985). *Group
Care Practice with Children*. London: Tavistock. Reprinted by permission of Tavistock
Publications.

out, on Mondays and Tuesdays these children were apt to have their difficult days, coinciding with the time she was off-duty. Numerous other valid suggestions were brought up, each one involving potential alterations in each worker's investment in time or personal energy. Workers also volunteered specific program suggestions for selected children and recommended different care practices for a particular sub-unit. These latter suggestions created both excitement and frustrations. A member of the administrative staff, in the midst of this lively discussion, wondered with serious concern whether or not these valid suggestions may not lead to a kaleidoscope of practices, and potentially a separate group care program for each resident! Another worker quickly added that the administrator was right; the suggestions would result in a unit with extremely poor organization. Someone else added ironically: "These kids could then get up at any hour of the day. Maybe then the evening shift can see how it is to get the youngsters to straighten out their rooms rather than always creating a mess." At this point, other workers voiced in turn their readiness for more personal involvement with the children. Several questioned with sincerity whether they could muster the energy for added personal care engagement — particularly with the difficult children under discussion. Somehow the perennial request surfaced about keeping the children's play areas free of office staff cars so that the children and care workers could play unhampered. This concern was pushed aside with embarrassed laughter and the meeting continued as before, by more or less acknowledging all input but dealing with none.

Towards the end of the allotted meeting time, a residential worker recommended a trade-off in more time with the kids in exchange for less paperwork. This suggestion, which received an affirmative sigh from many workers, reminded the agency director (who chaired the session) that he was about to take up the issue of recording with the care staff. He wanted their assistance in finding ways the agency could more effectively manage their recordings and to verify the residents' progress. He regretted that time had run out too quickly for this "lively and productive" staff meeting. The issue of alternative ways of recording was recommended as the major topic for next month's staff meeting.

What happened in this staff session seems to be merely an echo of what happens on the front lines of group care practice. In the treatment planning for each child, in the daily care activities, in the cooperation and stress of group care work, in program planning, and in the scheduling of staff, an inherent struggle exists between provisions of personalized care and institutionalized demands for organizational accountability. We also noted that the primary care issues, though central to service delivery and the agenda of this particular staff meeting, still remained sandwiched between organizational concerns. The scenario offered above articulates the major thesis of this chapter, which is that provision of *primary* (personal) care within a *secondary* (organizational) care context always presents a difficult course but it can also offer challenging opportunities.

## PRIMARY CARE WITHIN A SECONDARY CARE CONTEXT

### Care in Everyday Life

The care received by children growing up in their own families is directly impacted by the quality of care rendered to their immediate caregivers. Infants have their parent(s) "at their command, families to protect the mothers or alternate caregivers, societies to support the structure of families and traditions to give a cultural continuity to systems of tending and training" (Erikson, as quoted in Maier, 1978b, pp. 89-90). It is common knowledge that the quality of care and training of children is directly related to the sense of well-being experienced by their caregivers. Emlen's reminder, "if you care for children, then care for parents" (Garbarino, 1982, p. 234), can be broadened and applied to all types of primary caregivers: grandparents, babysitters, foster parents, day care and, of course, residential care workers. In fact, a decisive factor in group care work is whether there is or is not "ample care for the caring" (Maier, 1979, p. 172). Bronfenbrenner pointedly asks, "Who cares for those who care?" (Garbarino & Stocking, 1980, p. 3).

### An Ecological Perspective About Care

Validation of the above notion has recently been elaborated by Bronfenbrenner in his empirically grounded ecological formulations (Bronfenbrenner, 1979). An ecological system perspective applies not only to interpersonal interactions but also to the mutually reinforcing processes and events between larger and smaller systems.

Interconnectedness is part of the nature and pattern of life (Bronfen-brenner, 1979). In particular, we note that events in larger systems impact as much, if not more so, the nature of events in the relevant subordinate systems. In everyday life, for example, to cite Bronfen-brenner,

> a person's development is profoundly affected by events oc-curring in settings in which the person is not even present. . . . Among the most powerful influences affecting the devel-opment of young children in modern industrialized societies are the conditions of parental employment. (Bronfenbrenner, 1979, pp. 3-4)

The degree of work satisfaction, working hours, and take-home pay more strongly affect the degree of each parent's active and psycho-logical availability and the nature of parent-child interactions than his or her personal qualifications for parenthood.

We note that much of a child's life is determined by secondary life systems which involve neither the developing persons as active participants nor the young persons' caregivers in their role as the children's nurturers. Significant events occur that affect what hap-pens in the setting which contains the developing person (Bronfen-brenner, 1979, p. 25). It is important to note that members of the subordinate settings have little power to influence the very events which tend to influence strongly their own as well as the lives of care receivers (Bronfenbrenner, 1979, pp. 255-56). As illustrated, working hours, salaries or wages, and to an extent, work satisfac-tion, are beyond the control of the recipients. The labor market, policy makers, and other *settings of power* "control the allocation of resources and make decisions affecting what happens in other set-tings in the community or in the society at large" (Bronfenbrenner, 1979, p. 255). These decisions also reach into the lives of almost all individuals within their spheres — and subsequently impact the course of each family.

Applied to our immediate concerns, the nature of primary care in any children's center is strongly colored by the employment policy and the institution's pronouncements on the workers' roles within the total scheme. Such factors operate quite independently of the workers' personal and professional qualifications or the staff mem-bers' personal commitments to daily work tasks.

The ecological impact of secondary systems upon primary relationships is applicable to group care situations, regardless of whether the children are in care for part of, most of, or continuous 24-hour services. We noted in the staff meeting described above that a worker's personal readiness to adapt her/his working periods to the requirements of a particular group of children hinged on the program's readiness to adapt to particular working arrangements. One can assume with relative certainty that the decision would ultimately be made on the basis of how feasible it was for scheduling changes to be instituted within administrative considerations, in other words "making the least waves." It is unlikely that such a decision would be made on the basis of children's and workers' urgent need for each other.

At another point in the foregoing meeting, a clinical recommendation for greater individualization was immediately counteracted with the fear that increased attention to individual children's differential requirements would lead to a lack of clarity in oversight and would result in organizational "shambles." It is true that individualism in its extremes becomes the antithesis to organizational order, yet the reverse is also the case: organizational rigidity negates individuality, which is apt to receive less emphasis on organizational deliberations. Finally, we noted that a staff meeting, with an agenda focused upon the children's welfare, started and ended with organizational concerns. Service factors, such as whether recording for communication between staff would allow more intense therapeutic involvement, were easily overridden by administrative concerns. The professional dilemma of increased direct versus indirect service time became reframed into an organizational dilemma; the urgency of translating service gains into measurable standards of reporting. There is an ever present pressure to account for the program's efficacy to the next *larger* systems, namely the sponsoring and controlling systems. Altogether the issue before us is that primary, individualized care concerns tend to give way to those of secondary, organizational power.

The dominance of administrative over immediate child care concerns is not necessarily a peculiarity of the foregoing staff meeting. Rather it is inherent in the exchanges between two systems where the super-system or the organizational system substantially influences the norms, pace, limits, and flow of communication of its sub-systems. The sub-systems are those of the client, staff, group care, and physical domain systems. Each of the sub-systems, in turn, from time to time attempts to impact the organization. Only when persons associated with any one of the sub-systems marshall sufficient thrust to counteract organizational "necessities" do such sub-system efforts prevail. For instance, care workers could have jointly and in a determined manner insisted upon a more flexible waking-up time for children going to a school some distance away. They might have their breakfast ahead of the children attending the local school. The latter could proceed more leisurely, as they were also typically children who required more flexible time demands. It is possible that the straightening up of rooms could occur at varying points of the day. For some youngsters it is more important to start the day and get off to school with as little hassle as possible, whether their room is sufficiently tidied up or not. Such a thrust from the care staff might have led to an organizational change where workers were employed and supported for their flexibility and adaptiveness to situational demands rather than for allegiance and conformity to institutional practices. Moreover, such a thrust from a sub-unit could bolster administrative adaptiveness and readiness to justify to its own workers and the outside that children's centers are for adaptive living rather than providing a showpiece in housekeeping. Unmade beds at noon can represent sure signs that certain children and staff are working actively on other issues vital in the developmental lives of these particular children. (No apologies or regrets are necessary, if such conditions are part of acceptable agency standards.)

In general, the tendency is for organizational requirements to modify special individual care requirements. Such a dilemma can be witnessed when plans for children who are ready to engage in a wider range of activities are throttled when an *agency* does not perceive itself as being ready to branch out. Many activities beyond the perimeter of a group care center are prematurely curtailed for fear of unfavorable public relations. Other activities within the walls, such as appropriate exceptions for some children, variations in procedures, and programs for separate living units are discouraged, or, worse, not even considered due to fear of de-stabilizing the program's overall efficiency. The submergence of exceptions, special considerations, or a thrust towards greater diversity, all have a slight ring of truthful imperative. Where would the children, the staff, and the service be, if the stability of the agency or program were endangered? But is it really such an either/or dichotomy?

The very struggle between individual freedom for personal initiative and adherence to organizational norms, the desire to serve individual children, and to remain mindful of what others would say; and above all, the strain to become fully involved in child care ac-tivities while remaining a faithful peer to one's fellow workers, rep-resent mind-boggling and organizational nightmares. It is not unlike the everyday struggle of being a "good" parent as well as a full marriage partner; or a "good" sales person who fully meets a cus-tomer's interests as well as her/his own, as a business person. All these activities elicit conflicting requirements, a notion considered more fully below.

In group care practice it is a common occurrence that an intense involvement with one child readily creates a demand by other chil-dren for equal time. The result may be a rivalrous frown by cowork-ers with a possible warning against over-involvement or at least a curt reminder that not every staff member can afford such a heavy investment. Similarly, the impulse to deal with children according to the situation, viewing rules as being flexible or not applicable at a particular time, can easily be interpreted as a worker operating with-out standards or denying support to her/his fellow workers. It is also true that a search for common guidelines in the care of children may be continuously disrupted by the awareness that such common rules cannot apply logically to a number of children, or will not be carried out by some "notorious" care worker. In another instance, the hope that a token economy can provide a reliable and objective approach, rendering personal involvement unnecessary, is somewhat marred by recent data revealing that private, interpersonal negotiations over the allotment of a token may be more important than the token sys-tem per se.

The complexities just described spell out the interactional conflict between the individual's worker role and her/his larger system — the work group. Actually, this inter-system strain exists between all in-dividual and organizationally oriented processes and systems. Indi-vidual and peer group needs, situational and organizational proce-dures, clinical and bureaucratic considerations are in continuous interaction, meaning that one cannot deny the other. All are part and partners within the same larger whole. While this is so, in this struggle it is a fact of life that the supra-system largely determines the eventual outcome (Resnick, 1980). The credence which is ulti-mately given to work with each child, to staff co-ordination, and to the creation of specific care procedures is not so much decided by the children's and staff's ongoing requirements, as by the *organiza-tion's* capability and status to deal with these vexing issues. Child care issues, clinical considerations, and staff investments decline or flourish in the arms of the bureaucratic organization.

## BUREAUCRATIC AND CLINICAL ISSUES

It is taken for granted that much or most of an administrator's time (director, superintendent, principal, chief, or others) is necessarily absorbed with organizational concerns and the representation of her/his organization to the outside world (its respective suprasystem). It is not surprising that much of her/his time is consequently spent separated from the day-to-day concerns of the service. When she/he does devote time to any particular feature of the program, the impact of that agency administrator will be keenly felt and how she/he chooses to assess a particular program segment will also influence the direction and quality of care delivery of the center's staff. In a visit to one center for instance, is the administrator, with concerns about the number of children in service, likely to focus on whether things are "going smoothly," whether the hot water supply is sufficient, or the reasons why two window panes are broken again? In another example, the administrator's interests might focus upon the residents' progress, and, in particular, upon the difficulties and problems encountered by the staff, especially in the most recently emerging trouble spots. The former scenario of *administrative* emphasis is more common. That is understandable because this dimension relates to an administrator's working spheres. The latter foci of enquiry dip into the domain of care systems, also appropriate but more removed from the group care manager's view. It is no wonder then that care workers sense administrators' preoccupation with the "agency's" major management; consequently administrators' preoccupations readily become part of the operational norms of a staff team.

### The Clinical Aspect of Group Care Work

Practice in group care entails clinical work — that is, care provided on the basis of actual *observation of specific individuals' (child's) requirements* in contrast to a provision of group care on the basis of generalized expectations for members of a circumscribed group — a class of people.[3] *Clinical* means selected care for a specific individual in terms of her/his idiosyncratic situation on the basis of the group care worker's best professional understanding and skills.

## The Bureaucratic Aspects of Group Care Work

Practice in group care also entails bureaucratic performance. This framework inherently requires that a worker fulfills and enhances the service obligations of a particular organization, simultaneously delivering such service efficiently, regularly and impartially. Child care, when it is bureaucratically couched, means providing care of equal quality to all residents, without regard to personal discriminatory differences or personal whims. Bureaucratic service means performance by established norms, applicable as decreed or agreed, regardless of individual reservations or inconveniences. Both clinical and bureaucratic perspectives, that is *primary* and *secondary* care, have their legitimate claims for existence. Both systems seem to be diametrically opposing forces. Both exist within the same interactive field in group care practice with children. A closer look at this interlocking of primary and secondary care (or clinical and bureaucratic) systems may be helpful.

## A CONCEPTUAL LOOK AT PRIMARY (CLINICAL) AND SECONDARY (BUREAUCRATIC) CARE SYSTEMS

The individual and organizational strains and dilemmas mentioned above may be understood and explained through reference to system analysis (Parsons, 1964) and, in particular, Herman Resnick's explication (1980).

### Historical Vestiges

Group care centers, in many ways, possess some stark vestiges of pre-industrial economic society where kinship controlled the occupational system. Members of the kinship system virtually owed their lives to their place of work, with its intense face-to-face encounters, strong authority structure, and close kinship alliances. By contrast, modern society assures economic success through mobility, loyalty to the task rather than persons, and entails de-personalization of face-to-face contacts (Litwak & Szelenyi 1969).[4]

The interpersonal linking functions of the former kinship system are, in general, currently maintained by the family, but also by other modern primary systems: friendship, club, community or group, and group care centers. The ecological, economic, and political functions of kinship systems are now distributed over many modern structures such as government, worlds of business, the trades, and professions. This professional realm also includes the service delivery aspects of group care. The two contemporary spheres of everyday social functioning — the *interpersonal* and the *economic/political* spheres of group care practice — can be likened to a kinship economy.

### Sociological Manifestations

Parsons (1964) and Resnick (1980) establish that nowadays we are confronted with two distinctly separate *group* systems and system patterns of interactions. *Primary systems* comprise face-to-face small groups in close association like teams, cliques, and gangs as well as socially engineered primary systems. Such socially engineered systems might include communes, educational classes, military platoons, therapy and encounter groups, as well as day care or around-the-clock-care groups. *Secondary systems*, on the other hand, are organizational, usually large impersonal systems, for example: business, religious, professional, military, industrial, recreational, and other societal organizations, including group care service organizations.

Primary social systems are noted for their face-to-face association and co-operation among the members. They serve individuals and, at the same time, these individuals are fused into a common whole. Means and ends become intimately tied to one another within a primary system.

Secondary systems, by contrast, stand out as opposite but also complementary to primary group systems. Secondary group systems represent a larger whole, with an emphasis upon contractual, formal, and rational convenient relationships. People are linked with each other; nevertheless their involvement remains specialized and limited. Most striking, these systems function separately and apart from the individuals involved. Secondary settings, in contrast to primary ones, are not an end in themselves, but represent means to other ends (Resnick, 1980, p. 29).

Secondary orientations — such as formality, rationality, and structural emphases — find less favor in primary systems. In secondary systems, correspondingly, primary orientations — such as spontaneity, informality, and personalization — cause strain and are a sign of dysfunctioning. It is essential then to identify and discriminate between the respective variables and demands of primary and secondary groups.

### Variations in Emotional Demands

The expression of emotions in primary systems is expected and encouraged. Group members are expected to convey affect and to be emotionally supportive of each other. In secondary groups, a different norm is operative: emotional neutrality. The latter requires a withholding of personal emotions and relies upon an inconsequential acceptance of others. Emotional expression may deplete energy and lead to a diminishing involvement, or it may be transformed into obstacles for necessary co-operation. The norms of both systems create potential complications. In organizational settings, the demand for emotional neutrality is easily experienced as coolness or disinterest. The latter may lead to a reduction of energy input and to "merely attending to one's work."

It is no wonder that workers deeply involved in the care of children find much personal satisfaction in their practice; but they are simultaneously pulled by the need for neutrality and some may even consider deep emotional involvement as "improper professional" behavior. Other workers with greater emotional restraints are astonished to find children in care being less personally responsive to their semi-neutral behaviors, even though such workers seemingly attend to all details of group living. The administration is never apt to question the performance of the latter workers' practice; but emotionally expressive *co*-workers may criticize this care-giving performance as being "cold" and "uncaring." We observe that some workers attend *personally* and *affectively* to the children, deeming that fulfilling *care* requirements is central to group care practice; others conscientiously attend most judiciously to *service* demands, expressing harmonious caring within the organization. These competing expectations create an ever-present strain in primary systems which have an organizational mission. These factors have been pointed out emphatically by Wolins and Wozner (1982):

The logistic requirements of the well-oiled bureaucracy negated the demands of close, intimate interactions — the essence of people-changing activity. . . . The recipients of care become objects of the bureaucrat's manipulations and are denied control or participation in decisions that affect reclaiming and activity (p. 54).

As Goffman (1961) contends, the bureaucratic model is antithetical to reclaiming.

## STANDARDIZATION IN OPPOSITE DIRECTIONS

Primary group systems depend essentially upon *particularistic* standards. Only the person within each situation will know in which way a rule is applicable. It all depends upon the particular circumstances and the individuals involved. These notions are applicable to face-to-face interactions. In contrast, secondary group systems build upon *universalistic* standards. Rules apply to all in order to be fair to each. Uniformity in standards assures clarity, order, and authority of standards. Either standard — particularism or universalism — may lead to complications for its respective system. Standards purely adaptable to each situation may eventually obviate all standards, while an insistence upon general standards will deny individual requirements. This may be carried to the extent where uniform rules may eventually have little relevance for the person involved, rendering uniform regulations ridiculous.

In organizational life, particularistic considerations are immediately perceived as a threat to law and order, or favoritism unbecoming to an organization. In primary group life, universal rules are quickly resented as obstacles to individual initiative and differences. In group care practice, much energy is invested in working out applicable rules or standards for each living unit and child. These struggles, whether or not a set of rules is actually fair and applicable, can be understood by Parsonian concepts. Arguments for uniform getting-up time, for instance, are supported for their fairness, orderliness, and universal clarity for *all*. Counter-arguments could justify adaptive wake-up procedures citing fairness to particular children's circumstances or individual worker's preferences.

## SCOPE OF INTEREST

Primary group systems like their forerunners, the kinship systems, serve *manifold* interests. This multi-dimensional interest or preoccupation with many details, forges a homogeneous group prototype (i.e., a family, a commune, a friendship association, or a congenial living unit). Secondary systems, in comparison, concentrate upon *specific* interests in well-defined areas while serving a wide spectrum of purposes. It is not surprising that, in a case presentation for example, the organization-oriented workers can explain her/his *typical* work with specificity and technical detail. On the other hand, clinically oriented persons will likely preface their remarks with the explanation that their account is "atypical." They are apt to lose their audience with their mixture of details spiked with generalizations, unless their clinical accounting establishes a profile or constellation—that is a viable case report. A valid case presentation, by the way, evolves out of an interlinking of details into a generalized explanatory whole.

In another area of practice, we note that diffusion of worker or agency interests is frequently augmented by specific interests, such as an all-out push for greater physical order, for individual tutoring, or for a reliance upon group meetings. Each push tends to distort the program towards the selected, more narrowly specified area. In addition, while undergoing these "purges," workers and children tend to become classified according to their performance in the selected sphere of interest. It is no wonder that group care programs blossom or shrivel under specialized program reforms. Much depends upon whether such program alterations include both inherent group care realities: primary and secondary system demands.

## STATUS ALIGNMENT

A preference for *ascription*—the qualities owned by persons according to their positions in life—adds stability to primary group life. This is true so long as these qualities actually define the nature of face-to-face interactions. The following instances are a few of many variations: older and experienced staff are more competent; younger or new members require added guidance. Sex, ethnic, and other genuine differences are significant so long as they do not perpetuate stereotypes but represent affirmative differences instead. In organizational and primary systems, achievement or accountable competence defines status. Definition of status and change of status for organizational and primary systems have relevance in relation to system strains (Resnick, 1980) and contemporary struggles over changing societal norms (Maier, 1969, 1974). In group care practice, a continuous internal conflict exists as to how members' status is to be measured in their *ascribed* roles within their primary group position. For children, an example would be eldest, youngest, leader; or for workers, seniority, job classification, or personal achievements may apply. Competence requirements seem to encroach more and more upon primary as well as secondary group demands (Maier, 1974). Then, too, the recent awareness of sexism and racism in traditional primary group life — where reliance upon ascriptive values also perpetuated discriminatory practices — has furthered a shift to secondary system practices. To put it another way, there is a shift to award status by actual competence and achievements. This leaning towards competence rating in primary settings brings with it the danger of "hollow existence" for staff and residents alike. Are children and workers appreciated because they are familiar in one's life experience, because they are part of one's heritage, or because of their accomplishments and deeds (Resnick, 1980, pp. 40-42)?

A study of the foregoing variables highlights dynamic tension which is inevitable in both types of system, primary or secondary. Tension and repeated requirements of adaptation are particularly germane to group care settings, where the organizational service demands basically rely upon face-to-face interactions. System stresses, then, call attention to either adaptation towards organizational maintenance or clearer emphases upon children's and workers' primary care requirements. In either event, system strains can be viewed as dynamic rather than stultifying forces.

## TWO ORDERS OF PRIMARY GROUP SYSTEMS

Children and workers are frequently admonished to adhere to group norms "for the sake of everyone" or "for the sake of the group." Frequently, it is not clear whether "everyone" pertains to the group members or refers to the persons associated with the group's sponsorship, the group's supra-system. On the other hand, "for the sake of the group" might be a shorthand expression used for the wellbeing of the individual group members as persons. Another possibility could be "for the sake of the maintenance of a group" as a sub-unit of a larger system (Maier, 1978b, pp. 202-205). Each of these appeals serves different demands and different masters. Group care workers have to be clear in knowing with which primary group they are aligned at various points of their "practice."

If the group focus and concern of the moment pertain directly and personally to the individuals making up the group, then the interactions serve essentially the individuals' capabilities, enhancing interpersonal relations and self-verification. Care workers then have to deal with the group members' effectiveness in communication, interpersonal negotiations, and power juggling. Workers' group building efforts serve, essentially, as a source of individual identity formation. In practice, this would mean that a group planning session for an evening of fun would have to include an opportunity for *all* group members to share their wishes and expectations, searching for common denominators and give-and-take negotiations with regard to expectations which cannot be accommodated on that particular evening. Above all, the evening of fun has to stand as a joint group accomplishment so that members may verify that "I had a part in our having fun." In short, "for the sake of the group" in this context reflects individual group members' investment as well as a sense of group achievement.

In contrast, when concerns revolve around group building tasks which seek to maintain and to enhance the group as part of a larger whole, then efforts serve primarily a supra-system of which the immediate group is a part. An example would be care workers and children engaged in establishing their "citizenship" credibility, posing their group as a viable unit within a larger group care center. Concerns will typically reflect the mechanisms of control, establishment of norms, and value aspirations which are in tune with the larger system's expectations. Adaptation occurs not so much in tune with individual members' readiness but instead to the degree that everyone can stretch in adapting to the group's standards. Workers and children are challenged to find a fit. The group forgoes personal whims, shaping up in order that *the group* can gain or maintain a favorable place within a larger scheme.

## CARE WORKERS' STRAINS

The foregoing discussion of natural system uncertainties and differential but interlocking group-building factors may explain the many worlds in which group care workers operate. Yet an explanation never resolves day-to-day practice dilemmas. A *care* worker within an organizational context exists always in a dual world — in two contradictory systems. No wonder that "burn-out" is a rather common occurrence (Mattingly, 1977). Burn-out, rapid staff turnover, a high degree of personal frustration, perplexing diffusion in job descriptions as well as expectations can be traced to these contradictory work conditions. The work circumstances have inherent systemic difficulties; they have to be surveyed for their organizational facets rather than for signs of human frailties (Mattingly, 1977; Pines & Maslach, 1980). These complications emerge for all human service workers who are *employed* or *engaged* voluntarily to help individuals within the context of a service organization. In everyday family life, a parent comes close to such a dilemma when she/he shares in a child's discouragement or delight over school requirements. Is the parent subsequently to respond as a partner and spokesperson for the child and her/his family or the school system? Moreover, the group care worker is continuously required to function as the clinical (*individual*-care oriented) worker *and* as the agency's (organizational *service*-oriented — bureaucratic) worker. Nevertheless, solutions for some of these vexing situations may potentially be possible.

## POTENTIAL SOLUTIONS TO THE STRAINS BETWEEN CLINICAL AND ORGANIZATIONAL SERVICE DELIVERY

Child care within an organizational context does not necessarily have to lurch in different directions, frustrating both clinical or organizational operations. Clinical and organizational requirements do demand different efforts. They can be conceived as dialectic rather than counter-productive forces at the point where either system's pull constitutes a partial investment rather than a negation of the other sytem. In other words, clinical demands for continuous flexibility and basic care decisions in the hands of the group care workers can be recognized and carried out as basic organizational procedures. Organizational uniformity is established through decentralization of power and responsibility. Management and organizational supervision are called upon to oversee that care workers fulfill their *clinical* obligations to their clientele. At the same time the care workers can operate among themselves with a high degree of variation in style within the agreed care and treatment plans.

Parallel to such a clinical/organizational conceptual shift is the organizational stance which demands a universal program policy and which requires care workers and others to formulate concrete and communicable care and treatment programs. Such programs have to define both the definite outcomes expected (objectives) and also the actual care and treatment activities to be pursued with the children and their respective families. Care workers and their supervisory staff have then the opportunity and challenge of defining their territory and operations *within* these spheres of work (Bakker & Bakker-Rabdau, 1973). Many instances of organizational interference with child care decisions can be traced to the absence of clarity about the nature and boundaries of group care practice, in addition to the tendency of organizational requirements to permeate uniformly all parts of the service. Clear enunciation of care and treatment objectives and procedures could establish the extent to which group care works as a vital part of the organizational machinery.

The above suggestion to define primary care or clinical work within a secondary system or bureaucratic operation is consistent with an organizational perspective which views the parts as a dialectic whole. But the purpose here is not to give greater credence to bureaucratic considerations but rather to call attention to the organizational context which constitutes the *supra*-system within which clinical work proceeds. Group care workers may feel even greater commitment to their work with the children and, hopefully, a true identification with practice rather than yielding unnecessarily to bureaucratic demands. In reality it *is* the larger context — the organizational factors — which ultimately shape and determine the nature of group care practice. Consequently, group care work has to be formulated, operated, and evaluated from an organizational perspective. It is within such a perspective that personal (clinical) care and treatment can fully proceed and flourish within a well-organized agency program.

### Responses to Children's Emotional Demands

We postulated earlier that quality practice in group care demands close intimate interactions — the essence of people-changing activity — while bureaucratic practices are antithetical to care and treatment efforts (Wolins & Wozner, 1982, p. 54). Group care workers tend to be caught between these opposing demands such as being fully engaged with *all* children and being especially attentive to children who require individual adult involvement. The daily worker's dilemma is well known: provide a very personal "good night" to all and also provide quality involvement with a few individuals. These difficult time-chores are inherent in all caring care and do not represent an inadequacy in the organization or staff. The organizational issue is: In which way can staff be assisted to assure more quality time with the children or young people *plus* added time with some? Simultaneously, one needs to recognize as appropriate the children's wish for more attention and the workers' disappointment in not being able to deliver to everyone's satisfaction. Organizationally and clinically, caring efforts have to be objectively reviewed for the possibility of additional or alternative opportunities for personal, intimate interactions between the children and their daily care-givers. Clinically and organizationally, efforts have to be directed towards finding new opportunities for intimate and varied interaction between children and workers. For the latter, this kind of searching may lead to such practices as provision for intimate conversations before bedtime, rather than a mere get-together snack period; reading a story rather than a TV hour; a quick tussle, or other special quality time with workers. Another example would be the worker being available in the morning as a person for protests or laughter rather than as an organizer of chores and a manager of the long day ahead.

Bureaucratically, *individualized nurturing care* has to be conceived as the central ingredient of group care work with children who have experienced many separations and disruptions in their lives. Nurturing is not only required out of compassion and a humanistic belief that children and young people need love and affection, it is also based on scientific knowledge that children and young people want and will learn to care for and to love others when they have experienced genuine care themselves (Kobak, 1979). Organizationally, then, emotional involvement has to be defined as part and parcel of the work commitment for care workers. It has to be explicitly specified in each job description as an integral part of the daily ingredients of group care practice.

Another practice dilemma stems from the continuous personal and emotional demands placed upon workers in the face of administrative expectations that they must not get too deeply involved emotionally in their work. This admonition seems to originate from the organizational demand for objectivity. Emotional involvement, at the same time, is the group care worker's speciality (Barnes & Kelman, 1974). In many ways, group care workers find themselves in the same situation as parents who are overtaxed by children's never-ending and frequently incomprehensible demands. In fact, care workers, in a different way, find themselves akin to "abusive parents," who, as Durkin observes, "are chronically overstressed and undersupported, have incompatible demands made on them, and are alienated and relatively powerless to control their fate" (Durkin, 1982a, p. 5).

In tune with Durkin's pointed analysis, desired change cannot be accomplished by a frontal attack on the quality of a worker's involvement. Instead, personal stress can be reduced through institutional support and the establishment of manageable working conditions. In concrete terms, this would mean established working hours with periodic rest breaks in a location which assures separation from the work place. Also, it is essential to work out concrete, achievable care objectives rather than vague care expectations. A vague objective like "to help the children to manage well throughout the day" is absurd when these same youngsters can actually barely manage sufficient concentration to lace up their shoes. Above all, it means providing care workers with support and supervision for their *care* work rather than their managerial work per se so that their emotional involvement enhances rather than deters nurturing care. Such practices are psychologically sound, make clinical sense, and can be logically as well as bureaucratically arranged, managed, and appraised.

### *Standardization in* **Apparently** *Opposite Directions*

Clinical processes and organizational processes, as have been recounted earlier, proceed in opposite directions as if the two should never meet. Maybe a conceptual shift can link the clinical necessity to deal with individuals and small primary units in terms of their requirements with the organizational mandate for *universality*.

In group care practice, workers tend to stress vehemently the special needs of individuals and their separate living units, as if these needs were so unusual. Actually, individual requirements of people within their particular primary groups are derived not special, they represent merely the facts of life. Our difficulties are not so much from the children's special needs as from our inability effectively to formulate, communicate, and organize these requirements. Teachers have lesson plans and curricula. Nurses have charts and nursing procedures (Krueger, 1981, p. 4). Social workers, psychologists, and psychiatrists have case summaries, assessments and treatment plans with step-by-step interventive objectives and evaluations. What do other group care workers have? They have, at best, generalized statements, specifying acts of close control, unending patience, or the mandate of providing loving care. In some settings, they do have precise directions about how to award points and tokens for specific behaviors, but workers are left on their own to decide how they deal with the children and their group in general. These widely varied expectations are topped by the organizational expectation to maintain an orderly, smoothly run, contented group care center. The fact remains that from a clinical point of view there is no doubt that group care workers must have a *program* for each child in care and for the management of their unit-as-a-whole.

To augment general schemes, workers and their supervisors have to set up *personal care programs* akin to curricula in education. Such undertakings must be the *universal* practice of the service. The organization has to see to it that this kind of framework is maintained in order to assure fair and consistent care objectives for all. At the same time, the collective of children in care will be guaranteed, in principle, life-fulfilling activities according to idiosyncratic requirements. *Personal care* programs would then take up plans in the way educational plans specify the events of the day as a curriculum. In so doing,

> the entire nature of present definitions of childcare work in a residential programme . . . the grind of supervising kids ends. We are with them both individually and as they mesh together in the group. Control issues vanish and are replaced with content issues, highly relevant pieces of the total curriculum. (Barnes & Kelman, 1974, p. 19)

Bureaucratic verification of individualized care and treatment can be further refined by the very fact that every service receiver has individual requirements. The service deals with ordinary growth and developmental phenomena which for all children is anchored in the *interpersonal* interactions between caregivers and care receivers. Children are children, regardless of whether they receive family care or not. This truism is particularly relevant for the transmission of macro-systems values. "Children learn particular cultural values and particular moral systems only from those people with whom they have close contact and who exhibit that culture in frequent relationships with them" (Washington, 1982, p. 105).

Moreover, an extensive study of children successfully and unsuccessfully treated highlights that the most salutary change occurred when consistency existed in meeting clients according to their particular situations and their current understanding. Such results can be obtained even though it creates for the casual onlooker situations of uneven, inconsistent behavioral handling (Division of Youth and Family Service of the State of New Jersey, 1978).

### Interests on Different Ends of the Continuum

As outlined earlier, clinical considerations encompass a wide spectrum of the residents' lives. In fact, the more diffused the styles of workers interacting in a child's life, the more efficiently workers carry out their care obligations. It is also true, however, that organizationally a group care service has to be clear about its exact service mission and its use of resources. However, rigid adherence to a bureaucratic service mission, in turn, tends to stifle all those responses which seem appropriate in a creative clinical care and treatment program for children.

There seems to be a pull in two opposite directions. In one direction there is an effort to expand and deal with more when more is needed; in the other there is a gravitation towards holding the line within the province of the available resources, that is, to manage with that which is actually at hand. In holding to their respective directions both group care workers and organizational administrators are doing their respective jobs. In fact, at times, the workers in the group care center themselves become administrators and they themselves are apt to limit the use of resources in order to have enough to go around. But whatever the circumstances this struggle will be evoked between human and humane desires for an abundance of life and the bureaucratic necessity to control and to make do with that which is given in an economy of scarcity.

The organizational managers have the actual knowledge and control over the boundaries (just as in the living units, the group care workers have their sway). The organizational teams are the "gate-keepers" and the ultimate controls are without question in their hands. Having made a realistic acknowledgement of these factors, it is then important that group care workers relate themselves to the requirements of their practice and see to it that provision is made for those things they deem necessary for the children's development and enriched living experience. They are the ones who know what is needed. Organizational limitations, never-ending demands, public relations, and limited budgets are all legitimate pressures, and clearly enunciated reminders of them may be offered at periodic intervals, yet the necessity for additional resources, unexpected requirements, alterations and expansion in activities, as well as unforeseen circumstances, are also legitimate reasons for service delivery. All these demands would remain unnoticed and unattended by the service unless clearly articulated by care personnel.

Group care workers have to operate foremost and throughout as the representatives of care, ever ready to interpret the care requirements of children. Organizational wishes and restraints will always become readily known, due to indigenous power contained in supra-system demands. Workers' faithful and unchallenged acceptance of this power renders them "good servants" of the organization but diminishes their value as group care workers. The workers' pronouncements on the necessities for "their" children, including apparent luxuries, make them into responsible child care workers, and thereby into effective members of the organization. The distance between management and care practitioners must be shortened in order to make known and to secure what is needed for a life similar to that afforded to children in their own homes. Moreover, workers on the front lines, to follow Pina's astute observation, are the ones who discover innovative solutions. Their concerns can no longer be treated as exceptions when, in reality, they are a continuing feature demanding novel and urgent solutions (Pina, 1983, p. 3).

### Status Alignment

Employment on the basis of ascribed or achieved qualifications presents a dilemma either way. Group care as a profession or as a craft (Eisikovitz & Beker, 1983; Maier, 1983) demands training and competency achievement in terms of clinical *and* organizational work. The ascribed value of "being part of the children's lives" is another essential feature. The care-givers' role as vital participants in the residents' life development — to be the children's or young people's primary care persons in their everyday life — becomes a decisive variable in terms of staff selection, work, or time-off scheduling, and the workers' place within the center. Ascriptively, care staff *own* their place in the organization while the quality of their work has to be prescribed and appraised on the basis of actual achievement in providing interpersonal care services. This achievement is colorfully described by Durkin:

> one of the greatest joys of being a child care worker is that what you are as a unique configuration of personality traits, interests, skills, hobbies and how you have fun, etc. — that is, what you are as a person — gets full use on the job. (Durkin, 1982b, p. 16)

And it can be added that such personal qualities are used to meet the life requirements of the children as developing persons and members of a residential living-unit group. Then the group care worker will be a full professional within a bureaucratic organization: she/he can find personal satisfaction, using her/his own creativity as a professional.

## CLOSING COMMENTS

Provision of individualized (clinical) child care work within a group care (organizational) setting has been reviewed using a Parsons/Resnick "thinking screen." The latter explains the counter-pulls of primary and secondary system variables and processes. Resnick's conceptual analysis (1980) has been employed to understand some of the strains inherent in group care practice pursued as a clinical endeavor and, by contrast, as an organizational model.

Our purpose has been to conceive of group care practice as primary care or a clinical enterprise. *Primary care* is the essence of a group care worker's activities, implementing the children's developmental requirements, to obtain a close attachment with the children in care, and lastly, in order to foster a sense of permanency in the children's lives (Maier, 1982). The care-givers' work is defined as *clinical*, because their focus has to proceed on the basis of each child's individual requirements rather than to deal sociologically with the children as a class or group. At the same time, we must be mindful of the fact that such care is not being provided within a primary group system — the family, commune, or kinship network. Instead, it occurs in a socially engineered group care setting — a secondary organizational group. Organizational features place primary care in a different context and bring organizational demands in conflict with clinical realities.

In the second half of this chapter we have attempted to seek out potential ways and possible solutions for accepting inter-system strains as necessary ingredients of nurturing care within an organization. In fact, for many of these inter-system strains we neither have a solution nor want to provide solutions. The system strains seem to be part and parcel of the nature of contemporary living in modern, technological societies. Moreover, while the mutual "system wheels" turn, the partial intermeshing can be conceived as dialectical control processes which "grind" out a viable whole of ill-meshing but salutary encounters. Organizational demands may offer their own legitimate characteristics, such as minimizing or guarding against depletion of workers' own individual energies by yielding to children's endless personal requirements. The introduction of interpersonal neutrality within an organizational context may assist staff to maintain satisfactory work relationships with coworkers and supervisors while they are intensely involved with the youngsters in care. An ancient proverb can be paraphrased here: Give to the children what *is* the children's and to the organization what *is* the organization's!

In the spheres of standard setting and diversity of interests, the strains of the system or dialectic envelopment might include a scenario which can neither be accounted for nor resolved by workers or the organization. Indeed, this kind of tension may be representative of future life experiences anywhere. It is important for workers to deal with these events as part of a child's life experience. It is to be hoped that workers can transmit skills to children which allow them to reframe their experiences or at times to adapt to them, rather than by-pass or flatly accept restraints. This can be powerful intervention in group care practice.

Finally, this chapter brings together two spheres of life experience and two disciplines of knowledge that are rarely studied, viewed, and dealt with as one joint enterprise. This way of thinking requires that separate system-partners, by virtue of their division of labor and allegiances, become co-operators in their naturally conflict-ridden joint enterprise. These highly distinctive work approaches necessitate additional working orientations in order to incorporate the other system's realities (Resnick, 1983). In other words, personal care work within an organizational context demands more than appreciating and co-operating with other systems' demands. Viable group care practice may also require an evaluation and expansion of one's own theoretical stance and practice procedures. The next step is to find bridging concepts and linking practices with the immediate and wider worlds of which every child, young person or staff, every living-unit, however securely fenced off, and each service organization and their respective communities, are a part.

## NOTES

1. For simplicity, the terms "children" or "child" will refer to children as well as to adolescents or young people.

2. The major ideas underlying this chapter build upon Talcott Parson's formulation on "Pattern Variables" (1964), and in particular, Professor Resnick's lucid development of Parson's formulation (1980). I am personally indebted to my colleague, Professor Herman Resnick, for teaching me this rich material on primary/secondary system strains.

3. "A class of people" is here used sociologically – an empirically defined category of people as a distinct unit which is separate from other classes.

4. This factor is clearly visible in a number of highly applauded and well-known residential treatment programs which are operated akin to the norms of former feudal societies. We can list among others, Bettelheim's Orthogenic School (Bettelheim, 1950 and 1955; Neil, 1960; Mayer, 1960; Phillips, Phillips, Fixsen & Wolf, 1973).

# Chapter X

# The Child Care Worker

Child care workers are those persons who provide a major portion of round-the-clock care, supervision, and resources for children or youths in a group-life situation, whether for day care or residential care. They become the extension of the children's parents, by assuming immediate responsibility for nurturing care, socialization, and specific therapeutic requirements. The group situation is a socially engineered alternative to family living in which the child care worker functions as the instrumental leader. Child care workers then are both the children's link with the tasks before them and the world around them and society's guardians of the quality and direction of the care afforded to the children. Of all the staff working in child welfare settings, child care workers are most directly involved in the children's lives, in the latter's continuous encounters with the everyday issues of life as well as the variations created by the particular group-care program.

Individual child welfare programs use different terms to designate the child care person—cottage parent or houseparent, group counselor or group-life counselor, mental health worker or residential worker, teaching parent or teacher counselor. Although each title describes a specific aspect of residential care and child care functions, all can be viewed as variations of the general role of child care worker.

## FUNCTIONS

The functions of child care workers may be described as being equal to but unlike those of parents. Child care workers intervene in all aspects of a child's life, but do not replicate the parental role.

The tasks performed have instrumental and expressive components. Different programs vary in the instrumental tasks expected and the theoretical perspective associated with the expressive component related to the required tasks. For example, "getting children to sit down at mealtimes and eat their meals" is an instrumental task demanded of child care workers in all group care settings, while counseling with a child or the child's family on mealtime behavior might or might not be considered a "proper" child care function.

The delineation of tasks is related to the administration's conception of the child care worker's spheres of functioning. The child care worker can be responsible for group-life spheres per se or the individual child's group-life spheres. The expressive components of a child care worker's interactions with the children for making mealtime a mutual time of sharing and personal growth can be handled in various ways, depending on the worker's and the setting's care and treatment orientation. For example, emphasis might be placed on shaping behavioral expectations or on a child's finding satisfaction in the process of eating with others.

Child care functions can also be understood as service tasks that are comprised of direct and indirect aspects, with the instrumental and expressive child care functions inherent in each aspect.

### Direct Work With Children

Such work involves carrying out functions that help accomplish both the immediate and long-range objectives of the care that is instrumentally agreed on in a given setting. It takes the form of providing both everyday care and maintenance and individualized care and treatment. Everyday care includes the general child-rearing functions of physical care (provision of feeding, clothing, and rest), habit training (personal and interpersonal hygiene), first aid (health maintenance and restoration), self-management in interpersonal contacts (peer and adult relationships), and the introduction of new stimulations and variations in daily life experiences (planning new social contacts in the world of play, work, and routine). Individualized care includes the special provision of nurturing care, personal counseling, crisis intervention, tutoring, and family counseling, the introduction of specific therapeutic timing, activities, and personal role variations, and the application of behavioral change programs that arise out of an individual child's ongoing needs.

### Indirect Work With Children

This describes the carrying out of executive and managerial functions of a child welfare program within an individual child care unit. Such work involves management of the use of space and facilities and of the daily program of the unit (including provision of food, clothing, rest, routines, and controls as well as enriching daily activities and outside contacts) and leadership in overall planning of the use of group-life time, space, and content and of intra- and intergroup relationships. Also involved is implementation of the program's overall child welfare policies, which includes consultation and planning with other staff within the program and counseling and consulting with persons in the children's lives outside the program (teachers, parents and other pertinent community contracts), as well as writing and receiving reports evaluating the children's progress within and outside the unit's life.

The spread and variety of tasks asked of child care workers, combined with the fact that the children served have continuous, intense, and taxing individual demands, create extraordinary pressures on the workers. It is not surprising that the job turnover is high.

## THE WORKER'S PSYCHOLOGICAL POSITION

Child care workers function at the hub of the institutional wheel: they are the persons centrally responsible for the provision of care and treatment to the child away from family care. It is the child care worker who is with the child and who sees to it that the child's daily living requirements are fulfilled. Through the regular exercise of their caring functions and the control of resources available to the children, child care workers are the most powerful agents in the children's lives. Conversely, the children's everyday experiences of receiving the workers' personal attention as well as food and other necessities of life make the child care workers the central persons within their immediate daily lives (Portnoy, Biller & Davids, 1972).

The group care units constitute the basic service and organizational segments of a child welfare program. Thus the child care worker also has a key position in being able to modify the impact (both positive and negative) of other potentially important persons on the children's lives within and beyond the service program (the social workers, teachers, psychiatrist, and director of the program, as well as community people).

## THE WORKER'S ORGANIZATIONAL POSITION

Despite the important part child care workers play in the group-care units, they are apt to be among the lower-status persons — organizationally, economically, educationally, and socially — within their programs. They tend to be relegated to the lower echelon in decision-making. More often than not, they are bypassed in becoming full participants in staff or case conferences, in allocation of equipment and working (including office) space, and in representation to the outside world. They do not have power and status within the overall organization compatible to that they hold in the group care situation itself. Thus, the child care worker is apt to adapt to the immediate demands and values of the care unit rather than to the overall objectives and therapeutic directions of the total agency program (Polsky & Claster, 1968).

## THE WORKER'S PROFESSIONAL POSITION

Lacking an established professional reference group, child care workers depend for their vocational or professional image on the place of their employment. Child care work, long established as a profession in most European countries, can be described in the United States as a discipline-in-the-making. This trend is indicated by such developments as training programs and certification of child care work, the publication of a periodical (*Child Care Quarterly*) devoted to child care practice concerns, and the existence of associations of child care workers in two-thirds of the states, as well as the emergence of national organizations for child care workers (the American Association of Workers for Children and Professional Child Care Workers of America).

Whether child care work will become a discipline with professional standing or occupational commitments and whether it will become professionally or occupationally aligned with social work, nursing education, or a discipline of its own is yet not clear. Moreover, child care workers remain divided in their group affiliations; some lean toward membership in professional associations of their own or in the child welfare field, others toward labor or employees' unions, and some remain affiliated only with their place of employment.

## TRAINING OF CHILD CARE WORKERS

The trend toward professionalization of child care work has been intertwined with the emergence since the mid-1950s of educationally centered training programs. Institutions of higher learning in many states now offer courses on child care. These vary from short-term courses to fully accredited curriculums in community, two-year, and four-year colleges and in graduate divisions of universities. Some training programs emphasize the development of competence in workers already in the front lines of practice; others prepare workers, once trained, to enter the field of practice. There is debate over the establishment of degree ladders and the question of whether child care training programs should belong to community colleges or two- or four-year institutions of higher education. Yet, the basic issue for training, as for practice, remains: What constitutes the instrumental and expressive functions of child care? A clearer delineation of these functions will clarify the training requirements and the degree of eventual merger with established training programs for child development associates, day care personnel, social work, and psychosocial nursing (Beker, 1975).

## THE HISTORY OF CHILD CARE WORKERS

The ancestors of today's child care workers were the matrons of the orphanages and almshouses of the nineteenth century, who served as overseers of the children's moral training. In the first half of this century the preference in child welfare for foster home care caused institutional programs to designate first housemothers and later house-parents as the desired providers of care. "Family units," cottages or separate living units, replaced congregate living, and "residential care or treatment" became the preferred terms for around-the-clock group services. Child welfare's accent upon family living, with institutional care envisaged as a last resort after all other alternative services to family life had been exhausted, made the child care worker a less desirable agent for child rearing. Remnants of this perception still affect appraisal of the child care worker's role in the present-day scene.

With the shift in role and position, child care workers tended to model themselves after their more powerful professional colleagues in residential care programs—the social workers, psychiatrists, and educators. Child care workers, formerly viewed as surrogate parents, now tended to assume a perceived role as change (treatment) agents. Concerns about practice methods and skills replaced a previous preoccupation with personal attributes. These altered perceptions have facilitated the replacement of sixty hours or more a week of "parenting" by a forty-hour work week, as well as the recognition of the workers as members of a team and treatment agents in their own right.

These changes have raised questions about the kind of working orientation that would be most desirable. Should child care work proceed as a reeducation effort as in the RE-ED approach (Peabody College, Nashville, Tennessee), as a group socialization endeavor in line with the educateur model (Linton, 1971) as a behavior-rehearsal and citizen-training program as demonstrated in the work of Kansas' Achievement Places, (Phillips, Phillips, Fixsen & Wolf, 1974) or as a resource for basic everyday life experiences within an intense group-care situation as advocated in developmentally oriented programs (Nicholson, 1975; Trieschman, Whittaker & Brendtro, 1969; VanderVen, 1975)? Experiments with critical review of this wide array of group-care stances and techniques are now in progress.

## *THE CURRENT SITUATION*

Contemporary society's concern with achievement and interpersonal competence is reflected in the shift in the status of child care workers, who find themselves defined, more and more, as the major treatment agents in group-care programs. They counsel, reinforce behavior, guide group or milieu treatment sessions, manage token economies, engage in therapeutic encounters, the actual skills of living. Increasingly, child care workers are called upon not only to work with the children or youths in care but also to work with parents, the children's families, and other vital community contacts.

The trend toward group homes, five-day twenty-four-hour care, and day treatment programs—that is, community-oriented group care—has brought the child care worker further into the center of group care. In group homes or day care services, the child care worker is often the only staff person continuously on the scene. The recent emphasis upon behavioral training has redefined the child care worker's functions and experience into the area of expertise. It is the child care worker as the expert in child care who is the one to plan and counsel with the children's peers, teachers, and families. The child care worker has become a partner in the child's primary world. Parents are no longer compensated for. Instead, the child care worker serves as an extension of the parents — and the one to work with parents.

The actual number of persons currently employed in child care is unknown. An early 1970s estimate placed the number at 100,000 workers — 50 percent in child care institutions, 25 percent in programs for the retarded, 15 percent in correctional work, and 10 percent in work with the physically handicapped. In a New York City survey, 43 percent of the workers were under 30, most of them working with preadolescent children. In correctional centers with preadolescent and adolescent youths, 27 percent of the workers were under 30. A representative female child care worker would be in the 36-45 age range, married, and childless, with considerable past babysitting and nursing experience and with a distinct liking for children. A representative profile of the male worker would be a person in the 26-35 age bracket, married, and childless, with some years of college education, previous experience with children probably in community recreation programs, and a stated enjoyment of and ease with children (although he is guarded with adults) (Toigo, 1975). Staff turnover tends to be high in the first-year of employment (40 percent), leveling off to an average of two to three years of continuous service within one program.

A 1975 survey by the Child Welfare League of America, presenting a highly selective sample of child care programs and the only data presently available on a nationwide scale, reports a median salary of $7,314 for child care workers; this is equivalent to the pay of case aides and the lowest pay scale of all professional child welfare personnel. Five-sixths of the sample studied lived away from the institutional premises and without maintenance provisions as part of their employment arrangements. Salaries varied by region but had no significant relationships to educational background. Workers with a BA degree achieved a slightly higher range, and in general, persons trained in child care work received lower pay than those with no specific training for the work (Haring, 1975).

## THE FUTURE

Contemporary concern with providing care and increasing care services — day care, day program centers, group homes — combined with the potential for realization of national health and care assurance plans, places the activities of child care workers at the center of attention. Child care workers will be under pressure to define further the nature of their work. What is the unit of their work — the child alone or the child and his family? Do they work as an extension of the child's primary-life agents? Moreover, the child welfare field has to find new images for the service and training of child care workers, doing away with the distinction between day and twenty-four-hour care. A single group care worker is in the making.

Chapter XI

# Teaching and Training as a Facet of Supervision of Child Care Staff

In the supervision of child/youth care staff we are probably deal-ing with three areas of worker responsibilities. First, supervision serves to assist the care workers to fulfill their individual work as-signments on the most proficient level. Secondly, supervision be-comes functional while attending to tasks which the workers are not yet fully prepared to handle in any adequate way. In these instances, the supervisors have to provide "hurdling help" — helping workers to accomplish a task before the workers have actually learned how to master it. In these instances, a supervisor will advise or instruct a worker what to do in order that s/he will be able to navigate difficult circumstances with some semblance of survival. Essentially, the worker is assisted to handle an apparently insurmountable hurdle. There is often not time to have mastered such a care encounter or frequently in the case of group care situations, the supervisor taking responsibility along with worker, would not know exactly what is effective care for a particular situation and therefore they "wing it" together. The third area of supervisory work, the focus of the re-mainder of this brief essay, is the provision of professional training. *Supervision serves to assist child/youth care workers to become more effective in their work through an enrichment of skill and knowledge repertoire.*

Supervisors become the trainers, the teachers, of their care staff. In this aspect of their role supervisors have to shift from a reactive

This article originally appeared in *Journal of Child Care*, 2(4), 1985, 49-52. Reprinted by permission of the editors of *Journal of Child Care*, Woodpark Boulevard S.W., Calgary, Alberta, Canada.

stance dealing with problematic, worker-induced supervisory sessions' content, to a *pro*-active selected learning foci on the part of the supervisor. The supervisor is challenged to think through and to select appropriately the material which the supervisor wants his or her care workers to learn for the enhancement of their care work. Precisely what is it the worker needs to learn at the next supervisory session? What must s/he learn to *know* and to do?

Note the emphasis in learning is upon what to *do* and to *know* rather than "to be." The difficulty comes when we deal with what a person should be. For instance, we do not know how to help a person "to be less anxious," "to be freer," "to be honest." In contrast however, if we help a worker to handle chaotic mealtime more effectively by assisting the person with planning his or her table and seating arrangements, how to handle the passing of food or how to handle youngsters who have little sitting power, we may have achieved pertinent input. Once a worker understands a situation more clearly and has at least a beginning sense of efficacy for handling particular situations s/he will be apt "to feel freer," "less anxious," and can have the courage "to be honest" in his or her problematic encounters. In short, training has to focus on what skills and knowledge components care workers need to acquire rather than what kind of personal traits they must exhibit.

The workers' actual service capacities can be vastly enhanced by focusing upon what a worker is expected to learn to do in contrast to what the worker "is not to do." So frequently, we desperately try to instill a worker with what *not* to do. For instance, we may tell a worker, "Not to allow so much shouting and reaching across the table at mealtime." Such an input is wise but of little help! It still leaves the worker in a quandary over what to do. But to suggest, for example, the provision of at least two bottles of catchup on the table for hamburger might automatically allow for some table conversation; these recommendations constitute positive instructions. We continuously need to frame life events in such a way that workers can accurately look at their work situation describing what *is* going on rather than what is lacking in the situation. This kind of framework is applicable as well in looking at the children's behavior. Workers tend to describe what they do not like about the children's behavior in terms of what the youngsters are *not* doing. "Those kids," for example, "do *not* come off the playfield when I call them!" An account of negative behavior tends to describe what are the reporting person's expectations. However, when the worker can account for what the youngsters were actually doing (e.g., the four strongest kids were wrestling with each other, while all others were enthusiastic onlookers), potential solutions might be found. Then care worker and supervisor can explore together how to deal with such dilemmas. We urge supervisors to assist care workers to come to grips with what a child (or children) is doing and replace the typical account of what they are not doing—searching out together the next steps the child or children need to learn to master in order to move on in his/her competence development.

Finally, an essential feature of the teaching and training aspects of supervision is the decision whether supervisory work is aimed toward first-order or second-order change (Maier, 1984; Watzlawick, Weakland & Fisch, 1974). First-order change is progressive change which occurs continuously with added experience throughout life. Let's illustrate this as an early childhood experience when the infant gradually moves from crawling to toddling and eventually to adept walking. Much of our work with children relies upon such progressive, incremental changes. We see to it that the children improve—that they will do things better, faster, more skillfully and purposefully or, conversely, gradually dropping out the less desirable behaviors.

In another arena, *supervisors* hold the same expectations for incremental (first-order), gradual change when helping oversee their supervisees on the basis of added experience. (We are reminded of the occasional under-the-breath comment of many a supervisor, "They will learn someday!") This is a valid learning pattern.

Now let us look at second-order change. The latter builds upon incremental change but it depends upon a particular set of turning points within the progression of change. It is manifest by transformation that a substantive change has occurred. Using our earlier example, the infant seems one day to have become a toddler. In the above instance, incremental changes have reached a point where the change retrospectively creates a transformational image. The change creates for the person and its interacting environmental a *different* life condition and new socio-cultural expectations.

Additionally, if we were to examine closely the intent of much of child care work we would realize that most of our work with the youngsters is with a second-order change objective. We expect children within our care not merely to do better along their ongoing path of functioning. We also want them to manage, to feel, and frequently to conceive their life experience in a decisively different manner. They are placed in group care settings whether it is for twenty-four hours or partial day care services as transformational effort—a change not necessarily to do better but *to do differently*.

In the sphere of the *care worker's role* and his supervisor as well, second-order change perspectives are also important. Workers are not merely asked to do more or less in the way they tend to render care and to control others. In their group care work, they are asked to *transform* their everyday handling of life encounters and group management into situationally specific interactions. In other words, child/youth care workers should not expect to be "better" parents, teachers, peers, or adults. Instead, they as workers within their task commitments, need consciously (utilizing a second-order change) to proceed differently than in their everyday life patterns in order to be able to assist their charges.

As long as we envisage supervision in part as a teaching/training activity, much of the responsibility of the preparations, activities, and outcome evaluations shifts to the supervisor. The supervisors are the ones who have to assess *what* and *how* the supervisees can effectively learn.

Chapter XII

# Emerging Issues in Child and Youth Care Education: A Platform for Planning

Jerome Beker
Henry W. Maier

Teachers, practitioners, and researchers concerned with child and youth care and development have talked for a long time about professionalization—what it means, why we need it or why we don't, in what relationship to other professions, and the like (Beker, 1979, pp. 205-230). The differences are important but, at a deeper level, the field shares a commitment to a common effort, a common enterprise. Collectively, we have taken the lead in what Morris (1978) has identified as a broader, emerging professional concern with "caring," the process of caring, or "care work," which views nurturance as a helping modality with appropriate applications to the young, the aging, the disabled, the distressed, the isolated, and people in general (Maier, 1979). In this paper, the authors focus on several critical issues for the continued building of the professional discipline of child and youth care. We are concerned with what preparation for service in child and youth care means and how such preparation can best be conceptualized and delivered.

## INTERCONNECTEDNESS

A major theme that the field will need to confront, one that seems poised to take center stage with regard to a host of public issues and

This article originally appeared in *Child Care Quarterly*, 10(3), 1981, 200-209. Reprinted by permission of Human Sciences Press, Inc., 72 Fifth Avenue, New York, NY 10011.

private agendas in the 1980s and holds much promise for our work, is interconnectedness. More precisely, what is new is not the fact of interconnectedness but the recognition that it exists and must be harnessed in the service of our work. The old struggle concerned whether collectivism or individualism was the "true" mode of life; attention has more recently shifted to the interconnectedness between individuals and their social as well as physical environment. Ecological phenomena, the mutual relations between persons and their physical and social environments, are the ones that currently receive particular attention for their significance in the development of individuals and the quality of their lives. (Bronfenbrenner, 1979).

We have merely to remind ourselves of the events in Solzhenitsyn's (1971) *Cancer Ward*, where one person made a difference due to the interconnectedness between his or her actions and the environment when the person refuses to accept the prescribed role of patient; the whole treatment program is jarred as a result. Moreover, it now seems clear that the outcome of residential care is more influenced by the number of visits a child has with a family than by the internal quality of the residential program per se (Taylor & Alpert, 1973). Changes in sex roles impact the labor market; coffee drinking can influence the course of pregnancy; and Bronfenbrenner (1979) highlights that the welfare of children may be more intimately intertwined with the community's employment practices and the value systems of the child's life space than with the children's caregivers' direct child caring and child-rearing capacities. In every area, life turns out to be more complex than we had realized.

### Multidisciplinary Work

The awareness of interconnectedness is reflected in changing practice expectations and constraints. The focus has shifted from the boundaries between traditional professional disciplines to highlight multidisciplinary or generic approaches that focus on what needs to be done to ease a particular kind of problem or to best serve particular client groups (O'Connor & Martin, 1980). The child care field was out front on this one, and others are catching up. A major challenge will be to establish and maintain connections with allied disciplines so that existing and emerging knowledge and practice wisdom can be broadly applied by the wide variety of helping professionals for whom it may be appropriate.

## Community and Family Emphasis

Increasingly, as we learn more about the interconnected sources and conditions of developmental impact, the service arena for child and youth care workers will encompass community and family contexts. This requires new expectations and perspectives, new competencies, and new patterns of staff deployment to enable individuals with varying skills to complement each other's efforts. The implications for the education of practitioners are profound, and we have not yet done enough to meet the need. This is one of the changes that makes it increasingly difficult to view child and youth care work totally as a "craft" enterprise, as it has often been viewed in the past, although craftsmanship is an essential component. We all know good child and youth care craftspeople, and we have all seen some who flounder when more complex expectations are introduced. In the words of Louis Pasteur, "Chance favors the prepared mind."

## Social and Political Advocacy

Inevitably, as the locus of child and youth care work shifts to the community (Whittaker, 1979) and as we become increasingly sensitive to the interconnectedness between social conditions and human development, we will become increasingly involved in social and political efforts and issues. Effective advocacy will become crucial, both as a technique to establish social conditions that enhance child and youth development and as a way to model concern and participation to facilitate empowerment of the clientele. Ample precedent for such political involvement on behalf of the clients exists among educators and other youthworkers in Europe (Linton, 1971, 1973) and in some exciting ventures in this country.

As advocates, we will need to take account of the declining proportion of children and youth in our population as is projected for the years immediately ahead. It will not be easy to make arguments for the opportunity this will provide to serve young people more effectively and to arrange to have quality programs and systems ready for expected later increases in the population involved. It will be particularly difficult with decision-makers who seem more concerned with the number of dollars spent. But these are the arguments we must make if we are to be able to do the job. Here, too, the growing awareness of interconnectedness will have an impact, and we cannot know the changes in our service systems that will result. Declining numbers of children and youth may facilitate the earlier and more effective integration of many of them into the adult world. Thus, it may lead to lessened use of programs with which we are associated, even on a per capita basis. To the extent that this is a positive development, we, as responsible professionals, need to applaud and facilitate it.

### Legal Considerations

Another kind of interconnectedness with which the child and youth care field must be concerned is represented by the explosion in the influence of legal considerations in our work. Although we are perhaps most clearly and directly touched by liability issues and the rights of children including the "law guardian" phenomenon, we are also affected by affirmative action provisions, protection of research subjects, and on and on. We need to prepare those entering the field with the means for coping efficiently with such provisions and for effective advocacy to change those that are not consistent with our mission (Koocher, 1976; Rubin, 1972).

### Institutional Abuse

One emerging area of concern that bears special mention is institutional abuse. Importantly, attention has now been called to abusive practices that we all know have long existed in many child and youth care settings (Rubin, 1972; Child Abuse . . . , 1978; Hanson, 1981). Unfortunately, we did not act forcefully to eliminate such aberrations, which are really violations of our trust, before they became a public issue. We are now confronted with a public "black eye," one that is not totally unjustified. As a result, we have weakened our ability to deal with foolish nonsense that is being promulgated in the name of institutional abuse — and that obscures some of the more important needs in this area.

What seems most evident — although often not, unfortunately, to some of those who are promoting and funding work in this area — is the need to focus some of our attention on the factors that underlie abuse in institutional settings rather than simply to define and publicize standards and punish those who violate them. This means confronting the implications of the built-in, systemic reality that the work situation — starting with an eight-hour shift with difficult

youngsters—often places unrealistic expectations on child and
youth care personnel. This reflects the importance not only of preparing workers who will confront and challenge such systemic limitations, but also of providing behavior management alternatives and
ways to reduce fear and other stress. Thus, our educational programs should be able to reduce susceptibility to the pressures of
children who, frequently, come from abusing homes and who may
seek to provoke such responses. Such programs should also enable
workers to respond to provocative situations in ways that contribute
to the achievement of developmental goals, including the desire and
the capacity to challenge and to change the conditions of the service
environment when that is necessary to support sound practice. In
other words, frequently one of the most critical variables of abuse is
underfunding!

## CURRICULAR AND TRAINING ISSUES

These are some of the "new issues" in the field, or at least those
that have relatively recently assumed salience. More will undoubtedly arise. Beyond this, even the traditional base of knowledge and
understanding has not yet been operationalized in the form of a
generally agreed curriculum for preparing child and youth care
workers. With these additional inputs, we must again appraise our
educational programs for this complex and rapidly changing enterprise.

The more recent, functional awareness of the interconnectedness
of events, that life proceeds within open systems, requires us to develop educational programs that reflect holistic perspectives rather
than the more traditional, reductionistic ones. Attention will need to
shift from a preoccupation with the selection of course content and
the constellation of courses to be mastered to an emphasis on patterns of thinking and skills to be acquired in training that will enable
workers to interconnect their ongoing experience. How we organize
and deliver the material will be as important as what we include.

Such a focus transcends the old tension between "facts" that need
to be learned on the one hand and crucial sensitivities and "process
skills" on the other. That has ceased to be an issue because we
recognize that both are essential. Rather, it speaks to the need for
analytic, contextual thinking in place of traditional, linear patterns
(Maier, 1978a, pp. 1-13). Further, it is increasingly clear that both

child care work and preparation for it can no longer meaningfully consider children's life events simply in terms of the child's direct life experience — if they ever could! Child care activities need to be viewed in the context of, in Bronfenbrenner's (1979) terms, micro-mezzo-macro life spheres.

Nor can we reasonably continue with the accustomed additive pattern in curriculum-building, that is, simply to add another course when we become aware of another area that needs to be "covered." The crucial question is not simply what content — what course or program — should be included to embrace different and heretofore missing material that seems important. It must be broader. The curriculum and the process of teaching should be arranged so that the learner is required to deal effectively and integratively with the interconnectedness of what he or she is learning, and of life events. Learning to use what one knows contextually, and how to enhance contextual learning in others, is the most critical learning of all.

The recent expansion of law-related considerations such as efforts to apply due process to student disciplinary procedures provides a good example. Child and youth care workers need to know not only the changing procedures and constraints, but also how these factors affect the development of the young people in their care and how they — the workers — can relate to their clientele most effectively under the new conditions. The same holds for training in a new developmental/therapeutic technique, and in other areas.

### Learning and Teaching: A Contextual Approach

A useful corollary in the development of more effective child and youth care education might be that we should focus more on learning than on teaching. We know that not all we teach is learned. Specifically, we have witnessed that child care training courses frequently tend to be mini-exposures to child development, social work, or sociology, much of which may seem largely irrelevant to the work and concerns of practitioners in the field. Therefore, it is not learned, and not used. What is demonstrated to be relevant and essential, on the other hand, is learned, and what is learned is used. We know this from studies in child development. We all crawled and toddled until we learned to walk, then we walked. More to the point, we all used to take comments literally. But since we learned to think conceptually and contextually, we listen no longer to the spoken words but to the message and the questions raised.

How much of what is taught in our many programs is actually used by the presumed learner? And how much is applied contextually? Related to this is the need to focus on learners' ways of thinking about, conceptualizing, and approaching their tasks in learning and in practice, and how knowledge and skill are integrated in this process. If we focus on what is learned and, therefore, applied, we can feel confident that it was taught, although we may not always be sure at this point exactly what in the teaching process was critical. There is an analogy here to our outcome assessments of the young people in our care. We can recognize growth more easily than we can attribute it definitely to specific programmatic or outside influences. Here too, the "answers," if any, must be contextual. Our educational programs need to emphasize such non-linear, ecological thinking — including developmental perspectives — rather than more simplistic, linear modes. We are not, incidentally, alone in this; many allied professions are struggling, more or less effectively, with the same issues, and we have much to learn from, and to teach, our colleagues in this sphere (Kuhn, 1970).

Thus, the conceptualization of the teaching/learning process in our programs and in child and youth care practice itself should shift from one-dimensional, cause/effect thinking to multi-causal and interactional, that is, ecological or milieu-based concepts.

In the child and youth care field, we are accustomed to this viewpoint; it is no accident that the milieu notion is central in much of what we do within the group care environment. We need to extend this thinking more broadly, beyond the group care setting, into the community and into our thinking about the education of practitioners. In the latter arena, we need to develop programs that go beyond conventional teaching to model in their own operation the interconnectedness of life and the sensitivity to, milieu considerations that are organic to the work. Thus, educational programs for child and youth care work needed to model milieu teaching, planful intervention within the flow of life to facilitate growth-enhancing experience. We also need to provide alternative routes to mastery for students whom we expect to be able to recognize and nurture alternative developmental patterns in the young people with whom they work.

This perspective is, of course, in some ways more difficult and less comfortable than more traditional ones. Not only is it somewhat unfamiliar, although our awareness and use of milieu concepts in group care helps on this account, but there are no exact answers that apply "regardless." Instead, as Michael Cole has observed, "It all depends!" (Cole, 1979, p. x). How does one create an educational program to train practitioners if so much is conditional? It all depends!

Herein lies the challenge. We must find ways to help students learn how to work creatively and effectively and to stimulate positive growth and development in a world where so much is conditional but where "the Lord doesn't throw dice," as Einstein suggested; a world where events and conditions are systematic rather than chaotic, as chaotic as they may seem at times. Practitioners with a feeling for and an understanding of the systematic essence of their clients' lives despite apparent chaos can then apply their more specific knowledge and skill effectively. Tolerance for uncertainty, the courage to act on inevitably incomplete knowledge, and the strength to retrace and start again when that seems appropriate are all essential. As Michael Baizerman has suggested, we must be able to decide and act on what is indicated "for all practical purposes" at any given time, even though it may not be the final word.

## *Reliability First — Then Validity*

Finally, we are under a great deal of pressure to "demonstrate accountability," to show that our efforts are effective in producing competent workers or healthy development in young people. How can we assess the results of child and youth care education? How do we decide how good a job we are doing and when we need help? In research terms, the question is posed as one of validity: Do the interventions "work," do they produce the desired effects? And can we connect particular outcomes, specific influence on learners, to particular program elements?

As has frequently been observed in relation to outcome studies in relation to group care and other helping processes, however, we are ill-equipped to answer such questions in a meaningful way (e.g., Durkin & Durkin, 1975). This holds for education in child and youth care work as well. Even the most convincing evidence that students have turned out well, for example, leaves us at a loss when we try to establish reasons definitively. Was the selection process critical? The orientation? Individualized curricular planning? The coursework? Field placements? Relationship with a faculty member? Or the interconnectedness of these elements — and how can we replicate that? We do need to respect our intuitive notions and professional judgment, of course, but these seem somehow inadequate when we are faced with external requirements that we justify, "objectively," our need for support.

The fact is that we do not "know," in the sense that we can demonstrate it statistically, what makes the difference, even though we think we can often recognize it when it occurs. Even then, we cannot really replicate it, except perhaps in ways too gross and too vague to be much help. In research terms we are faced with reliability questions that must be resolved before we can approach questions of validity in a meaningful way. "The basic issue confronting the helping professions," Egan (1975) suggests, "is *reliability*, not validity" (p. 1-2).

It is essential, therefore, that we take the lead in interpreting conscientiously what can and cannot realistically be done as we respond to accountability expectations. We will need to depend on our own professional judgments and those of our colleagues, using more systematic, "objective" approaches where we can. Most important, it is essential that we identify for ourselves and for others why we propose to do what we do, and that we develop a convincingly integrated web of construct validity that will permit us to proceed with confidence and integrity where we cannot adduce systematic evaluative techniques and findings. We know that there are no exact answers, and that we must learn as we move ahead in a series of increasingly accurate "best approximations" that hold "for all practical purposes" until we learn even more.

## SUMMARY AND CONCLUSION

The major theme to which we need to attend in planning for enhanced child and youth care work education is that of interconnectedness. Increasingly, effectiveness in working with children alone or in groups will not be enough, as the locus of understanding and effort shifts to the family, the community, and even broader efforts along advocacy lines. Educational programs for child and youth care workers need to reflect interconnectedness and a rapid rate of change — not only by providing students with appropriate tools, but also by modeling the kinds of approaches that are involved. The milieu concept, so long central in our thinking about our practice in the field, has much to do with the education of child and youth care practitioners as well. Serious and meaningful assessment of our efforts will require a combination of conceptual analysis and qualitative and quantitative techniques, with emphasis on careful attention to reliability in place of premature attempts to establish the trappings of validity.

There are those among our colleagues who view it as a bit too audacious for us to be talking about such changes in curricula at a time when resources for education are declining and support for new and expanded educational programs is hard to find. Many of us have chosen to move ahead anyway, focusing more on the needs of our young people than on the reservations of our contemporaries. The field has been developed and sustained to date through commitment, enthusiasm, adherence to principles in place of expediency and, above all, dogged persistence — all reflected in a great deal of hard work. We believe that if the need and the quality can be demonstrated, we will be able to enlist the necessary support. Our common interest in children and our child welfare programs will be worthwhile if the enthusiasm, the quality, and the intensity of our work can be sustained and directed effectively, even in a period of declining resources.

It all depends . . . on us!

# References

Ainsworth, F. & Fulcher, L. C. (Eds.). (1981). *Group Care for Children: Concept and Issues*. London: Tavistock; New York: Methuen.

Ainsworth, M. D. (1969). "Object Relation, Dependency and Attachment: A Theoretical Review of the Infant-Mother Relationship." *Child Development, 40*(4), 969-1025.

Ainsworth, M. D. (1972). "Attachment and Dependency: A Comparison." In Geriwitz, J. S., *Attachment and Dependency*. Washington, DC: Winston, pp. 97-136.

Ainsworth, M. D. (1974). "Mother-Infant Interactions and the Development of Competencies." In Connoly, K. J. & Brunner, J. (Eds.), *Growth of Competence*. New York: Academic Press, pp. 14-15.

Ainsworth, M. D., Bell, B. M. & Stayton, D. (1974). "Infant-Mother Attachment and Social Development: Socialization as a Product of Reciprocal Responsiveness to Signals." In Richard, M. P. (Ed.), *The Integration of the Child into a Social World*. Cambridge, England: Cambridge University Press, pp. 99-135.

Ainsworth, M. D. & Blehar, M. C. (1978). *Patterns of Attachment*. Hillsdale, NJ: Erlbaum

Allen, D. M. (Ed.). (1973). *Training for Residential Work*. London, England: Central Council for Education and Training in Social Work.

Allerhand, E., Weber, R. E. & Haug, M. (1966). *Adaptation and Adaptability: Bellefaire Follow-up Study*. New York: Child Welfare League of America.

Arieli, M., Kashti, Y. & Shlasky, S. (1983). *Living at School: Israel Residential Schools as People-Processing Organizations*. Tel Aviv, Israel: Ramot Publishing.

Bakker, C. & Bakker-Rabdau, M. K. (1973). *No Trespassing: Explorations in Human Territoriality*. San Francisco: Chandler and Sharp.

Bale, T. (1979). "Saying Good-bye in Residential Treatment." *Child Welfare*, *58*(9), 586-596.

Bandura, A. (1977). "Self-Efficacy: Toward a Unifying Theory of Behavioral Change." *Psychological Review*, *84*(2), 191-215.

Bardwick, J. M. (1974). "Evolution and Parenting." *Journal of Social Issues*, *30*(4), 39-62.

Barker, R. G. (1968). *Ecological Psychology*. Palo Alto, CA: Stanford University Press.

Barnes, F. & Kelman, S. H. (1974). "From Slogan to Concepts: A Basis for Change in Child Care Work." *Child Care Quarterly*, *34*(1), 7-23.

Beker, J. (1972). *Critical Incidents in Child Care*. New York: Behavioural Publications.

Beker, J. (1975). "Development of Professional Identity for the Child Care Worker." *Child Welfare*, *54*(6), 421-431.

Beker, J. (1979). "Training and Professional Development in Child Care." In Whittaker, J. K., *Caring for Troubled Children: Residential Treatment in a Community Context*. San Francisco: Jossey-Bass, pp. 205-230.

Beker, J. & Maier, H. W. (1981). "Emerging Issues in Child and Youth Care Education: A Platform for Planning." *Child Care Quarterly*, *10*(3), 200-209.

Belsky, J. (1980). "Future Directions for Day Care Research: An Ecological Analysis." *Child Care Quarterly*, *9*(2), 82-99.

Belsky, J. & Steinberg, L. D. (1979). "What does Research Teach Us about Day Care: A Follow-up Report." *Children Today*, *8*(4), 21-26.

Benning, R. J. (1981). *Secure Treatment: An Analysis and Outcome*. Salem, OR: Oregon State Publications. (Unpublished report.)

Berkman, W. A. (1979). "Co-Parenting—An Outgrowth of a Boarding Home Program for Handicapped Children." *Children Today*, *8*(4), 10-12.

Bertcher, H. (1973). "The Child Care Worker as a Role Model." *Child Care Quarterly*, *2*(3), 178-196.

Bettelheim, B. (1950). *Love is Not Enough*. New York: Free Press.

Bettelheim, B. (1955). *Truants from Life*. New York: Free Press.

Bettelheim, B. (1967). *The Empty Fortress*. New York: Free Press.

Bettelheim, B. (1974). *A Home for the Heart*. New York: Knopf.

Birnbaum, D. (1973). "Some Observations on the Dilemmas and Pressures of the Child Care Job." *Child Care Quarterly*, 2(2), 87-97.

Bowlby, J. (1969). *Attachment and Loss*, Vols. I and II. London: Hogarth Press.

Brazelton, T. (1977). "Effects of Maternal Expectations on Early Infant Behavior." In Cohen, S. and Comoskey, T. J. (Eds.), *Child Development*. Itasco, IL: F. E. Peacock, pp. 44-52.

Brazelton, T. B. Quoted in Hersh, S. P. & Levin, K. (1978). "How Love Begins Between Parent and Child." *Children Today*, 7(2), 2-6, 47.

Brazelton, T. B. (1981). *On Becoming a Family*. New York: Delacorte Press.

Brazelton, T. B., Koslowski, B. & Main, M. (1974). "The Origins of Reciprocity: The Early Mother-Infant Interaction." In Lewis, M. & Rosenblum, L. A. (Eds.), *The Effects of the Infant on Its Caregiver*. New York: John Wiley, pp. 49-76.

Bronfenbrenner, U. (1970). *Two Worlds of Childhood*. New York: Russell Sage Foundation.

Bronfenbrenner, U. (1976). "The Family Circle: A Story of Fragmentation." *Principal*, 55(5), 11-24.

Bronfenbrenner, U. (1977). "The Fracturing of the American Family." *Washington University Daily*, October 5, p. 5 (summary of a lecture).

Bronfenbrenner, U. (1979). *The Ecology of Human Development*. Cambridge, MA: Harvard University Press.

Bronfenbrenner, U. & Weiss, H. B. (1983). "Beyond Policies without People: An Ecological Perspective on Child and Family Policy." In Zigler, E. F., Kegan, S. L. & Klugman, E., *Children, Families, and Government: Perspective on American Social Policy*. New York: Cambridge University Press, pp. 393-414.

Broussard, E. (1976). "The Neonatal Prediction and Outcome at 10 and 11 Years." *Child Psychiatry and Human Development*, 7(2), 85-93.

Browning, M. & Stover, O. (1971). *Behavior Modification in Child Treatment*. Chicago: Aldine-Atherton.

Brunner, J. S. (1970). *Poverty and Childhood*. Detroit: Merrill Palmer Publications.

Burmeister, E. (1960). *The Professional Houseparent.* New York: Columbia University Press.

Byers, P. (1972). *From Biological Rhythm to Cultural Pattern: A Study of Minimal Units*. New York: Columbia University Press. (Unpublished PhD dissertation.)

Cameron, J. R. (1978). "Parental Treatment, Children's Temperament, and the Risk of Childhood Behavioral Problems: 2. Initial Temperament, Parental Attitudes, and the Incident and Form of Behavioral Problems." *American Journal of Orthopsychiatry*, 48(1), 140-147.

Capelle, R. G. (1979). *Changing Human Systems*. Toronto: International Human Systems Institute.

Carlebach, J. (1983). "Foreword." In Arieli, M., Kashti, Y. & Shlasky, S., *Living at School*. Tel Aviv, Israel: Ramot Publications, pp. 7-8.

Chess, S. & Hassibi, M. (1978). *Principles and Practice of Child Psychiatry*. New York: Plenum Press.

Child Abuse and Neglect in Residential Institutions (1978). *Selected Readings on Prevention, Investigation, and Correction*. Washington, DC: National Center on Child Abuse and Neglect, Department of Health, Education and Welfare.

Clough, R. (1982). *Residential Work*. London: Macmillan Press.

Cole, M. (1979). "Introduction." In Bronfenbrenner, U., *The Ecology of Human Development*. Cambridge, MA: Harvard University Press, pp. VII-X.

Condon, W. (1975). "Speech Makes Babies Move." In Lewin, R. (Ed.), *Child Alive*. New York: Doubleday, pp. 75-85.

Conte, J. (1978). *The Use of Time Out Procedures in Group Care Facilities for Children: A Literature Review and Cautionary Note*. Seattle, WA: School of Social Work, University of Washington. (Manuscript for publication.)

Craig, E. (1973). *P.S. – You're Not Listening*. New York: Signet Books.

Damon, W. (1977). *The Social World of the Child*. San Francisco: Jossey-Bass.

Damon, W. (Ed.). (1978). *Social Cognition*. San Francisco: Jossey-Bass.

Datan, N. & Ginsberg, L. (Eds.). (1975). *Life-Span Development: Psychological-Normal Life Crises*. New York: Academic Press.

Davis, A. (1981). *The Residential Solution*. London: Tavistock.

Denholm, C. J., Pence A. & Ferguson, R. V. (1983). *The Scope of Professional Child Care in British Columbia*. Victoria, BC: School Child Care, University of British Columbia.

Dennison, G. (1970). *The Lives of Children*. New York: Random House.

DeNoon, B. (1965). "Horses, Bait, and Chocolate Cake." In Maier, H. W. (Ed.), *Group Work as Part of Residential Treatment*. New York: National Association of Social Workers, pp. 88-95.

Division of Youth and Family Service of the State of New Jersey (1978). *The Impact of Residential Treatment*. New Brunswick, NJ: Institute for Criminological Research, Rutgers University.

Dupont, H. (1978). *Affective Development: A Piagetian Model*. Eighth Annual Interdisciplinary International Conference on Piagetian Theory and the Helping Professions, Los Angeles, University of Southern California. (Unpublished paper.)

Durkin, R. P. (1982a). *The Crisis in Children's Services: The Dangers and Opportunities for Child Care Workers*. Second National Child Care Workers' Conference, Banff, Alberta. (Unpublished paper.)

Durkin, R. P. (1982b). "Institutional Child Abuse from a Family Systems Perspective: A Working Paper." *Child & Youth Services*, *4*(1), 15-22.

Durkin, R. P. (1982c). "No One Will Thank You: First Thoughts on Reporting Institutional Abuse." *Child & Youth Services*, *4*(1), 109-113.

Durkin, R. P. & Durkin, A. B. (1975). "Evaluating Residential Treatment Programs for Disturbed Children." In Guttentag, M. & Struening, E. L. (Eds.), *Handbook of Evaluation Research*, Vol. II. Beverly Hills, CA: Sage Publications, pp. 275-339.

Ebner, M. J. (1979). "Hard Hats vs. Soft Hearts: The Conflict between Principles and Reality in Child and Adolescent Care and Rx Programs." *Child Care Quarterly*, *8*(1), 36-46.

Egan, G. (1975). *The Skilled Helper*. Monterey, CA: Brooks/Cole.

Eisikovitz, Z. & Beker, J. (1983). "Beyond Professionalism: The Child and Youth Care Worker as Craftsman." *Child Care Quarterly*, *12*(2), 93-112.

Elkind, D. & Weiner, I. B. (1978). *Development of a Child*. New York: John Wiley.

Emlen, A. (1977). *If You Care About Children, Then Care About Parents*. Nashville, TN: Address to the Tennessee Association for Young Children (November).

Epstein, Y. M. (1981). "Crowding Stress and Human Behavior." *Journal of Social Issues*, *37*(1), 126-144.

Escalona, S. K. (1968). *The Roots of Individuality in Infancy*. Chicago: Aldine.

Fanshel, D. (1975). "Parental Visiting of Children in Foster Care: Key to Discharge?" *Social Service Review*, *49*(4), 493-514.

Fixsen, D. L., Phillips, E. L. & Wolf, M. M. (1973). "Achievement Place: Experiments in Self-government with Pre-delinquents." *Journal of Applied Behavior Analysis*, *6*(1), 31-47.

Forbes, D. (1978). "Recent Research on Children's Social Cognition: A Brief Review." In Damon, W. (Ed.), *Social Cognition*. San Francisco: Jossey-Bass, pp. 123-139.

Freedman, J. L. (1975). *Crowding and Behavior*. New York: Viking Press.

Freud, A. & Dann, S. (1951). "An Experiment in Group Upbringing." In Eisler, R. S. & Freud, A. (Eds.), *The Psychoanalytic Study of the Child*, Vol. VI. New York: International Universities Press, pp. 127-168.

Fulcher, L. C. (1983). *Who Cares for the Caregivers? (A Comparative Study of Residential and Day Care Teams Working with Children)*. Sterling, GB: University of Sterling. (Unpublished PhD dissertation.)

Fulcher, L. C. & Ainsworth, F. (Eds.). (1985). *Group Care Practice with Children*. London: Tavistock; New York: Methuen.

Furman, E. (1982). "Mothers are There to be Left." In Solnit, A. J. & Eisler, R. S. (Eds.), *The Psychoanalytic Study of the Child*. New Haven: Yale University Press, pp. 15-28.

Furth, H. G. (1980). *The World of Grown-ups: Children's Conception of Society*. New York: Elsevier.

Garbarino, J. (Ed.). (1982). *Children and Families in the Social Environment*. Chicago: Aldine.

Garbarino, J. & Stocking, S. H. (1980). *Protecting Children from Abuse and Neglect*. San Francisco: Jossey-Bass.

Givens, D. (1978). "Social Expressivity During the First Year of Life." *Sign Language Studies*, *20*, 251-273.

Goffman, E. (1961). *Asylums*. New York: Anchor Books.

Goffman, E. (1971). "The Territories of the Self." In *Relations in Public Places*. Glencoe, IL: Basic Books, pp. 18-61.

Goldsmith, J. M. (1976). "Residential Treatment Today: The Paradox of New Premises." *American Journal of Orthopsychiatry*, *43*(3), 425-433.

Goocher, B. E. (1975). "Behavioral Applications of an Educateur Model in Child Care." *Child Care Quarterly*, *4*(2), 84-92.

Green, J. W. (Ed.). (1982). *Cultural Awareness in the Human Services*. Englewood Cliffs, NJ: Prentice-Hall.

Hall, E. T. (1969). *The Hidden Dimension*. New York: Anchor Books.

Hammond, J. W. (1973). "Child Care Workers as Helpers to Parents." *Child Care Quarterly*, *2*(4), 282-284.

Hanson, R. (1981). "Institutional Abuse of Children and Youth." *Child & Youth Services*, *4*(1-2), 3-45.

Haring, B. (1975). *Salary Study – 1975 – CWLA*. New York: Child Welfare League of America.

Harlow, H. & Menus, C. (1977). "The Power of Passion of Play." *New Scientist*, *10*(2), 336-338.

Harris, R. J. (1980). "A Changing Service: The Case for Separating 'Care' and 'Control' in Probation Practice." *The British Journal of Social Work*, *10*(2), 163-184.

Hartup, W. W. (1979). "Peer Reactions and the Growth of Social Competence." In *Primary Prevention of Psychopathology*, Vol. III, Social Competence of Children. Hanover, VT: University of Vermont Press, pp. 150-170.

Hedin, D. (1982). "Chapter on Youth Outreach." In Beker, J. & Eisikovitz, Z. (Eds.), *Knowledge Utilization in Residential Child and Youth Care Practice*. (Manuscript for publication.)

Helmreich, R. I. & Collin, B. E. (1967). "Situational Determinants of Affiliative Reference Under Stress." *Journal of Personality and Social Psychology*, *6*, 79-85.

Henry, J. (1957). "The Culture of Interpersonal Relations in a Therapeutic Institution for Emotionally Disturbed Children." *American Journal of Orthopsychiatry*, *27*(4), 725-734.

Hersh, S. P. & Levin, K. (1978). "How Love Begins between Parent and Child." *Children Today*, *7*(2), 2-6, 47.

Horejsi, C. (1979). "Applications of the Normalization Principle in the Human Services: Implications for Social Work Education." *Journal of Education for Social Work*, *15*(1), 44-50.

Horowitz, M. J., Duff, D. F. & Stratton, L. O. (1970). "Personal Space and the Body Buffer Zone." In Proshansky, H. M. et al. (Eds.), *Environmental Psychology: Man and his Physical Setting*. New York: Holt, Rinehart & Winston, pp. 214-220.

Inbar, M. (1976). *The Vulnerable Age Phenomenon*. New York: Russell Sage Foundation.

Inbar, M. & Adler, C. (1977). *Ethnic Integration in Israel*. New Brunswick, NJ: Transaction Books.

Jones, F. R., Garrison, K. C. & Morgan, R. F. (1985). *The Psychology of Human Development.* New York: Harper and Row.

Kagan, J. (1974). "Family Experience and the Child's Development." *American Psychologist, 34*(10), 886-891.

Kagan, J. (1977). "The Child in the Family." *Daedalus, 106* (Spring), 33-56.

Kagan, J. (1978). *The Growth of the Child.* New York: Norton.

Kazdin, A. E. (1977). *The Token Economy.* New York: Plenum.

Keniston, K. (1968). *Young Radicals: Notes on Committed Youth.* New York: Harcourt and Brace.

Kessen, W. (Ed.). (1975). *Childhood in China.* New Haven, Yale University Press.

Kirigin, K. A., Braukman, C. J., Atwater, J. & Wolf, M. M. (1978). *An Evaluation of the Achievement Place Teaching-Family Model of Group Home Treatment for Delinquent Youths.* Lawrence, KA: Department of Human Development, University of Kansas. (Unpublished manuscript.)

Kobak, D. (1979). "Teaching Children to Care." *Children Today, 8*(2), 6-7, 34-35.

Koocher, G. (1976). *Rights and the Mental Health Profession.* New York: John Wiley.

Krueger, M. (1981). *Some Thoughts on Research and the Education of Child Care Personnel.* Milwaukee: University of Wisconsin. (Unpublished paper.)

Kuhn, T. S. (1970). *The Structure of Scientific Revolutions.* Chicago: The University of Chicago Press.

Lee, D. (1978). "Round-the-Clock Teaching-Parents." *Practice Digest, 1*(3), 14-16.

Letulle, L. J. (1979). "Family Therapy in Residential Treatment of Children." *Social Work, 24*(1), 49-51.

Lewis, D. K. (1979). *Work with Children.* Beverly Hills, CA: Sage Publications.

Lewis, M. & Rosenblum, L. A. (Eds.). (1974). *The Effects of the Infant on its Caregiver.* New York: John Wiley.

Lindheim, R., Glasser, H. H. & Coffin, C. (1972). *Changing Hospital Environments.* Cambridge, MA: Harvard University Press.

Linton, T. E. (1971). "The Educateur Model: A Theoretical Monograph." *Journal of Special Education, 5*(2), 155-190.

Linton, T. E. (1973). "The Educateur: A European Model for the Care of 'Problem Children.'" *International Journal of Mental Health, 2*(1), 1-88.

Litwak, E. & Szelenyi, I. (1969). "Primary Group Structures and their Functions: Kin, Neighbors, and Friends." *American Sociological Review*, *34*(4), 465-481.

Long, N., Stoeffler, V., Krause, U. & Jung, C. (1972). "Life-Space Management of Behavioral Crises." In Whittaker, J. K. & Trieschman, A. E., *Children Away from Home*. Chicago: Aldine, pp. 256-266.

Maas, H. S. (1979). *Social Development and Social Loss*. Berkeley, CA: University of California. (Unpublished paper.)

Maas, H. S. (1980). "The Child's Responsibility to Society." In Freeman, D. S. (Ed.), *Perspectives on Family Therapy*. Vancouver, Canada: Butterworth, pp. 201-214.

Maas, H. S. (1984). *People and Contexts*. Englewood Cliffs, NJ: Prentice-Hall.

Maccoby, E. E. & Masters, J. C. (1970). "Attachment and Dependency." In Mussen, P. H. (Ed.), *Carmichael's Manual of Child Psychiatry*, Vol. II. New York: John Wiley, pp. 73-157.

Magnus, R. A. (1974). "Parent Involvement in Residential Treatment Program." *Children*, *3*(1), 25-27.

Maier, H. W. (1963). "Child Care as a Method of Social Work." In Child Welfare League of America, *Training for Child Care Staff*. New York: Child Welfare League of America Publications, pp. 62-81.

Maier, H. W. (1965). "The Social Group Work Method and Residential Treatment." In Maier, H. W. (Ed.), *Group Work as Part of Residential Treatment*. New York: National Association of Social Workers, pp. 26-42.

Maier, H. W. (1969). "When Father is no Longer the Father." *Journal of Applied Social Studies*, *1*(1), 13-20.

Maier, H. W. (1971a). "The Child Care Worker." In Morris, R. (Ed.), *Encyclopedia of Social Work, 1971*. New York: National Association of Social Workers, pp. 111-114.

Maier, H. W. (1971b). "A Sidewards Look at Change." *Social Service Review*, *45*(2), 123-136.

Maier, H. W. (1974). "A Sidewards Look at Change and What Comes into View." In *Social Work in Transition: Issues, Dilemmas, and Choices*. Seattle, WA: School of Social Work, University of Washington, pp. 138-147.

Maier, H. W. (1975). "Learning to Learn and Living to Live in Residential Treatment." *Child Welfare*, *54*(6), 406-420.

Maier, H. W. (1976). "Human Functioning as an Interpersonal Whole: The Dimensions of Affect, Behavior and Cognition." In *Teaching for Competence in the Delivery of Direct Services.* New York: Council on Social Work Education, pp. 44-49.

Maier, H. W. (1977). "Child Welfare: Child Care Workers." In Turner, J. B. (Ed.), *Encyclopedia of Social Work, 1977.* Washington, DC: National Association of Social Workers, pp. 130-134.

Maier, H. W. (1978a). "Piagetian Principles Applied to the Beginning Phase in Professional Helping." In Weizmann, R. & Brown, R. et al. (Eds.), *Piagetian Theory and the Helping Professions.* Los Angeles, CA: University Press, University of California, Ch. 1, pp. 1-13.

Maier, H. W. (1978b). *Three Theories of Child Development* (3rd revised edition). New York: Harper and Row.

Maier, H. W. (1979). "The Core of Care." *Child Care Quarterly,* *8*(4), 161-173.

Maier, H. W. (1980). Wanted: Information on Children in 24-Hour Group Care Services. World Mental Health Conference: *Residential Treatment for Children and Adolescents.* Vancouver, BC: World Federation of Mental Health (Unpublished report.)

Maier, H. W. (1981). "Essential Components in Care and Treatment Environments for Children and Youth." In Ainsworth, F. & Fulcher, L. C. (Eds.), *Group Care for Children: Concepts and Issues.* New York: Methuen; London: Tavistock, pp. 19-70.

Maier, H. W. (1982a). "The Space We Create Controls Us." *Residential Group Care and Treatment,* *1*(1), 51-59.

Maier, H. W. (1982b). "To be Attached and Free: The Challenge of Child Development." *Child Welfare,* *61*(2), 67-76.

Maier, H. W. (1983). "Should Child and Youth Care Go the Craft or the Professional Route?" *Child Care Quarterly,* *12*(2), 113-118.

Maier, H. W. (1984). "A Simple but Powerful Concept Poses a Challenge for the Teaching and Learning of Social Work Practice." *Social Work Education,* *4*(1), 17-20.

Maier, H. W. (1985a). "Personal Care within an Organizational Service Context." In Fulcher, L. & Ainsworth, F. (Eds.), *Group Care Practice with Children.* New York: Methuen; London: Tavistock, pp. 21-47.

Maier, H. W. (1985b). "Teaching and Training as a Facet of Supervision of Care Staff." *Journal of Child Care,* *2*(4), 49-52.

Maier, H. W. (1986a). "Human Development: Psychological Basis." In Minahan, A. (Ed.), *Encyclopedia of Social Work* (18th edition). New York: National Association of Social Workers, pp. 850-856.

Maier, H. W. (1986b). "Personal to Societal Perspective: How Children and Youth Conceive their World beyond the Residential Settings." In Kashti, Y. & Arieli, M. (Eds.), *Residential Settings and the Community: Congruence and Conflict*. London: Freund Publishing House.

Maier, H. W. (1986c). "Developmental Foundations of Child and Youth Care Work." In Beker, J. & Eisikovitz, Z., (Eds.), *Knowledge Utilization in Residential Child and Youth Care Practice*. (Book manuscript for publication.)

Maier, H. W. (1986d). *Dependence and Independence Development throughout the Human Life Span: Implications for the Helping Professions*. Seattle, WA: University of Washington. (Manuscript for publication.)

Maier, H. W. (1986e). *Are there Vulnerable Age Phases of Transition?* Seattle, WA: University of Washington. (Manuscript in preparation.)

Mattingly, M. A. (1977). "Sources of Stress and Burn-out in Professional Child Care Work." *Child Care Quarterly, 6*(2), 127-137.

Mayer, M. F. (1958). *A Guide for Child Care Workers*. New York: Child Welfare League of America.

Mayer, M. F. (1960). "The Parental Figures in Residential Treatment." *Social Services Review, 34*(3), 273-285.

McDonald, D. J. (1978). "Children and Young Persons in New Zealand Society." In Koopman-Boyden, P. G. (Ed.), *Families in New Zealand Society*. Wellington: Methuen Publishers, pp. 44-56.

Mehler, F. M. (1979). "Houseparents: A Vignette." *Child Care Quarterly, 8*(3), 174-178.

Mehrabian, A. (1976). *Public Places and Private Spaces*. New York: Basic Books.

Monane, J. H. (1967). *A Sociology of Human Systems*. New York: Appleton-Century-Crofts.

Mordock, J. B. (1979). "Evaluation in Residential Treatment: The Conceptual Dilemmas." *Child Welfare, 58*(5), 293-302.

Morris, R. (1978). "Social Work Function in a Coming Society: Abstract Value, Professional Preference and the Real World." *Journal of Education for Social Work, 14*(2), 82-84.

National Day Care Study (1979). *Final Report: Children at the Center: Summary Findings and Policy Implications of the National Day Care Study* (Final Report: Vol. I.). Cambridge, MA; Abt Associates.

National Institute of Child Health and Human Development (1968). *Perspectives on Human Deprivation: Biological, Psychological and Sociological.* Washington, DC: National Institute of Child Health and Human Development, Department of Health, Education and Welfare.

Neill, A. (1960). *Summerhill: A Radical Approach to Child Rearing.* New York: Hart Publishing.

Nicholson, M. L. (1975). "Child Care Practice and the Passions of Today: Some Propositions." *Child Care Quarterly, 4*(2), 72-83.

O'Connor, G. & Martin, P. Y. (1980). *The Social Contexts of Practice in Human Services.* Tallahassee: Florida State University.

Oxley, G. B. (1977a). "A Modified Form of Residential Treatment." *Social Work, 22*(6), 493-498.

Oxley, G. B. (1977b). "Involuntary Clients' Responses to a Treatment Experience." *Social Casework, 58*(10), 607-614.

Parsons, T. (1964). *The Social System.* New York: The Free Press.

Pecora, P. J. & Gingerich, W. J. (1981). "Worker Tasks and Knowledge Utilization in Group Care: First Findings." *Child Welfare, 60*(4), 221-231.

Phillips, E. L., Phillips, E. A., Fixsen, D. L. & Wolf, M. M. (1971). "Achievement Place: Modification of the Behaviors of Pre-delinquent Boys within a Token Economy." *Journal of Applied Behavior Analysis, 4*(1), 45-59.

Phillips, E. L., Phillips, E. A., Fixsen, D. L. & Wolf, M. M. (1973). "Achievement Place — Behavior Shaping Works for Delinquents." *Psychology Today, 7*(1), 74-79.

Phillips, E. L., Phillips, E. A., Fixsen, D. L. & Wolf, M. M. (1974). *The Teaching Handbook.* Lawrence, KA: University of Kansas Press.

Piaget, J. (1951). *Play, Dreams and Imitation in Childhood.* London: Heineman.

Piaget, J. (1975). *The Child's Conception of the World.* New York: Littlefield.

Pina, V. (1983). "Comment: Isolationism is Dead: Survival Mandates Flexible Systems, *Newsletter of the Child Care Learning Center*, 5(2), 3.

Pines, A. & Maslach, C. (1980). "Combating Staff Burnout in a Day Care Center: A Case Study." *Child Care Quarterly*, 9(1), 5-16.

Plank, E. (1973). "Play Activities." In *Working within Hospitals* (revised edition). Cleveland, OH: Case-Western Reserve University Press.

Polansky, N. R., Ammons, P. W. & Weathersby, B. I. (1983). "Is there an American Standard of Child Care?" *Social Work*, 28(5), 341-346.

Polsky, H. W. (1962). *Cottage Six*. New York: Russell Sage Foundation.

Polsky, H. W. & Claster, D. S. (1968). *The Dynamics of Residential Treatment*. Chapel Hill, NC: University of North Carolina Press.

Portnoy, S. M., Biller, H. B. & Davids, A. (1972). "The Influence of the Child Care Worker in Residential Treatment." *American Journal of Orthopsychiatry*, 42(3), 719-722.

Powell, D. (1978). "The Interpersonal Relationship between Parents and Caregivers in Day Care Settings." *American Journal of Orthopsychiatry*, 48(4), 680-689.

Proshansky, H. M., Ittelson, W. H. & Rivlin, L. G. (Eds.). (1970). *Environmental Psychology: Man and his Physical Setting*. New York: Holt, Rinehart & Winston.

Radloff, R. & Helmreich, R. L. (1968). *Group under Stress: Psychological Research in Selab II*. New York: Appleton-Century-Crofts.

Redl, F. & Wineman, D. (1957). *The Aggressive Child*. New York: Basic Books.

Resnick, H. (1980). "A Social System View of Strain." In Resnick, H. & Patti, R., *Change from Within*. Philadelphia: Temple University Press, pp. 28-45.

Resnick, H. (1983). *The Political Dimension in Social Welfare Organizations: The Missing Ingredient in Social Work Education*. Seattle, School of Social Work, University of Washington. (Unpublished manuscript.)

Robinson, H. B., Robinson, N. M. & Wolins, M. (1976). *Early Child Care in the United States of America*. New York: Gordon and Breach.

Rodriguez, D. T. & Hignett, W. F. (1981). "Infant Day Care: How Very Young Children Adapt." *Children Today*, *10*(6), 2-6.

Rubenstein, J. & Howes, C. (1979). "Caregivers and Infant Behavior in Day Care and in Homes." *Developmental Psychology*, *15*(1), 1-24.

Rubin, S. (1972). "Children as Victims of Institutionalization." *Child Welfare*, *51*(1), 6-18.

Runstein, H. (1983). *Rethinking Learning Environments for Children in the "Vulnerable Age" Six through Twelve*. Seattle, WA: School of Social Work, University of Washington. (Unpublished paper.)

Rutter, M. (1979). "Review: Maternal Deprivation, 1972-1978: New Findings, New Concepts, New Approaches." *Child Development*, *50*(2), 283-305.

Sable, P. (1979). "Differentiating between Attachment and Dependency in Theory and Practice." *Social Case Work*, *60*(3), 138-144.

Schaefer, C. E. (1977). "The Need for Psychological Parents by Children in Residential Treatment." *Child Care Quarterly*, *6*(4), 288-299.

Schaffer, H. R. (1977). *Mothering*. Cambridge, MA: Harvard University Press.

Schaffer, H. R. & Emerson, P. E. (1964). "The Development of Social Attachments in Infancy." *Monographs of the Society for Research in Child Development*, *29*(3), 5-77.

Schwartz, W. (1971). "The Practice of Child Care in Residential Treatment." In Mayer, M. F. (Ed.), *Healing through Living*. Springfield, IL: Charles C Thomas, pp. 38-71.

Scott, J. P. (1958). *Animal Behavior*. Chicago: University of Chicago Press.

Seaburg, B. A. (1971). "Arrangements of Physical Space in Social Work Settings." *Social Work*, *16*(4), 43-49.

Segal, J. & Yahraes, H. (1978). *A Child's Journey*. New York: McGraw-Hill.

Seidl, F. W. (1977). "Conflict and Conflict Resolution in Residential Treatment." *Child Care Quarterly*, *6*(4), 269-278.

Sivadon, P. (1970). "Space as Experienced: Therapeutic Implications." In Proshansky, H. M., Ittelson, W. H. & Rivlin, L. G. (Eds.), *Environmental Psychology: Man and his Physical Setting*. New York: Holt, Rinehart & Winston, pp. 27-37.

Smart, M. S. & Smart, R. C. (1977). *Children: Development and Relationships*. New York: Macmillan.

Solzhenitsyn, A. I. (1971). *The Cancer Ward*. Harmunsworth, England: Penguin Books.

Sommer, R. (1969). *Personal Space: The Behavioral Basis of Design*. Englewood Cliffs, NJ: Prentice-Hall.

Spergel, I. A. (1971). "Street Gang Work." In Morris, R. (Ed.), *Encyclopedia of Social Work*. New York: National Association of Social Workers, pp. 1486-1494.

Sroufe, L. A. (1978). "Attachment and the Roots of Competence." *Human Nature*, *1*(10), 50-57.

Sroufe, L. A. & Waters, E. (1977). "Attachment as an Organizational Construct." *Child Development*, *48*(4), 1184-1199.

Stea, D. (1970). "Space, Territory and Human Movements." In Proshansky, H. M., Ittelson, W. H. & Rivlin, L. G. (Eds.), *Environmental Psychology: Man and his Physical Setting*. New York: Holt, Rinehart & Winston, pp. 37-42.

Taylor, D. A. & Alpert, S. W. (1973). *Continuity and Support following Residential Treatment*. New York: Child Welfare League of America.

Thomas, A. & Chess, S. (1977). *Temperament and Development*. New York: Brunner/Mazel.

Thomas, A., Chess, S. & Birch, H. G. (1964). *Behavioral Individuality in Early Childhood*. New York: New York University Press.

Thomas, A., Chess, S. & Birch, H. G. (1968). *Temperament and Behavior Disorders in Children*. New York: New York University Press.

Toigo, R. (1975). "Child Care Manpower Development: A Literature Review." *Child Care Quarterly*, *4*(1), 6-17.

Trieschman, A. E., Whittaker, J. K. & Brendtro, L. K. (1969). *The Other 23 Hours*. Chicago: Aldine.

Turiell, E. (1978). "Social Regulations and Domains of Social Concepts." In Damon, W. (Ed.), *Social Cognition*. San Francisco: Jossey-Bass, pp. 45-74.

VanderVen, K. (1975). *The Development Child Care Model of Education: The Baccalaureate Program in Child Development and Child Care*. Pittsburgh: University of Pittsburgh Press.

VanderVen, K., Mattingly, M. A. & Morris, M. G. (1982). "Principles and Guidelines for Child Care Personnel Preparation Programs." *Child Care Quarterly*, *11*(3), 221-244.

Vygotsky, L. (1978). *Mind in Society*. Cambridge, MA: Harvard University Press.

Washington, R. O. (1982). "Social Development: A Focus for Practice and Education." *Social Work*, *27*(1), 104-109.

Waters, E. (1978). "The Reliability and Stability of Individual Differences in Infant-Mother Attachment." *Child Development*, *49*(6), 483-494.

Watzlawick, P., Weakland, J. W. & Fisch, R. (1974). *Change*. New York: Norton.

Wax, D. E. (1977). "Human Ecological Perspectives within a Residential Treatment Setting for Children." *Child Care Quarterly*, *6*(1), 51-60.

Webster, C. D., Somjen, L., Shoman, L., Bradley, S., Mooney, S. A. & Mack, J. E. (1979). "The Child Care Worker in the Family: Some Case Examples and Implications for the Design of Family-Centered Programs." *Child Care Quarterly*, *8*(1), 5-18.

White, M. S. (1979). *Focus on Parental Visitation in Foster Care: Continuing Involvement within a Permanent Planning Framework*. (Project under the Child Welfare Services Training Grant Team 9038 T21 — research in progress). Minneapolis: School of Social Work, University of Minnesota.

White, R. W. (1972). *The Enterprise of Living: Growth and Organization of Personality*. New York: Holt, Rinehart & Winston.

Whittaker, J. K. (1969). "Program Activities." In Trieschman, A. E., Whittaker, J. K. & Brendtro, L. K., *The Other 23 Hours*. Chicago: Aldine, pp. 100-120.

Whittaker, J. K. (1979). *Caring for Troubled Children*. San Francisco: Jossey-Bass.

Whittaker, J. K. & Garbarino, J. (Eds.). (1983). *Social Support Networks: Informal Helping in the Human Services*. New York: Aldine.

Whittaker, J. K. & Trieschman, E. (Eds.). (1972). *Children Away from Home*. Chicago: Aldine-Atherton.

Wilson, T. (1977). "Creating a Diversified Activity Program in a Small Psychiatric Institution for Children." *Child Care Quarterly*, *6*(4), 248-258.

Wineman, D. (1959). "The Life Space Interview." *Social Work*, *4*(1), 3-17.

Winnicott, D. W. (1965). *The Family and Individual Development*. London: Tavistock Publications.

Wolf, M. M., Phillips, E. L. & Fixsen, D. L. (1974). *Achievement Place: Phase II*. Bethesda, MD: National Institute of Mental Health.

Wolf, M. M., Phillips, E. L., Fixsen, D. L., Braukmann, C. T., Kirigin, K. A., Willner, A. G. & Schumaker, J. (1976). "Achievement Place: The Teaching-Family Model." *Child Care Quarterly*, 5(2), 92-103.

Wolf, M. & Proshansky, H. (1974). "The Physical Settings as a Factor in Group Function and Process." In Jacobs, A. & Spradlin, W. W. (Eds.), *The Group as an Agent of Change*. New York: Behavioral Publications, pp. 206-227.

Wolins, M. & Gottesmann, M. (Eds.). (1971). *Group Care: An Israeli Approach*. New York: Gordon and Breach.

Wolins, M. & Wozner, Y. (1982). *Revitalizing Residential Settings*. San Francisco: Jossey-Bass.

Wrenn, C. G. (1972). "The Nature of Caring." *The Humanist Educator* (June), 167-172.

Wylde, S. R. (1979). "Arthur: A Creative Reward Program for Acting-out Children." *Child Care Quarterly*, 8(3), 220-226.

Yawkey, T. D. & Bakawa-Evenson, L. (1977). "Planning for Play in Programs for Young Children." *Child Care Quarterly*, 6(4), 259-268.

Youniss, J. (1980). *Parents and Peers in Social Development*. Chicago: The University of Chicago Press.

# Index